The

OFFSHORE
MONEY BOOK

he

OFFSHORE
MONEY BOOK

ARNOLD L. CORNEZ, J.D.

International Publishing
Chicago

Second Printing

ISBN: 0-942641-72-8

Dedication

This book germinated from the development of a personal and business relationship with my dear friend. What we lacked in acumen of the offshore world, we made up for with energy, enthusiasm, camaraderie, fine dining and humor.

We traveled the world together: Tokyo, Hong Kong, Shanghai, Beijing and Puerto Vallarta; then to France, Switzerland, Austria. We made five trips to Luxembourg. We never found the proverbial pot of financial gold, but we did find a deeper friendship.

We learned so much in the offshore school of hard knocks, where tuition is even more expensive than Harvard Medical School. The experience provided the impetus for me to make a transition to my third career (following engineering and law) as an offshore private advisor and consultant in an effort to harness this newfound knowledge.

Thanks, Mel, for the experience of a lifetime. It was worth it all.

Melvin Nissinoff died in 1995 at the young age of 57. I'll always miss him.

Arnie

Table of Contents

Acknowledgments xiii

About the Author xv

A Note from the Author 1

1 An Introduction to the Reluctant American 11
    Terminology 11
    Are *You* a Reluctant American? 13

2 Getting Started: Recognizing and Overcoming
   Your Concerns 19
    The Structures...20
    The Participants 22
      The Question of Trust...23
    The Costs of Setting Up an Offshore Structure.................25
    International Services, Set-up and Servicing.....................26

3 Why Go Offshore? 29
    Reasons to Stay Onshore 29
    Reasons to Go Offshore...30

4 Where and How Do I Place My Assets? 35
    Guidelines for Evaluating Offshore Options.....................36

A General Discussion of Some International Financial
   Centres 44
Selected Tax Havens of the World..................................48
Legal Issues and Terminology..56
   Spendthrift Clause..56
   The Statute of Limitations 57
   The Choice of Governing Law 58
Transferring Assets..58
   APT Costs..59

5 What Structure Do I Use?...61
   Basic Offshore Entities..62

**6 The Caribbean Style of an International Business
   Company: An Exempt Company...............................71**
   What Can an IBC Do?..72
   IBC Features 74
      General Considerations 74
      Tax Regimen...75
      Simplicity and Flexibility of Operations.....................75
      Quality of Communications 75
      Language..76
      Legal System 76
      *Costs: Registration Fees and Domecilliary and
         Management Fees* 76
      Privacy 76
      Choice of Name Restrictions.......................................77
      Monetary Controls 77
   Applying for Company Formation and Agreement...........77
   An IBC Comparison Checklist 78
   Other Forms of Companies..84

7 The Offshore (Foreign) Asset Protection Trust 85
   Trusts 101 85
   The U.S. Living Trust..87
   The Evolution of the Trust 89
   Who Needs an APT? 92

The Parties to the APT 94
Other Trust Nomenclature..98
   The Rule Against Perpetuities.......................................98
   Rights of Settlement...99
   Different Types (Classes) of Creditors 99
   The Statute of Elizabeth 100
   Forced Heirship 101
   Choice of Law 101
   In rem jurisdiction..102
   Actionable Fraud and the "Badges of Fraud" 102
   Duress Provisions 104
   Settlor in Contempt of Court......................................105
   Flight Provisions: The "Fleet" Clause or the
     "Cuba" Clause...106
   Enforcement of Foreign Judgments 106
Costs 106
Technicalities..108

8   Offshore Banks and Banking Services 109
Offshore Credit or Debit Cards 109
General Banking Rules...110
Private and Numbered Accounts 111
   The Chop Block Account..112
   The Sparbuch (Savings) Account 114
Monetary Policies and Exchange Controls.......................115
Private Banking 115
   Your Personal Private Bank 116
Privacy 117

9   Annuities 121
General Background 121
   Going Offshore–The Swiss Annuity 122
   The Private Annuity 123

10 Other Structures and Strategies............................ 127
Offshore Exempt Companies..127
   An OS Company Limited by Guaranty.........................127

A Company with a Limited Lifetime...........................128
The Contract Hybrid Company.................................128
Demystifying Residence: Domicile, Citizenship
and Passports 129
Renouncing U.S. Citizenship...133
Typical Second Citizenship Acquisition Programs....136
The Living Trust 138
The Family Limited Partnership (FLP) 138
The Weakness of the FLP as an AP Tool...................141
An FLP Checklist 143
Real Property Equity Stripping: An Asset
Protection Tool 144
The Unincorporated Organization or Unincorporated
Business Organization 145
Proprietary Triple Trust Structure 145
Contemporary Three-Tier Structure 148
The Pure Trust 150
Defined...150
The Business Trust 154
The Pure Equity Trust 154
Fraudulent Trust Characteristics 155
Providing for a Child in a High-Risk Profession.............155
Offshore Charitable or Private Foundations....................156
Bankruptcy, with an Asset Preservation Plan..................156

11 Tax Treatment, Ramifications and Deferral 159
Offshore Taxes 101 159
Tax Implications for U.S. Persons 162
Tax on the U.S. Trustee...163
Special Tax Concession by Local Jurisdictions.........163
Excise Tax 163
Taxes on Annuity Proceeds...163
*U.S. Taxes on the IBC Investing in the
U.S. Stock Market*..164
The High Tax on Renouncing U.S. Citizenship..........164
IRS Requirements for an Offshore Principal Office 165

Applicable IRS Forms 166
Classifying Tax Havens Based on Tax Attributes...........170

12 Offshore Communications and Privacy 173
Privacy 173
Encryption 177

13 The Captive Insurance Company............................179
Captive Insurance Defined 179
Costs 183
Typical Statutory Requirements......................................183
Global Insurance Resource on the Web 184

14 Conclusion: Applying What You Have Learned.....185
A Case Study: Putting the Pieces Together.....................185
A Test for the Reader 187
Avoiding Offshore Scams: "Greed-O-Nomics" 101 188
    The Nigerian Scam..190
    The Prime Bank Note, Prime Bank Guaranty and
        Roll Program Scam...193
Farewell to the Reluctant American 197

Appendix A: "CyberShore"™ Resources on the
Internet 201
Offshore Related Sites on the Internet 201
    World Wide Web Search Engines................................202
    Pretty Good Privacy (PGP)™ 203
    Privacy Publications and Web Sites 203
    General Offshore Materials.......................................204
    Tax Information..206
    Asset Protection 208
    Offshore Banking and Credit Cards 208
    E-cash Companies..210
    Global Business, General 210
    Media 212
    Couriers 213
    Estate Planning..213

Appendix B: Glossary of Terms and Abbreviations .. 215

**Appendix C: Some Offshore and Onshore
Publications of Interest 233**

**Appendix D: Some Selected and Representative
Offshore Service Providers 241**

Appendix E: What to Do with Offshore Assets.......... 247
1995 World Investment Report 247
Offshore Stock and Commodity Markets 248
The "New" Time Sharing: Vacation Ownership.............252
Offshore Mortgage Financing 255
Other Examples of OS Investment Opportunities 255

Index 257

Acknowledgments

This was a team effort, and most of the people involved didn't even know they were part of my team. The credit for this book should go to the hundreds of people who have most graciously or unknowingly generously shared their priceless knowledge and "secrets" with me over the last 10 years. At first, I was the insatiable dry sponge and filter, and this book is the essence of the efforts of those years, my "give back" to you. From grape juice comes Cognac; from potatoes comes Absolut®; and from a sifting through my notebooks and lifetime experiences for grains of knowledge comes *The Offshore Money Book*.

During the final, formative months, the following persons onshore and offshore directly contributed to this work, and my acknowledgments are in order.

Vernon K. Jacobs, CPA, CPU, Editor, *The Jacobs Report on Asset Protection Strategies,* Prairie Village, Kansas. My unending thanks for critiquing the entire book, especially with your major emphasis on the complex issue of taxes in Chapter 11.

Michael F. Quarles, JD and LLM candidate, Villanova University of Law and School of Commerce and Finance, Villanova, Pennsylvania. Thanks for a comprehensive total review of the final draft.

Michael Hatcher, Editor, *The Financial Privacy Report,* Burnsville, Minnesota. Mike provided a grueling critique of the entire draft, leading to a much improved version.

David Lesperance, Attorney at Law, Hamilton, Ontario, Canada. My thanks to Dave for a major rewrite of the Chapter 10, on second passports and citizenships.

My thanks also to:

Charles A. Cain, MA, ACIB, Trustee and Director, Skye Fiduciary Services Limited, Ramsey, Isle of Man.

James R. Allen, EA, San Jose, California.

Michael G. Christiani, MBA, Avon, Connecticut. Portfolio and Asset Manager.

Ronald H. Ruiz , Dr. Juris., Zug, Switzerland. Offshore Consultant.

William Storie, William R. Storie & Company Ltd., Hamilton, Bermuda.

Robert Giffin, Attorney at Law, Santa Rosa, California.

And last, but certainly not least, to J. My thanks to my loving wife of nearly 30 years. Judie was editor-in-chief, unabashed critic and distant comfort during the periods of necessary solitude for the research and drafting of *The Offshore Money Book*–everything my best friend needed to be.

♥,
Arnie

About the Author

Mr. Cornez has the ideal formal education for the new high-tech world of global finances. With degrees in electrical engineering and law, as an interdisciplinarian, he merges the offshore world into one functioning entity. He has done so for over 10 years, and during this time has acquired a worldwide network of quality associates and friends.

As a world business traveler, he easily flows from a discussion on qualifying a stock for trading on the Luxembourg stock exchange to creating a captive insurance company in the Turks and Caicos Islands; from a private bank in Vanuatu to an exempt company on the Isle of Man.

He has been quoted in the prestigious *Barron's,* appeared on Public Broadcasting's TV show *Frontline,* spoken at numerous seminars and taught at the university level the subject of doing offshore business on the Internet.

Arnie loves fine wines and dining and enjoys sharing both with his wife, his three married children and their expanded families.

Arnie may be contacted by e-mail to:
`offshore@bahamas.net.bs`
Or by air post to:
PO Box CB 13039, Nassau, the Bahamas CB 13039.

A Note from the Author

"You cannot discover new oceans unless you have the courage to
loose sight of the binding shore."
Anonymous

To set the tone for this book, allow me to state outright that it is regrettable that there is a public misperception that "sunny climes are for shady people." I write in such environs of public misconception and attempt in this book to counter it. Misconception breeds fear of the unknown and fear begets your reluctance. Hence, I use the title *The Offshore Money Book: A Comprehensive Guide for Reluctant Americans.* If the title of this book has a familiar ring to it, you are dating yourself. In 1958, authors Bill Lederer and Eugene Burdick penned the bestseller, *The Ugly American.* It described a stereotype portrayed by the wealthy, rude, arrogant, unskilled and demanding Americans representing the United States (U.S.) abroad, which created a negative image worldwide. With due apologies to the authors, the title for this book now appears particularly *apropos, as* the stereotype of the American now going offshore is one of being timid and misinformed. Unfortunately, the offshore professional must first patiently educate the inexperienced, reluctant American before they can work together. This book serves that professional's need as well, and I hope it is favorably received in the offshore community.

While the typical European child is multilingual and is raised in an environment where he or she may see a parent traipsing off to another country for business purposes just for the day, Americans by contrast are culturally and linguistically limited. Americans (including our U.S. Congress, with its "fortress America" hang-up) are seen from offshore as provincial and isolationists. Germans love to vacation and some "live" to travel the world. At times I hear more German and German accents than English as I motor through Yosemite.

Foreign nationals, other than the reluctant American (RA[1]), are also more inclined and comfortable in investing world-wide. The RA continues to self-restrict, at least in the geographic scope, by staying at home. French and German business owners avoid what they perceive to be confiscatory income taxation by their respective countries by using offshore companies (conduits) to earn and retain a significant portion of the profits on each transaction (earnings stripping) through "upstreaming."

Blame it on the negative press, the media and intimidation by the IRS. Blame it on being uncomfortable with the concept of an offshore bank or brokerage firm. Blame it on not knowing the strange vocabulary: nominees, trust protectors, company, members, control of assets, remote vesting, choice of law, family protective trusts, IBCs,[2] APTs and so on. Or blame it on all of the above. That defines the mission of this book. Folks, we're going to work on your "reluctance" problem. You need to psychologically adapt, to adjust and think globally, as the remainder of the world presently does. Let's catch up! I can probably help those of you who are ready for a progressive solution.

I have concluded that the mystery of the offshore financial world to the RA is primarily cultural and environmental, but it's rapidly changing. Negative press that perpetuates the attitude that going offshore is for tax cheats, criminals, money launderers and drug lords and is illegal per se certainly doesn't help. Negative portrayals of tax havens, such as in John Grisham's novel, *The Firm* don't help the image of the tax shelter either.[3] Yet, there are

---

[1] In some other tax literature you will encounter the abbreviation RA being used in reference to a resident alien.

[2] Abbreviations are listed in the Glossary, Appendix B.

[3] "You're an idiot, Tarrance. That money spent less than ten minutes in the Bahamas. You can't trust those corrupt fools down there." From *The Firm*, by attorney and author John Grisham.

thousands of honest, hardworking professionals managing more than US$5 trillion dollars in global funds in the world's international financial centres (IFCs) on a daily basis. Banking, asset and portfolio management, trustee and company management income derived from these services has far surpassed the income from tourism[4] in many countries that were formerly just vacation destinations. There is a race among tax havens to elevate their stature in the world financial community, to become characterized more as an international banking and financial centres, not just third-world tax havens.

Among the many questions asked of me during the mutual due diligence period where the prospective client and I evaluate each other (yes, it's a two-way street), is "How can I trust those people offshore? Are they going to run off with my money?" Or such blunt variations as "I trust you Arnie, but you're no kid, and what happens if something happens to you [read here: death, disability, dementia; I've been accused of this last by my spouse already, but it's only selective hearing] or Alzheimers (God forbid!)."

I am going to vet[5] you quite thoroughly since I don't want to be drawn into any unsavory or illegal scheme. Is there an undisclosed "smoking gun" in your future? Do you have an undisclosed hidden agenda? Life is too short to play tax evasion or frustrate-the-creditor games.

On the other hand, I have a different set of concerns in addition to protecting you; that is, protecting *me* as a service provider. I certainly would like to earn fees[6] for advising you, but planners engaged in asset protection and international estate planning for clients face unique risks of complicity and criminal

---

[4] Curiously, although the U.S. Virgin Islands is a tax haven to U.S. nonresident aliens (NRAs), that profit center has yet to be developed. Tourism, not international finances, was the source of a $1 billion income in 1995, providing employment to 85 percent of the total work force.

[5] Vetting is the process of qualifying prospective clients to determine if they are good candidates for asset protection and international estate planning.

[6] Some service providers are now quoting fees on a "value added" basis. In other words, how much did they save you with their tax and estate planning?

liability.[7] A professional planner or service provider then, will not (should not) assist an unqualified settlor. My offshore associates and I require letters of reference for you from your attorney and CPA (see Forms 1-A and 1-B and Form-2).

FORM 1-A: Letter of Reference–An Example

(*ON LAW FIRM LETTERHEAD*)

Dated

To Whom It May Concern:

I am an active member of the State Bar of California in good standing and a member of the federal bar in California. I am entitled to practice in all California courts as well as some federal courts in California.

NAME has requested that I write this letter for his confidential use. I have known *NAME* for _____ years, since 19_____. Our relationship has been [select one, *exclusively professional\ professional and social*].

I have found *NAME* to be of very high character, fair in his business dealings and I am not aware of any unconscionable conduct on his part. [*Please add any further comment that is complementary here.*]

I would be pleased to provide any further references upon written or telephonic request through *NAME* to maintain the privacy of this communication.

It is a pleasure to be able to assist *NAME* by providing this private letter of reference.

Sincerely yours,

[*signature of attorney*]

[*etc.*]

---

[7] ⬚ Under state laws and U.S. federal statutes, offshore financial planners and other professionals who may have inadvertently participated in "aiding and abetting" under 18 U.S.C. §2, have become part of a "conspiracy" and/or "conspiracy to defraud" under 18 U.S.C. §371, have made "false statements" under 18 U.S.C. §1001, may be participating in conduct characterized as "money laundering" under 18 U.S.C. §1956 & 1957, may be encouraging "bankruptcy fraud" under 18 U.S.C. §152, or "mail fraud" under 18 U.S.C. §1341, or be involved in the "obstruction of justice" under 18 U.S.C. §1503 and/or 1505 "predicated offenses" under 18 U.S.C. §1961, et seq. under the RICO racketeering statutes. Wow!

FORM 1-B: Letter of Reference–An Example

(ON LAW FIRM LETTERHEAD)

Date

CONFIDENTIAL

To Whom It May Concern:

    I have had the privilege of knowing *NAME* personally and professionally for over eight years. I have advised him as an individual and represented business with which he was affiliated. My personal experience with the man indicates that he is both capable and professional as well as of good moral character. I have the highest regard for Mr. *NAME*, and regardless of the endeavor, he would come with my personal recommendation. Should the need arise, I would be happy to discuss further and confidentially the specifics of my relationship with Mr. *NAME* upon which these observations are made.

Sincerely yours,
[*signature of attorney*]
[*etc.*]

FORM 1-2: Letter of Reference–An Example

(ON CPA FIRM LETTERHEAD)

Date

To Whom It May Concern:

    I am an active Certified Public Accountant in California and in good standing with all licensing and regulatory agencies.

    NAME has requested that I write this letter for his confidential use. I have known *NAME* for _____ years, since 19_____. Our relationship has been [select one, *exclusively professional\ professional and social*].

    I have found *NAME* to be of very high character, fair in his business dealings and I am not aware of any unconscionable conduct on his part. [Please add any further comment that is complementary here.]

    I would be pleased to provide any further references upon written or telephonic request through *NAME* to maintain the privacy of this communication.

    It is a pleasure to be able to assist *NAME* by providing this private letter of reference.

Sincerely yours,

[signature of CPA][*etc.*]

All this legalese aside, nothing can make a point as well on the issue of confidence in the offshore professionals, or get so deeply into your own heart, as when your daughter tells you the same thing. "Dad, I feel comfortable about it, except what is going to happen when you're not around any longer?"

Yet, somewhere around US$5 trillion dollars[8] (including countless billions from Americans) is professionally entrusted to offshore asset and portfolio managers, trustees, bankers, nominees, assets protectors, etc. Who really knows how much "flight capital"[9] is out there? These numbers are generally estimates from others that are perpetuated. I know of no agency that has an accurate means of keeping count.[10] The level of capital flight from the U.S. increases as a lack of confidence in government grows, as government grows without bounds, as the cost of government grows out of control, as the federal deficit grows without the ability of Washington to cap it. Flight is also precipitated further by greater concerns over invasion of personal privacy, as more and more powerful computers begin linking databases never accessible before. Where will it end?

Rampant litigation, outrageous jury awards and threats of confiscatory direct and indirect taxes continue. I am not a historian (just ask my high school teachers; I'm safe since they all are in that great high school in Heaven, looking down at me and still nodding) but some gems I recall are of interest.

The concept of trusts may have all started with the Egyptian Pharaohs, was refined in the early Greek or Roman days, also under Islamic law, and further developed in 1400s when the English Crown attempted to nationalize (confiscate for "taxes") land from their wealthy citizens. They cleverly responded by transferring it to the Church and renting it back for a peppercorn a year. Even the Crusaders did their "estate planning" (with trusts) before they left on their mission for the Church–or was it really the

---

[8] Assuming that the world's population is 5.75 billion people, then the average offshore assets in the world's tax havens would be $870 per *person*.

[9] See Appendix B for definitions of many terms in this book.

[10] I've been advised that the IMF keeps tabs of the money at the banks in the tax havens but have not been able to confirm such.

Crown? In more modern times, overly aggressive tax collection (Venezuela collects pots, pans or anything that can be carried off by the tax collector as a tax payment), political instability and war create "flight capital." Stronger currencies exacerbate the "flight to quality" currency. They say that flight capital from the U.S. is accelerating at a surprising rate (not to me). When the price of gold climbs, does the capital flow to the offshore trusts increase as well? And the phenomenal growth continues. American CPAs and tax lawyers have also attempted to stay legal (be tax compliant), protect their client's assets (and derrière) and stay one step ahead of Congress and the tax collector. The outflow of cash from the U.S. to offshore entities (Swiss annuities, business investments, etc.) is growing exponentially. The reasons are numerous, and this book attempts to address that issue, as well.

But this book is primarily an attempt to demystify offshore finance for the RA; to give you the self-confidence you need by expanding your working knowledge of creative international estate planning, mechanisms and the new offshore vocabulary for family wealth conservation. As a businessperson, you need to react to global opportunities or perish at the hands of your competition. Globalization is here now! You need to respond to worldwide opportunities and markets. As you go international, you will face a unique set of problems not encountered by onshore companies.

Another new vocabulary has arisen in the global business community. The following terms will become part of your lexicon: transfer pricing, advanced pricing agreements, branch profits, anti-conduit financing rules, earnings stripping, etc.

This book does not present the offshore bank as a panacea for all your offshore needs, because that simplistic solution doesn't work for most RAs. Nor is the offshore bank, the family limited partnership or the family protective trust a totally "bulletproof or boilerplate" solution. Each of you has a different agenda. There is no such thing as "one size fits all," a "cookie cutter" or a "mass production solution" or a "kit." If you accept that statement as a major premise, you have mastered Step One. I discourage you from utilizing a consultant that forces the square peg into the round whole.

Step Two is the realization and acceptance that going offshore may *not* be the solution for you. What are you trying to achieve by going offshore? A Nassau company formation acquaintance disclosed to me that about one half of the Bahamian companies formed are not around the second year. If it is not possible, not practical, not economically feasible, why go? If all your wealth is tied up as equity in U.S. real estate, your options are more limited. See the concept of "equity stripping" (Chapter 10) or exchanging the highly appreciated real property for an offshore "private annuity" (Chapter 9).

During the course of drafting this book, I reaffirmed that the steps for going offshore are not necessarily purely objective. Consequently, it could drive the objective part of your brain "crazy." It's not simply a matter of taxes or fears of being a potential litigation target. Accept that there is more than one correct plan for doing so. Exactly how you ultimately structure your offshore vehicle may vary from advisor to advisor.[11] Recognizing this element of subjectivity, my first disclaimer is in order. Yes, there are several ways of proceeding; they probably will all work, but one may be better for you. Let's hope this book helps you identify the "best" way or, at least, that after reading this book you will be able to ask the right questions. The only so-called "dumb" questions are those you don't ask. This book will help you formulate questions to ask your OS professional.

Also, this book is *not* a list and description of tax havens, offshore banks and professionals, sources for offshore credit cards, tax avoidance techniques, etc. However, I have alternatively identified many tax havens and provided a key point analysis for you as an educational exercise. A comprehensive look at the world's major tax havens would take a book in itself and other authors, Hoyt Barber,[12] Anthony Ginsberg[13] and Adam Starchild,[14]

---

[11] As an example, a Southern California lawyer who is active in the field of APTs and published a book on the topic uses the British Virgin Islands (BVI) for them. Since BVI does not have a "trust act," I wouldn't go there.

[12] Barber, Hoyt L., *Tax Havens*, 1993, McGraw-Hill, Inc.

[13] Ginsberg, Anthony S., *Tax Havens*, 1991, Simon & Schuster.
    🖥 http:www.butterworths.com.au.catalog/t0783.htm

[14] Starchild, Adam, Scope International Ltd., see Appendix C.

to name only three, have previously done a fine job on the topic of tax havens. Although somewhat dated, they remain fine reference books.

Halfway through the writing of this book I had misgivings of pretension. I must confess that I don't know everything about going offshore. However, my personal resolution was, since I probably knew more than you and had brilliant associates to guide me, I could teach you or at least guide you, if you let me.

This book comes with due apologies to other pundits in the field just in case I may have misstated something. Please send me a note and I'll remedy the problem in time for future revisions–this project is intended to be an evolving, ongoing process with an update service (use the sign-up form at the end of the book).

Communication to me by e-mail would be preferred, to: offshore@bahamas.net.bs or via "snail-mail" to PO Box CB 13039, Nassau, Bahamas CB 13039. Thanks.

To further assist those of you who are computer literate (or want to be) and can "surf" the Internet, I've included some relevant World Wide Web (WWW) sites and marked them with the symbol ⌨ throughout the book. I also refer you to Appendix A for a more comprehensive listing of "CyberShore™" sites. A caution is in order: Although the Web sites were confirmed at the time of drafting this book, they seem to change often. If the Universal Resource Locator (URL) address is no longer current, you should do a Savvy Search, Yahoo or Lycos Web search. (See Appendix D for their URL addresses, as well as other WWW "search engines.") The world is going high-tech, and if you still think that Java™[15] is only coffee, you'd best get on-line!

For you "hands-on" paralegals who want to know everything, I have taken some of the legal terms and tax issues unique or applicable to the offshore lexicon and attempted to define them in everyday English for you. These items are marked with the symbol ▣.

⌨ http:www.au.com/offshore/books/

[15] A computer language utilized on the Internet which can be used to download programs off of the Net as required. Java can be embedded into the computer operating system. Java is a ™ of Sun MicroSystems, Inc.

Occasionally, attributes that, in my subjective opinion I believe are favorable, are identified as such with a plus sign (+). Conversely, negative attributes are marked with a minus sign (-). For example: long statute of limitations (-). Complex issues such as double taxation under multinational tax treaties, although accepted as a reality of life, must be ignored in this book because of their complexities as well as limitations of space and personal knowledge. The subject of the formation of an offshore mutual or hedge fund is also beyond the scope of this book.

I may have been overly ambitious in this book. For the first time, to my knowledge, an author has attempted to integrate the trilogy of international estate planning, financial planning and asset protection into one book and as *one subject, "Offshore Economics," which it rightfully should be.* Most prior authors have treated each of these three subjects in a partial vacuum. I trust I have not disappointed you in this first-time effort.

Simpler issues, such as how to legally outmaneuver the tax authorities euphemistically called loopholes are addressed. All tax issues are indeed very important, but since they would require a more in-depth tax analysis and explanation than is appropriate in this primer, I deem their complexity beyond its scope. After all, I'm the author and I have license to say so. Perhaps that will be the topic for my next book . . .

Arnie, an *Un*reluctant American
May 1996
Completed in Lake Tahoe, Nassau, and "Provo,"[16] Caicos

---

[16] The "belongers" (similar to a Kamaaina in Hawaii, a difficult status to acquire) name for Providenciales, Caicos Island.

1
An Introduction to the Reluctant American

Terminology

Let us discuss terminology at the onset. I could use the terms foreign, offshore, transnational, global, international, transworld, multinational, and so on in this book, and I do. I'm not yet ready for the "global village." My preference is the modern term offshore and believe that it is the word being generally utilized by the global community. I will even use the abbreviation OS from time to time. Offshore is an international term meaning not only out of your country (jurisdiction) but possibly out of the tax reach of your country of residence or citizenship. The term foreign carries confusion and I prefer avoiding it except in Chapter 11 where it is appropriate in the U.S. taxing and IRS reporting scenario.

For example, a Delaware corporation operating in California is characterized by the State of California as a *foreign corporation* doing business in California. The Internal Revenue Service (IRS) uses a number of tests to label a trust as a *foreign trust*. Three of the tests are:

1. Geographical. A trust not having a U.S. situs (country of domicile or country whose laws govern the trust as a foreign trust (See Chapter 11).
2. Residence of the trustee.

3.   Location of the trust's assets.

All the IRS forms (see Chapter 11) for reporting transfers offshore, parties to an offshore trust or offshore ownership of corporations are couched in terms of "foreign" trusts, beneficiaries of "foreign" trust, and so on. The terminology is inconsistent. What you say and the terms you use depend upon whom you are speaking with and the subject at hand. I will attempt to use the word foreign when referring to IRS tax forms and U.S. taxes for consistency with the Internal Revenue Code.

Further compounding the terminology problem is the U.S. mutual fund industry's use of the terms global fund and international fund. A global fund is defined as a fund that invests in the U.S. and offshore, while an international fund only invests offshore.

Ironically, OS doesn't necessarily mean some island jurisdiction. Austria, Liechtenstein,[17] Ireland,[18] Monaco, the U.S., Switzerland, Luxembourg, the Netherlands, Gibraltar and Andorra, to name a few, are considered to be offshore and to be tax havens by some. It depends on who you are, where you reside, your citizenship, your source of income and your objectives. It further depends upon favorable tax treatment under double tax treaties.

The IRS has labeled approximately 30 jurisdictions as being used to reduce tax liabilities and restructure income. They are low by at least 50 percent in that there are more than 60 tax havens, all competing for your OS business. In addition to the more commonly known or high-profile tax havens, the IRS includes Bahrain, Grenada, Nauru, the Turks and Caicos Islands (TCI) and Vanuatu.

---

[17] On a per capita basis, Liechtenstein is one of the world's richest countries.
[18] Ireland is unique in that it is the only EC country that, as an incentive for tax haven business, offers tax free benefits to nonresident companies. It also offers you citizenship if you have an Irish grandparent.

Are *You* a Reluctant American?

You are an RA if one or more of the following items apply to you:

1.   You believe that only tax cheats and criminals need to place some of their estate offshore for privacy and financial peace of mind. Estate as used here encompasses your assets; that is, your wealth. You don't have to be very wealthy–or dead–to have an estate.

2.   You have used the same domestic (U.S.) attorney and Certified Public Accountant (CPA) for 20 years and you won't go to the bathroom without calling him or her first. This book encourages regaining (reclaiming) your financial privacy. You need to practice what I have defined as "professional diversity." This book also encourages another new concept for achieving privacy, which I have labeled as "geographic diversity." It's very likely that your existing professionals are very competent in what they have done for you to date, but most are fearful of sending you offshore and are probably not honest enough to tell you so. They most likely know little of dealing with business matters on an international scale. They too are worried about malpractice lawsuits against them and their philosophy is to discourage what they don't fully understand to avoid potential liability rather than to encourage exploration and open themselves up to the risks of personal litigation. They may be very comfortable professionally and not wish to take on a new and very complex topic, namely asset protection using offshore vehicles.

      The initial planning, strategizing, structuring, integration with estate and financial planning and creative methodology are at the heart of asset protection and the most difficult phase by far. The easy part is putting the structure in place.

      Presently, there is no current professional obligation upon an estate planner or other professional to encourage the esoteric area of asset protection strategies. I predict that it will change! However, the more "modern" attorney, offshore consultant, service provider and CPA is thinking offshore as a further integrated estate planning and asset protection (AP) tool and not as an independent technique in a vacuum. They have added the terms APT and the IBC to their everyday vocabulary (more on these terms below). Financial greed may also preclude your current professional from sending you offshore where they will lose control over some of your financial matters and perhaps eventually lose even you as their client.

3.   You can't trust anyone offshore with your money. How many U.S. banks appear on the list of the largest 20 banks in the world? Few. Some offshore banks have higher reserves than U.S. banks. Very professional, proud, and honest people are working in the offshore community. They are also at your service. How do we get into your "circle of confidence?"

4.   You need to have your every asset in your own name and be the "king of the mountain." You are a "control freak."

5.   You can't enjoy the beneficial use of a French Chalet or a Lexus without actually being on title and owning it.

6.   You're going to take it all with you when you die.

7.   You don't think we live in a "sue crazy" society where groundless suits are filed or you don't believe that *you* are at some risk of litigation (the "ostrich syndrome") and of an unpredictable judgment for damages against you. You don't believe that the complexity of our legal system (overwhelming regulations and litigation) and taxing structure don't hold you hostage to the legal profession, CPAs and the IRS.

You are no longer an RA–you have arrived at the next level of learning and awareness–when:

1.   You can practice living low profile. You don't need to brag about your offshore assets at cocktails parties. (You can

also sleep well and not worry about it.) You can discretely and legally conceal part of your wealth offshore, away from prying eyes, potential litigants and computer data bases. You can't conceal it *all,* since that would constitute a fraud against your future creditors or claimants.

2.   You are comfortable with professional and geographic diversity for your wealth conservation and management. You accept that law-abiding people go offshore with some (not all) of their wealth.

3.   You accept that there are other stock exchanges offshore providing excellent investment opportunities not afforded to U.S. persons. (See Appendix E.)

4.   You fantasize about spending some of your retirement[19] time in a Caribbean condo or in Monaco and having your grandchildren visit you there.

5.   You're tired of the slow erosion of your personal privacy and you want to do something about it.

6.   You recognize that it is not only the other person who gets sued, that litigation is rampant and it is not going to get better under the present U.S. legal system. With a surplus of imaginative attorneys creating new theories of liability, you want to plan ahead for that contingency. This is especially important if you are in a high-risk profession and have the

---

[19] ⌨ Offshore retirees face an unusually heavy tax burden if wanting to remain active in the U.S. voting process. You can't vote unless you are a "resident" of some state. You then subject yourself to the laws of that state.

potential problem of being uninsured or *under*-insured against a "runaway"[20] jury verdict.

7.   You accept that there is a *new trilogy*. You must consider estate planning, financial planning *and* asset protection and not operate in vacuum where one element is missing.

8.   You can intelligently discuss the subjects of offshore incorporation (IBC), use of nominees, departure tax or expatriation planning, global estate planning, asset protection trusts (APT), wealth preservation and conservation, and asset and portfolio management services.

9.   You, like most Americans find the income tax system unfair and incomprehensible; it is Byzantine. You believe that the IRS is "out of control." You are aware of the differences among the terms tax avoidance, tax evasion and the cute term, betwixt the two, tax "avaison." You know that the IRS has a Tax Haven department (see Figure 1-1) and monitors tax haven activities, but you are in compliance and can sleep nights. You know where the fuzzy line is between tax avoidance and tax evasion and tread carefully. (I suspect that the IRS purchases all the books on going offshore, too! I got a call one day from an IRS purchasing agent to buy our books and she even wanted to put the purchase on the IRS's credit card.)

10.   You are not a control freak and do not need to make every decision personally. *If you are, no one can help you!*

---

[20] 📖 During early 1996, a weakened tort reform bill was passing through the Congressional process. The Senate resisted major tort reform that would have provided long overdue, sweeping reform to the nation's tort litigation system. The needed overhaul failed. What remained was a cap on punitive damages for egregious conduct of $250,000, or two to three times the actual damage award, whichever is greater.

FIGURE 1-1: Receipt Stamp: IRS Tax Haven Office

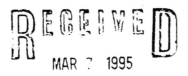

MAR 7 1995

TAX HAVEN EG1312
SAN JOSE, DISTRICT
INTERNAL REVENUE SERVICE

11.   You recognize that through knowledge you acquire power. What you learn from this book by keeping an open mind may change your life forever!

12.   You feel insecure that the U.S. national debt is five trillion dollars, give or take a few billion (who seems to care in Washington, DC?), and this domestic monetary crisis makes you hedge your personal finances.

13.   You will become more computer literate and harness the vast offshore resources available on the Internet. Just sample some of the 💻 sites identified in this book and you certainly will concur that it was well worth the time and financial investment to get on line.

14.   You recognize that there is a litigation explosion and finally, that *even you can be a potential target.*

2
Getting Started: Recognizing and Overcoming Your Concerns

There is more to going offshore than the act of merely opening up a private and personal offshore bank account or forming an offshore corporation. That's no big deal! Open a copy of *The Economist* and read all the advertisements from offshore banks wanting your money and company formation firms offering to create an instant international business company (IBC) or exempt company for you. The big deal is that it should all be part of a bigger plan, a total structure that won't be obsolete in a few years and can accommodate the inevitable changes occurring in your personal life (divorce, marriage of children, birth of grandchildren, etc.) and your global business needs. One Bahamian company formation service advises me that after the first year, one half of the new corporations formed there by his company are dormant or abandoned.

• A Chinese philosopher[21] once said that "A journey of 1,000 miles must begin with the single step." The first step is to identify your concerns.

• What do you do? You can more easily find out what to do than how to do it. You need to "buy" those "how to" services from a qualified professional for your peace of mind.

---

[21] Lao-tzu, 640-531 B.C.E.

- Who do you use for the different roles—the trustee, the nominee, the asset manager, the trust protector?
- How well do you trust them?
- Where do you go? What's the difference between a tax haven and an international banking centre (IBC)?
- What are the costs? How much to set it up and sustain it in subsequent years?
- Who will provide the international formation and annual services?
- What type of banking services are required; i.e., public vs. private banking?
- What type of flexibility is needed when establishing and administering the trust?

If you've started and are already offshore, ask yourself the following questions:

- Why did you go offshore?
- Is it legal?
- Is it the best structure for you for what you need and will need to accomplish in the future?
- What do you do? How do you "fix" what is already in place offshore if it is "broken"—i.e., it is not the best structure for you.

The Structures

I use my own planning terminology in this book. I might state that the final "operating structure" is composed of individual "entities" or "boxes." For example, the first entity (box one) is owned by box two and box two flows into box three, that is, a three box or three entity structure.

Every entity has its place. The structure could flow from onshore to offshore and back again using boxes or entities that can be one or more of the following:

- The international business company (IBC) or an exempt company, a company incorporated within a tax haven but not authorized to do business within the country of incorporation. The IBC or exempt company is intended for global operations.
- The asset protection trust (APT).
- The family protective trust, same as the APT.
- The family settlement trust, same as the APT.
- The private bank (not for general public banking).
- The traditional annuity.
- The annuity variation entitled the private annuity.
- The private family or charitable foundation.
- The captive insurance company.
- The limited duration or life company.
- The company limited by guaranty, the guaranty/hybrid company.
- The real estate family limited partnership (FLP), a variation of the limited partnership (LP) for providing asset protection for the "crown jewel"[22] real property asset.
- The offshore mutual or hedge fund.
- The limited liability company (LLC).
- The Nevada corporation with bearer shares.
- Time share resorts.
- The unincorporated business organization (UBO or BO). Don't use it! A company treated for tax purposes as a trust. Neither fish nor fowl.
- The business trust organization (BTO), the pure trust, or the so-called Massachusetts Trust; not recommended by your author.
- The common law or pure trust as a tax avoidance strategy; not recommended by this author.

---

[22] A crown jewel is generally an office building, shopping center or apartment house with highly appreciated value. It generally doesn't include the family residence because it is not business oriented.

The Participants

Continuing on with our definitions, the role of the *offshore trustee* remains the same as that of his or her traditional onshore counterpart. However, the use of *nominees* is not a traditional U.S. mechanism. Offshore nominees are utilized as shareholders and/or directors and/or officers of an IBC for the ultimate in privacy. *Caveat: If nominees own and control an IBC, it's not yours.*

The role of *trust protector* is unfamiliar to most Americans. In simple terms, the protector is the watchdog of the trustee and the trust assets. It could be a company, committee or an individual. The risk of using an individual in this function is that upon the disability or death of that individual, the trust is without a protector. I would strongly suggest that you not create an APT or a FPT without including a trust protector. Depending upon the *trust deed* (the trust agreement), various powers are given to the protector. The protector may legally discharge the trustee, replace the trustee, and veto the proposed actions of the trustee. When in doubt, the trustee seeks the consent of the protector. When an action that is not in the normal course of trust business is required of the trustee, the trustee will seek the concurrence of the protector. A very powerful role indeed! The protector should not be given excessive powers such that it may be considered as a co-trustee and may even be a U.S. person. Some writers believe that using a U.S. person as a protector is dangerous since the U.S. courts can exert much more influence over a U.S. person.

The *asset* or *portfolio manager* has a traditional role. He or she is appointed by a written contract with the IBC or the APT. It can be a fully discretionary account, or limitations can be imposed by the contract under the terms of the APT or by the officers of the IBC. Fees to the asset manager can be based on performance achieved or on a percentage of the valuation of the estate under his or her management. However, asset management can be obtained from quality offshore brokerage houses, which only charge the traditional brokerage fees and perhaps a small percentage of the portfolio as a discretionary management fee.

The OS trustee is usually an individual or small trust company licensed and regulated by the tax haven. This is directly contrary to the domestic U.S. concept of using a commercial trust company such as the trust department of a bank. There is no difficulty in securing a high-quality, professional individual to act as the trustee for the OS trust, but this person will not assume the liability for U.S. IRC compliance and will hire an expert familiar with U.S. tax filing requirement.

The Question of Trust

Mistrust is probably the biggest deal killer for most RAs. *If you can't trust your offshore professionals, nothing can help you!* I am not a salesman trying to talk you into going offshore. My agenda is to raise your comfort level with the concept of going offshore so that you at least reach a point where you will allow yourself to trust offshore professionals; to heed their counsel and follow their advice.

Your trust and level of confidence is raised by a combination of the following factors:

1.   Selecting offshore professionals is not a matter of picking out a name in the yellow pages of the Isle of Man telephone directory, as you customarily select onshore services. They are there, though in fact, so many are listed, you'd be overwhelmed at first, but the phonebook does provide some guidance. I usually "borrow" one from each country I visit.

2.   You may initially rely on a referral from a U.S. consultant, but true comfort comes with time. Taking small steps and gradually building upon them as your acceptance level increases.

3.   You could act on your visceral feelings after listening to a speaker at a seminar.

4.   Traditional standards of due diligence still exist.

5.   Go to the offshore consultant who is an established expert or writes a notable newsletter (one in which you can believe and find comfort) for advice. If the consultant is not concerned about putting his or her advice in writing for the whole world (and the IRS) to see, it should be credible.

6.   Stay away from the promoter who offers a flat price of "X" dollars for running you off to an island in the South Pacific regardless of your personal and special needs. One size never did and never will suit all. You are all like distinctive snowflakes with your unique facets of life.

7.   Stay away from the promoter who promises exorbitant OS returns on your money. Don't lose sight of the fact that high returns come from higher financial risks or even scams. You don't have time to earn it back again! There is no magic about going OS that will earn you the highest rate of return with low risk. Retain your guidelines and conservatism.

8.   Don't abandon those traditional safeguards and standards of selecting domestic professionals. Don't compromise. If you don't like them, don't use them no matter what you have been told by others. Prepare for a long-term relationship. Prepare too for the possibility of your second generation working with a second generation of offshore (OS) consultants. Consider what happens if you become disabled or when you are deceased. Could your spouse or significant other (or am I politically incorrect and should I be using the term "life partner?") work well with the offshore consultant? I encourage, as an absolute minimum, the dinner meeting with the reluctant spouse who doesn't care to get involved in financial matters so that there is at least a modicum of communication, a social relationship in effect and some agreement with respect to the final offshore decisions.

In many cases spouses are unaware of what is happening financially in a family partnership. This leaves the tremendous burden of educating the survivor to the OS consultant–clearly, not a role we relish. If your spouse truly doesn't have an aptitude for investment management, then at least, if possible, share your plans with a financially astute child. Doing so will give you the comfort of knowing that the financial dynasty will continue in the event of disability or death.

The Costs of Setting Up an Offshore Structure

I see OS APTs for sale from Belize[23], Central America, for only $200.00. Here, like anywhere else, you really can't get more than you pay for.[24] A no-frills Bahamian IBC can cost as little as $875. But what do you have after you purchase it? Be honest with yourself. You very likely have no basis of reference to evaluate the quality of the product being offered to you. You can't just buy OS products in a vacuum. I repeatedly tell my clients that you should never buy OS products at "sale" prices. (For further details, see Chapter 7.)

For a trade-off study and a fully up-and-running, turn-key structure consisting of an APT and IBCs, with all the bells and whistles, all nominees in place, bank account, brokerage account, and so on you will pay between $15,000 to $25,000. If your gut reaction to the above numbers is alarm, then going offshore may not be economically feasible for the size of your estate (your net wealth), or you have a false sense of the *value added* phenomena and the costs of going OS the correct way. You are purchasing the expertise that goes into creating a legal, tax compliant and functional offshore structure. Besides, the U.S. dollar is still way down in value worldwide with respect to most major world currencies and doesn't buy as much as it used to. Have you traveled to Europe lately? I use the "Snickers Test" and surprisingly, it works. When a candy bar sells for 50 cents at full price in the U.S. and for 85 cents in Nassau, the "RA cost of living

---

[23] The former British Honduras, though neither very British or Honduran.

[24] My Dad used to tell me that he could get a "good deal" for those who might believe that oat feed is expensive if they didn't mind if it went through the horse first.

index" tells me that it is 70 percent more expensive for food in the Bahamas. Easy to do. U.S. candy bars are popular and for sale worldwide, even in Moscow.

The OS structure could be done in phases. It may not be necessary to put it all in place the first year. This would then defer some of your set-up costs but may subject you to some unnecessary risks. *Staging is not generally recommended unless absolutely necessary.*

Also, get a handle on the second year costs, or subsequent years' costs. Your OS consultant should be able to give you an estimate of these costs within 10 percent.

International Services, Set-up and Servicing

The U.S. is characterized as the most litigious[25, 26] society in the world. Frightening, isn't it? Since this is not a misconception, it has spawned an entirely new defensive industry–the so called "asset protection" specialty.

Numerous professionals and companies, onshore and offshore, are all competing to set-up your structures. Offshore operations are a source of both initial revenue and continuing revenue from ongoing annual fees. A word of caution is in order: Once company nominees are put in place, it is extremely difficult, when compared to the U.S. legal system, to replace them. Registered agents and nominees don't readily want to relinquish their roles and future income, but with perseverance, they will eventually and reluctantly do so.

---

[25] If you doubt this statement, can you advise me why the City and County of Los Angeles have more judges than the entire nation of France?

[26] Two companies in the U.S. *buy* a portion of a winning judgment obtained from a lawsuit, but at a deep discount. San Francisco's Judgment Purchase Corporation (Judgment) operates in four East Coast states, as well. Judgment may pay only $100,000 for a $250,000 piece of a million-dollar judgment. If the judgment survives on appeal, Judgment has a windfall of $150,000. Judgment has the possible affect upon the legal system of financially supporting the appellate process and prolonging litigation as opposed to a settlement being reached during the appellate waiting period.

Don't confuse the substitution of nominees in the IBC with the absolute right in a trust indenture to discharge the trustee, even without cause. You need to clearly distinguish between the attributes of the exempt company (IBC) and the trust (APT).

3
Why Go Offshore?

"The dog with a bone is always in danger."
Old African proverb

We all have different agendas, we think. Yet, if you would or could speak confidentially with others who are similarly situated, you would find much commonality in the considerations for going OS as well as in the concerns that precipitate such thinking. Simply speaking, it is more difficult for a creditor to access offshore assets. In an offshore court of a tax haven, the judges generally grant lesser (or no) punitive damages than is the case in the U.S. Let's initially discuss why you *don't* want to go offshore.

Reasons to Stay Onshore

• The U.S. government insures your funds on deposit with U.S. banks. There is no equivalent of America's FDIC or FSLIC banking protection[27] anywhere else in the world. If an offshore bank account is represented by the bank as being "insured," it is with a private insurer. Your protection is only as good as the financial reserves of the insurer. On the positive side, consider that in many international financial centres (IFCs), banking regulators require higher bank reserves than are required in the U.S. This makes for a "safe" haven as well as a tax haven.

---

[27] Some people believe that the FDIC and FSLIC insurance encourages banks to take higher risk investments. This reduces reserves and causes excessive disintermediation. This in turn puts more pressure on bankers to offer depositors higher yields and assume higher risks.

• U.S. stock brokerage accounts are insured by the Securities Industry Protection Corporation (SIPC), an agency of the federal government, against losses (for example, your broker running off with your money). Many brokerage houses supplement this with private insurance.

• Many offshore people consider the U.S. (i.e., Nevada, Delaware, Wyoming, Utah) to be "their" tax and safe havens.

• The U.S. is the most politically stable country in the world with only two major political parties, regular elections and with a safe and currently financially sound and insured banking system.

• The maximum income tax rate in the U.S. is lower than in many other industrialized countries.

• The rate of inflation is relatively low.

• Your estate planning and financial planning can often be met by "onshore" planning. There is a "surplus" of *on*shore planners.

• There are no express exchange controls in the U.S.–though many indirect controls and disclosure requirements are imposed– permitting you to wire transfer any amount of funds offshore. The privacy of such wire transactions is an issue addressed elsewhere in this book.

• U.S. currency remains strong and freely convertible to other world currencies, and the "Ben Franklin" is the unofficial currency for most of the world.[28] More $100 bills circulate outside the U.S. than inside, by a ratio of about two to one.

Reasons to Go Offshore

At this point you might ask, "If the U.S. is so good, why go offshore?" The answers are in this book, and I believe that is your principal reason for reading it.

---

[28] The C-note is the de facto currency of Russia. It is estimated that $16 billion worth of $100 bills circulated in Russia in preference to the ruble (or is it rubble?). Russia had ruble recalls in 1991 and 1993 with very short exchange periods. The U.S. currency has never been devalued or recalled since its inception in 1861.

There is a myth perpetuated by the press and the IRS that people only go offshore for illegal purposes or to hide something. Wrong!

To try to identify all your individual concerns and the reasons why you should want to go offshore with some of your assets would be almost impossible. However, we can identify some of the major factors. Some may appear redundant, but this list was created in an attempt to encompass as many common concerns as possible.

- A quest and hunger for renewed personal privacy and confidentiality. With faster, higher speed computers tying together more and more databases, there will ultimately be no financial (or personal) privacy left in the U.S.
- Concerns for financial security for you and your entire, extended family for your lifetimes, and perhaps for your financial dynasty.
- Fear of the future. Is the Environmental Protection Agency going to charge you for removing contaminated soil on that parcel you sold in 1990 at a clean-up cost of $1,000,000?
- Rampant litigation, vexatious litigants, predator plaintiffs and attorneys and runaway jury verdicts in the U.S. Are you the next victim?
- Concerns with the U.S. Government. Is the U.S. going bankrupt? Is it there already? What will be the long-term effects upon you (increased taxes, etc.) to balance the budget in 7 to 10 years and "eventually" clear up "our children and our grandchildren's" deficit?
- Fears with respect to the U.S. banking system as bank after bank is swallowed up in megamergers.
- Hidden and confiscatory taxes; crippling, oppressive and costly governmental regulations; and red-tape from mediocre bureaucrats.
- The possibility of divorce and related problems or the expenses of a prolonged separation. Protection from the conduct of an imprudent spouse.

- Potential business failure, insolvency or bankruptcy.
- Anticipation of debilitating illness and its financial drain.
- Provisions for your retirement.
- Providing for your spouse and progeny during your lifetime and after your death.
- Providing for a disabled spouse or child, an insolvent child with poor money management skills, a relative, friend, or such after your death.
- Protection of a lump-sum disability award (personal injury, workman's compensation, no-fault settlement, etc.) against future claims by creditors.

Certain interests don't want to see your assets go offshore:

- Your friendly banker and, in general, the American banking system. As the level of flight capital grows, the corollary is true: There are fewer dollars in the U.S. banking system. A staggering two-thirds of the $100 bills in commerce circulate offshore! Banks make money on the arbitrage between what they pay you for the use of your money and what they charge others to rent money. They also make money by providing banking and financial services and transactions. As money flows offshore, logically, the U.S. banks[29] will be making less money.
- Your onshore professionals, who know little or nothing about going offshore, will discourage you to protect themselves and to retain you as a client.
- The Internal Revenue Service. As funds legally flow offshore, the IRS loses its ability to monitor and audit the day-to-day activities of people who are wrongfully perceived to be evading taxes by the mere act of going offshore.
- Credit reporting bureaus, databases and credit card issuers. There is also money to be earned by selling demographics; your credit report and buying habits are marketable assets. As more and

---

[29] With the U.S. banking merger and acquisition mania, U.S. banks are among the *most* profitable in the world.

more transactions go offshore, the database on you becomes less accurate and complete. You have beaten "Big Brother"–the system doesn't know *all* about you.

• Plaintiff's counsel. To sue or not to sue you, that is their question. It has got to be worth their while. The best way to determine if you are the next victim is to run an asset search on yourself to determine if you're worth suing. If your assets are not in your name, you could discourage litigation against you. If the assets are not in your name *and* also offshore, those assets could also not be subject to being sold to satisfy a runaway jury verdict and judgment against you.

• Law enforcement officials who abuse the forfeiture laws to generate "funding" for their agencies. When your assets aren't in the U.S., they aren't available to seize.

In short, onshore assets and investing is not the only game in town.

4
Where and How
Do I Place My Assets?

"Sunny climes are for shady people."
F. Scott Fitzgerald, in Tender Is the Night,
in reference to Monaco.

The offshore location you select is called the situs, the tax haven, the jurisdiction, the venue or the international financial or banking centre (IFC) throughout this book. Herein, all these terms mean essentially the same thing. However, IFC is certainly more prestigious a term for a situs than a tax haven in a "third-world" country.

The title of this chapter poses two of the four most frequently asked questions:

1.   How do I trust the offshore service providers?

2.   Where is the best location for my offshore assets and business operations?

3.   What if something happens to my trusted service provider?

4.   How do I retrieve offshore assets if I need them?

Answering questions 1 and 3 is one of the missions of this book. Answering question 2 takes a whole chapter (Chapter 4), but I have developed a checklist of factors to consider in selecting the right tax haven for you, just to get you started, below. Question 4 is your "final exam."

There is no best reply as to where to go because that depends upon the client's needs. Is it for personal reasons, or business reasons or both? Is it for a trust and/or an IBC? For creating and managing an offshore mutual fund you should go elsewhere and split the two functions between two jurisdictions.

I recently attended a program on asset protection planning presented by the California Continuing Education of the Bar. A speaker identified six preferred jurisdictions: the Cook Islands, the Cayman Islands, the Bahamas, the Turks and Caicos Islands, Gibraltar and Cyprus. It really depends upon what you're trying to achieve. Some are great for an IBC; others are better for APTs.

Guidelines for Evaluating Offshore Options

Here is my set of situs evaluation yardsticks, presented in no special order of priority.

1.   General reputation or quality of the tax haven.
Choose a haven that has a high reputation worldwide for providing quality international financial services (see the author's subjective ratings below). Some countries had successful economies before the U.S. was formed. Look for well regulated local institutions and professionals and sufficient safeguards to monitor the quality of banking services and professionals. Further, choose a country that provides business friendly legislation and which has been a haven for many years, not a "Newbie" to the field. Select a haven in which only "white" money and "clean" business is encouraged, where banks operate under strict rules. You might find yourself stigmatized on account of the situs you have chosen.

Because the level of flight capital is increasing worldwide, not just from the U.S., but from Hong Kong, Canada and the states of the former Soviet Union, to name a few, offshore business has become very competitive. New tax havens are springing up like mushrooms after the rain. How many of you ever heard of the following jurisdictions, let alone tried to find them in a world atlas without an index–Vanuatu, Niue (see below), Cook Islands, Nevis and St. Kitts, (see Chapter 10),

Anguilla and Aruba? They all compete with each other for the economic gains from your money going into their tax havens. As businesspeople, the local politicians appreciate how your money can improve their banking industry, their GNP, their economy and their employment opportunities for their local people. Good jobs keep their brightest young people home rather than relocating to another tax haven seeking employment opportunities. And conversely, better jurisdictions attract better professionals from other jurisdictions.

2.   ⌘ Choice of governing law.
I prefer tax havens that utilize a legal system based upon British common law, precedents and the doctrine of equity as the basis for their legal system. It is called the Westminister Model. I find it preferable to countries that alternatively use statutory adaptations—a highly codified body of civil laws—such as Liechtenstein and the French Territories. These, I admit, are subjective criteria. It is your comfort level that needs to be satisfied.

3.   Principal language.
My personal preference is that English speaking Americans who can't converse at a highly sophisticated and technical level in another tongue remain in the English speaking jurisdictions. I can be swayed, though, under the right circumstances. Can you read legal documents drafted in another language?[30] If not, stay in the English speaking havens; there are many high-quality jurisdictions to choose from. If you speak fluent Spanish, you

---

[30] ⌨ English has evolved as the de facto language of the Internet. The full potential of the Internet for use by the RA will not be realized until this language barrier is overcome. Picture this, if you will, and it is real. By the time you read this book, you may be able to communicate in French, Spanish, German or Italian using technology called Barcelona. It is an on-the-fly language translator that converts written documents into another language. A company named Globalink is developing the technology and teaming up with that stock market star performer Netscape. Barcelona will become a global e-mail language translator platform. Dare I say that soon it won't matter what principal language in which you write, it all will be in English to you?

could use Costa Rica, Panama or the Canary Islands. Otherwise, don't add to the complexity of your education and decision-making process by considering a situs where language is an impediment to your achieving your offshore goals. If Dutch is your language, try the Netherlands Antilles, Curaçao ("Island of Business") or Aruba (where Papiamento is also spoken).

4.   Use an independent country or a very stable dependent territory .
There are conflicting views on this subject.

  a. Select a jurisdiction that is an independent country and cannot be pressured by its parent jurisdiction to comply with an offshore court order. Don't select one that will be required by the parent country to implement laws that are unfavorable to the settlor (although I find this unlikely because of the fierce competition among the tax havens for flight capital and a hunger for the ability to provide very profitable banking services).

  b. Others prefer the protection afforded by the Queen; they feel the "British Colours" provide stability to the country. For example, the Cayman Islands and the Turks and Caicos Islands have their military defense guaranteed by the Crown (+) and their banking systems are subject to review and audit by the Bank of England (+), making them much stronger than Antigua.

5.   Seek excellent, high-quality communications.
Nothing can be as frustrating as working late to send an e-mail message to Costa Rica before you leave for home and find out the next morning that it bounced back because of an Internet server being unable to connect or being timed-out. Or getting a fax from the Cook Islands with its most important copy garbled from noise on the line (Figure 4-1 is an example of a fax transmission with two garbled lines).

  Communications problems such as these can cause a full business day delay. One could always telephone but there are times when it is incumbent that the terms or conditions be in writing and unequivocal. What price for quality communications? This is not the place to skimp on costs.

FIGURE 4-1: Garbled Fax Transmission

FAX LETTER

DATE: January 16, 1996

 TO: Arnie Cornez

FROM:

SUBJECT: Your instructions dated January 10, 1996

    1. Fax to
sent these faxes ╭   Will that be OK? Also for the
fax advising

    2.d. I can wire   so I can
keep the number reasonably round. I am proceeding on this assumption.

➤   3. Global Group bank account. Barclays has a new Interbien form
to be completed when
of the business,   of the transactions
and the annual volume.
"offshore investment and tax consulting"; the purpose of the account is
"to collect fees" but you'll have to help me out with the last two. ◀

    5.
                         is you typed.

    I guess that's it for now. Looking forward to seeing you in
February.   Awaiting your reply.

                         Regards,

Always go with first-class, high-quality equipment and long-distance telecommunications service providers.

You will need varied forms of telecommunications to transact your worldwide business offshore, including the following:

a. Voice communications by telephone. If you feel compelled to use a "roam" phone, use high-quality, 900 MHz, digital phone. The cheaper analog phones operate at 46/49 MHz and are very noisy. They can easily be monitored with inexpensive equipment; like the old party lines; they are not secure. The 900 MHz units, being digitized, are not easy to snoop upon. If you are willing to pay around $1,800 per phone you can get high-quality voice encryption from Cylink or Motorola.

b. Facsimile (fax) communications. Always use the fine mode to assure higher quality reception. Although it seems like it will be more expensive, in the long run it will save you money and time. Cylink also offers a fax encrypter.

    c. Modem-to-modem data transmission. Don't push the curve–offshore lines are of poorer quality than you can expect in the States. Even though you may have just installed this red-hot, 28.8 Kbps modem or you now have an ISDN connection, run at 9,600 and you'll be happier with your connections. Cylink offers a data encrypter of bank communications quality and security.

    d. Internet communication, including e-mail, encrypted e-mail using Pretty Good Privacy™ (PGP) (see Chapter 12 and Appendix A) and the new voice communications over the World Wide Web (WWW or Web). PGP is omnipotent in the Internet and has become the de facto standard for private, secure e-mail communications. If you are computer savvy, you can download (using file transfer protocol, or FTP) PGP off of the WWW. If you're not, you need a relatively user friendly PGP program; one is commercially available (in the U.S. and Canada only) from ViaCrypt, Phoenix, Arizona; phone, (602) 944-0773; fax, (602) 943-2601; e-mail, info@viacrypt.com; and 💻 http:www.viacrypt.com for Windows and the Mac. They also have the reputation of providing excellent product support for their commercial customers.

    e. Voice scramblers and encryption. Voice scramblers provide some degree of privacy against eavesdroppers and hackers but not at the same level obtained by full encryption. Don't confuse a voice scrambler with encryption–encryption is much better. High-quality, very secure, full encryption devices for voice, fax and data are available from many suppliers, for example from Cylink Corporation, Sunnyvale, California, (408) 735-5800.

    f. Wire transfers. These fulfill the need for expedient money transfers and are available in most major world currencies. U.S. dollar wire transfers are all consummated in New York City.

6. *Seek tax havens in a "user-friendly" time zone.*
Consider the advantages of a "friendly" and convenient time zone. Do you mind getting up during the middle of the night to call your offshore trustee or asset manager? How many hours are you willing to fly to visit your offshore banker? Summer is only "one day long" on the Isle of Man but generally all year long in the Turks and Caicos, the Caymans Islands, the Bahamas, the Canary Islands and the Caribbean.

7. *Political and economic stability.*
What is the strength and stability of the central government? Will a change in the governing political party affect the stability of your offshore structure or the safety of your money? Is the county susceptible to violent political swings, military coups or invasion? Does it have a reputation for massive corruption?

A carefully drafted APT will provide for these contingencies with appropriate language in the trust deed. Several events may occur. The trustee may resign and/or the trust may be recandled (moved and reactivated) in another tax haven. The precipitating conditions could be actually enumerated in the trust deed, expressed in the letter of wishes (sometimes referred to as a side letter) or be discretionary with the trustee. Most tax havens welcome and will adopt "clean orphan" trusts.

8. *Information exchange and the level of privacy.*
What is the level of information exchanged between the U.S. and your tax haven for routine tax matters? What tax and assistance treaties exist between the U.S. and the tax haven of interest? The Mutual Legal Assistance Treaty (MLAT) provides for the exchange of information among member countries for suspected criminal matters but it excludes tax crimes such as U.S. tax evasion.

The issue of tax treaties is an extremely complex matter requiring the assistance of a tax expert or an international tax specialist. Your CPA is unlikely to be really familiar with this topic (see Chapter 11).

9. Currency regulations or exchange control.

None is preferential; minimal may be acceptable. Look for the ability to obtain asset preservation by utilizing currency diversification as is done with Swiss annuities. Countries such as the Bahamas, the British Virgin Islands (BVI) and the Turks and Caicos Islands (TCI) use U.S. dollars (USD) freely and with USD designated banking accounts.

10. Tax regimen.

Tax treatment on income tax, foreign source income, nonresident treatment and special tax concessions are complex issues (see Chapter 11).

11. Quality of local professionals and the financial services industry.

The soundness of your OS structure is only as good as the professionals who create and currently manage it and its infrastructure. Look for an educated work force; an abundance of fairly priced, qualified attorneys, banking facilities, chartered accountants, asset and portfolio managers, consultants, company managers and trustees is essential. You don't shop offshore for professionals by letting your fingers do the walking in the Aruba Yellow Pages. You use referrals through existing personnel and other professional relationships.

I suggest that you use residents of the jurisdiction who have been there so long that they are no longer considered outsiders. They don't want to lose their work permits and become exiles, so they are more likely to be trustworthy.

12. Long-term economic and social stability.

Select a jurisdiction with a high per capita income. Look carefully at the business and political climate to see how it might affect you. Even the Cook Islands had their little political scandal in 1995 that made some offshore consultants nervous, including your author. Haiti was a stable economy until two things happened: The clampdown on U.S. importation of foreign made goods which used child labor and the takeover (invasion) of Haiti by U.S./U.N. forces in 1994. Now its economy is in shambles.[31]

13.   *Local customs and social environment.*
Religion, politics, labor movements, social life, work ethics, business customs, general crime, drug involvement and such are further factors. These can only be ascertained through reading the local newspapers, speaking with knowledgeable locals and, best of all, living in the country during an evaluation period.

14.   *Acquisition of second passport or citizenship.*
A second citizenship, second passport, tax residence, tax domicile, real estate ownership, securing a work permit, operating a "local" business, or ultimate retirement site are essential considerations that would have an influential effect on the selection process (see Chapter 10).

15.   *OS operating entity.*
What you require from your OS structure very much determines where you go. Clearly, if it is a self or captive insurance company, one utilizes Bermuda, the Caymans or Guernsey. Even the Turks and Caicos Islands are seeking to emerge[32] in this area.

For example, some havens encourage types of companies to.locate there by enacting special preferential laws. These jurisdictions are generally in Switzerland, Luxembourg, the Netherlands and Liechtenstein. Similarly, in the Caribbean, the Netherlands Antilles, as a holding company situs, attracts IBCs.

---

[31] As reported in the local media, politicians utilized their influence to structure busines deals for their personal financial benefit.

[32] Reports indicate that far more new captives are being formed in the Turks and Caicos Islands (TCI) than Bermuda. TCI takes a low-fee approach and targets the smaller captives.

16.   Banking.
Which international banks have correspondents in your other operating countries to facilitate transactions? Which banks don't have operating branches in the U.S.? For the ultimate in privacy, those with U.S. operations should not be utilized.

17.   Real estate.
What are the costs of offshore real estate ownership, both for acquisition and annually? While the costs are outrageous in the Caymans, in Costa Rica you get more for your money. What are the limitations as to ownership; who can take title?

18.   Local politics.
What anticipated trends in future local legislation may affect what you are doing? Is the tax haven stable, with conditions changing slowly, or is it on the leading edge? Are they subject to outside (U.S.) influences and pressures of "cooperation" with U.S. authorities?

A General Discussion of Some International Financial Centres

A general discussion of the attributes of tax havens follows, to provide you with a sense of what is important in the evaluation and selection process. Following this discussion is comparative information and a mélange of selected IFCs.

Belize, Central America. Belize, the former British Honduras, is not yet in the same league as the Bahamas, Bermuda, Costa Rica and the British Virgin Islands (BVI). It has a long way to go to reach the higher level of performance and professionalism provided elsewhere, to effectively compete; however, they have enacted APT legislation. It is at a lower tier in the OS world's listings of tax havens, not yet an international financial centre. You should want and need more than a tax haven.

As a retirement location in Central America, some dislike it and others think it's great! Belize brings in the retiree's money and creates economic gains for the locals. There really are only two Central American retirement locations on my OS list, Costa Rica and Belize. Between the two, I still prefer Costa Rica. (Spanish language and local laws vs. English common law issues). It has been reported that close to 25,000 Americans have retired in Costa Rica, which is a brief 2.5 hour flight to Los Angeles, Houston or Miami.

Belize is a relative newcomer to the world international financial scene and has much to learn, including how to create the correct political and regulatory climate to attract flight capital and offshore consultant's business. Their regulators appear to be ineffective. The Internet is awash with offers for US$200 Belize trusts, and they are being sold in a multilevel marketing (MLM) scheme. Noncompliant claims of U.S. tax-free income abound. This affects me negatively. You can't get an efficacious and worthwhile trust deed for $200! You don't want a trustee who sells gelato (isn't that Italian, you ask?) on the beach during the day and writes his or her trusts at night. I'm concerned for those who may be deceived with a false sense of accomplishment and protection but in reality are left holding a weak, nonpersonalized trust–a boilerplate document. And what about those $850 second-year trustee fees that they don't mention?

Niue, an example of an obscure tax haven. Located in the South Pacific, just east of the International Date Line, lies the British Commonwealth of Niue. Although a self-governing territory it ultimately comes under the jurisdiction of New Zealand (as do the Cook Islands, another, more popular tax haven). Permits *oral* trusts (simply amazing to a common law academician!). Written trusts must be registered with the Registrar (-).

Niue has tried to assure security by copying the typical IBC style of legislation as used in many Caribbean jurisdictions (+). Its trust laws are still not clear (-). Of interest is that any one of three languages may be used in drafting the IBC documents:

English, Chinese or Cyrillic.[33] Take a Cyrillic document to your U.S. lawyer to explain it to you!

However, the bottom line is that it would still be cheaper to create a company in the Bahamas. The fees in Niue would be about the same as in the BVI.

Nevis, a corporate tax haven. Within the Caribbean Federation of St. Kitts and Nevis one finds the independent state of Nevis. Incentives are provided with total company tax exemption and freedom of exchange controls–this jurisdictions seeks the world's tax haven business. With fast company formations (in one hour), expeditious statutory requirements and competitive pricing, Nevis is attracting the offshore community.

Dominica, West Indies, Caribbean, another example of an obscure tax haven. In the West Indies, between Guadeloupe and St. Lucia, off of the beaten track, with a low profile, a friendly business-oriented government, Dominica wants your tax haven business. Still relatively underdeveloped, its government is always interested in discussing business ventures providing mutual benefits.

South Africa. Although not considered a tax haven as such, following are a number of factors that make South Africa an attractive investment destination as a "gateway" to Southern Africa.

1. Lack of capital gains taxes.

2. A "moderate" level of income taxes.

3. A very sophisticated financial community.

4. Low level of corruption.

5. Favorable tax treaties with many countries.

---

[33] Cyrillic is an old Slavic alphabet based on the Greek. It is still utilized in Bulgaria, Russia and other Slavic countries.

6.   A strong domestic market and access to the greater Southern Africa Market.

Notice how the same parameters continue to appear when evaluating a jurisdiction!

Vanuatu, the South Pacific, is one of the fastest growing industrial environs in the Pacific Rim. It is catering to an explosive growth in this region for tax havens. It offers the ability to create private banking at a relatively low cost, either for one's own business or personal needs or for providing merchant banking services. One of the principal reasons for locating here is economic: The country is still small and seeking entrepreneurs, so the establishment costs are cheaper and the regulatory agencies are more cooperative.

Guernsey, located off of the Normandy Cherbourg peninsula. Although Guernsey trades with the EC, it is outside of the "EC directive" intended to harmonize the old financial directives of the EU and thus can be unique. It is part of the British Isles but not the United Kingdom. It was given the right to domestic self-government. Politically stable because there are no political parties, it has a low tax regimen. There are no inheritance taxes, death duties, capital transfer taxes or VAT. With an abundance of professionals and a well regulated financial environment, it attracts IFC business from the global community. Its 73 banks from 17 different countries and 30 captive insurance companies are certainly a testimonial to its position as an IFC.

Nevada, USA. Following are some of the tax-haven type characteristics that make Nevada a U.S. tax haven for Americans (holding offshore assets that have returned) and foreigners. Wyoming is also popular with the Germans for similar characteristics.

1.   No corporate income taxes.

2.   No taxes on corporate shares.

3.   No franchise taxes.

4.   No personal income taxes.

5.   No information-sharing agreement with the IRS.

6.   Nominal annual fees.

7.   Minimal reporting and disclosure requirements.

8.   Names of stockholders are not of public record. This indirectly permits bearer shares.

9.   Officers and directors may be non-U.S. persons.

10.   A director need not be a shareholder.

Selected Tax Havens of the World

The following list includes the author's subjective ranking, on a scale of 1 to 10, for the RA and is presented in alphabetical order. No haven was given a score of 10 because no haven can be all things to all people.

Please note:

APT = asset protection trust or statutory trust, dependent upon the haven's trust act or ordinance.

BWI = British West Indies.

IBC = exempt company or international business company, as appropriate, depending upon the exempt company act or ordinance of the haven.

NR = not ranked.

NWI = Netherlands West Indies.

- Alderney. NR. A tax haven.
- Andora. NR. A tax haven.
- Anguilla, BWI. 6/10. General: British Dependent Territory, low profile, banks monitored by the Bank of England; have enacted APT legislation.

- Antigua and Barbuda, BWI. 6/10. General: low profile, highest per capita income in the Eastern Caribbean, no exchange controls, no information exchange agreements with any other country, no income taxes, English Common Law jurisdiction. IBC: have Offshore Corporate Law, strict confidentiality.

- Aruba, NWI. 5/10. General: Dutch legal system, known for lavish casinos (suspected of money laundering for Columbia), off the coast of Venezuela, banking privacy eroded by new laws, entitled Melding Obgebruikelijke Transacties, requiring banks to report any "unusual transactions," thus creating much paperwork; the Freezone is also under investigation involving money transactions.

- Austria. 8/10. General: excellent banking privacy (+), a gateway to transacting business in the former Soviet Union.

- Bahamas. 8/10. General: an independent country (1973), third oldest democracy in the world, tourism provides for more than 50 percent of its gross national product, over 400 banks and trust companies (+), same time zone as Eastern zone (+), have enacted APT and the International Business Companies Act (patterned after the successful BVI Act) legislation (+), no income taxes, no recognition of foreign judgments, fourth largest in international banking, new, stronger, criminal legislation with respect to money laundering. IBC: no requirement to retain books in jurisdiction, total privacy at Company Register. APT: two-year statute of limitations (S/L) for fraudulent transfers to the APT; rule against perpetuities is based on a "wait and see test" (-) (see Chapter 7).

- Bahrain. NR. A tax haven.

- Barbados, BWI. 6/10. General: low profile, no recognition of foreign judgments. APT: has enacted APT legislation. IBC: attractive jurisdiction, double tax treaty with the U.S.

- Belize. 5/10. General: shaky politically and economically, no recognition of foreign judgments (+). APT: no statutory recognition of creditor "classes" (+); have enacted APT legislation (+).

• Bermuda. 8/10. General: British Dependent Territory, insurance capital of the world (+), good infrastructure (+), least expensive location for an OS mutual fund (+), no income tax, withholding tax, capital gains tax, capital transfer tax, estate duties or inheritance tax (+), no recognition of foreign judgments (+), no binding effect upon choice of law (-). APT: has enacted APT legislation (+), permits a 100-year vesting period (+), provisional abrogation of the Statute of Elizabeth (see Chapter 7) (+). IBC: good site for IBCs (+).

• British Virgin Islands, BWI. 8/10. General: British Dependent Territory, good location for an OS mutual fund (+), banks monitored by the Bank of England, special tax laws (such as no taxes). IBC: strong IBC jurisdiction (++), total privacy at Company Register (+), permit bearer shares. APT: weaker trust laws (-), have not enacted APT legislation (-).

• Canary Islands. 6/10. General: attempting to become an IFC, has created a Special Canary Zone (SCZ). IBC: has implemented new company laws, nonresident companies pay only a 1 percent annual tax, no local members permitted–for OS business only.

• Cayman Islands, BWI. 8/10. General: British Dependent Territory, English common law jurisdiction, largest offshore IFC in the world, 600 banks (monitored by the Bank of England) 18,000 IBCs, good locale for an OS mutual fund (+), no personal or corporate income taxes, no capital gains, inheritance or gift taxes, long statute of limitations, higher incorporation costs than Bahamas and BVI (-), no recognition of foreign judgments, no tax treaty with the U.S. (+). IBC: require meetings to be local (-), governmental register of directors, no corporate name restrictions (can use S.A., Ltd., Corp., Inc., etc.), no privacy at Company Register. APT: have enacted APT legislation (+), with laws that are considered models for other banking jurisdictions; a unique feature of their APT laws is that there need not be a full nexus for the trust in that the trustee and trust assets may be situated in another jurisdiction. Only a creditor in existence at the time of creation of the APT has standing to sue (future creditors are without standing). Their six-year statue of limitations (-) on the ability for a creditor to attack transfers of assets to an APT is a major negative factor (-). It appears that a U.S. bankruptcy trustee would not have standing to enforce a derivative creditor right, and only the actual creditor could file an action in the Caymans against the trustee (+); considered more susceptible to U.S. influence (-), long (150 years) perpetuities period (+).

- The Channel Islands (see Guernsey and Jersey). 8/10. General: lower tax rates, some reluctance to implementing APT legislation, no transferability of trusts (-). Exempt from many EU regulations.

- Cook Islands, South Pacific. 6/10. General: recognizes the concept of community property (+), considered more susceptible to U.S. influence through New Zealand (-), standard of proof for fraud is the U.S. criminal burden of proof "beyond a reasonable doubt" (+) (but will the Cook Islands' courts uphold this position?). APT: a Pacific Rim leader, having a somewhat overly aggressive trust protectionist statute some characterize as "hostile" to creditors, no recognition of foreign judgments, have enacted APT legislation (+) and have a special APT called the international trust, shortest statute of limitations on fraud limitations (two years from the date the claim arose) (+) **or**[34] one year from the date of transfer of the asset to the trust to the APT (+), have the strongest anti-claimant laws (+)[35] (in that there need not be a full nexus for the trust—the trustee and trust assets may be situated in another jurisdiction). Only a creditor in existence at the time of creation of

---

[34] The word "or" has created a problem with the Cook Island Trust Act. The Act doesn't state which of the two events comes first—the two years from the date the claim arose "**or**" the one year from the date of transfer of the asset to the trust to the APT. The issue is currently under appeal to the Privy Council, House of Lords, England.

[35] The U.S. judgment creditor must file a *new* action in the tax haven alleging **fraud in the transfer**. The time for filing may have run under the local, shorter statue of limitations against fraudulent conveyances. The fraud being attacked is the judgment creditor's assertion that the assets were transferred to the APT with the primary motivation of the transferor being to "defraud, hinder or delay a creditor or to put assets beyond the reach of a claimant." Or, with further allegations, that the transfers made the transferor insolvent. Some tax havens that have enacted statute of limitations on challenging the asset protection trust include: Bahamas, Bermudas, Cayman Islands, Cook Islands (shortest), Cyprus and Mauritius.

the APT has standing to sue (future creditors are without standing), their six-year statute of limitations (-) on the ability for a creditor to attach transfers of assets to an APT is a major negative factor, giving them a high profile because of these features (-), sometimes used as a final flight jurisdiction because of these characteristics: for example, they provide retroactive protection of "immigrant" (recandled) trusts, permit a 100-year perpetuity period, and permit a quasi-charitable trust. The Cook Islands are actively promoted in the Southern California area as a panacea by service providers.

• Costa Rica. 7/10. General: a stable Central America democracy, best retirement country in Central America (+), classified as a low-risk investment jurisdiction based on political, financial and economic factors (+), considered more susceptible to U.S. influence (-), Information Exchange Agreement with the IRS has eroded banking privacy (-).

• Cyprus. 7/10. APT: no recognition of foreign judgments (+), has enacted APT legislation but still considered a raw, untested jurisdiction; the jury is still out.

• Dominica, BWI. 5/10. (See full paragraph above.)

• France. NR. General: not a tax shelter, at the time this book was written, France was weakening banking privacy by seeking to impose bank disclosure requirements in response to civil officials, without disclosing any cause for the inquiry, for money transfers to other countries in amounts over FFr100,000 (approximately US$20,000) (-). France is also seeking means to clamp down on tax evasion. APT: the law of trusts are not recognized as a legal concept in this jurisdiction (-).

• Gibraltar. 8/10. General: British Dependent Territory, highly stable since 1713, but potential problems with Spain, no recognition of foreign judgments, full exemption from income tax and estate duty (+). IBC: register of IBC members must be kept in Gibraltar (-), no changes of shareholders or beneficial ownership without consent of local authorities (-), shareholders and directors of IBCs are of public record, requiring nominees (-). APT: has enacted favorable APT legislation (+), APT is not registered by each transfer in to the trust (-), two-year statute of limitation on fraud (+), uses an objective test for fraudulent intent and not the "badge of fraud" test (was the settlor solvent at the time of transfer?) (+) (see Chapter 7).

• Granada, BWI. NR. General: A tax haven, Americans are very popular here.

• Guernsey. 8/10. General: one of the better equipped IFCs (+), but not a Common Law jurisdiction (-). (See full paragraph in text).

• Hong Kong. NR. General: lower tax rates (+), British dependent territory, but the jury is still out until after China takes possession of Hong Kong in 1997. (Only a policy of laissez-faire will save Hong Kong.)

• Ireland. 7/10. General: has established (1987) an International Financial Services Centre (IFSC) in Dublin, full EC member, good locale for management of an OS mutual fund (+), costly jurisdiction for formation of an OS mutual fund (-), double tax agreement with the U.S., local government believes there is misuse of their IBCs. IBC: called Irish-non-resident companies, newer companies must disclose the beneficial owners (-), requires using a second entity, either a trustee owner or a second IBC that issues bearer shares, tax rate not more than 10 percent.

• Isle of Man. 8/10. General: downgraded from 10 since it is not an APT jurisdiction and has higher establishment and annual costs (-), excellent regulatory monitoring (+), a safe haven, 20 percent income and corporate taxes, no capital gains or inheritance taxes. IBC: higher incorporation costs (-). APT: has not enacted APT legislation (-), has not overridden the Statue of Elizabeth (-).

• Jersey. 8/10. General: excellent IFC, no exchange control restrictions (+), low income tax of 20 percent since 1939, excellent regulation of banking and financial services industries (+), not a Common Law jurisdiction (-). (See full paragraph on Jersey above.)

• Labuan. 5/10. Newcomer in the South Pacific.

• Liberia. NR. A tax haven.

- Liechtenstein. 7/10. APT: provides an excellent form of a codified trust, one of the best and most flexible trusts, called the "family foundation," and also private foundation structures called the Stiftung.
- Luxembourg. 7/10. General: outrageously costly locale for an OS mutual fund (-).
- Madeira. 7/10. General: special tax concessions for preferred businesses, has promising free trade zone.
- Malaysia. 6/10.
- Malta. NR. A tax haven.
- Marshall Islands. 6/10. General: an independent country. APT: have enacted APT legislation (Trust Act 1994), trust must be registered with the Registrar (-), must have two local trustees (-).
- Mauritius, Republic of. 7/10. General: Mauritius is a gateway to India and South Africa, utilized as a situs for mutual funds. APT: has enacted APT legislation.
- Monaco. NR.
- Monserrat, BWI. 5/10. British Dependent Territory. More famous for their volcano eruptions than as a tax haven.
- Nauru. 5/10. A tax haven. Low-cost private banks.
- Netherlands Antilles. 8/10. General: good locale for an OS mutual fund, opening a new Free Trade Zone, the Hato FTZ, providing special tax breaks, good source for second passports for retired people (+). IBC: curiously, the Japanese trust the Dutch more than the British, excellent for holding companies (+).
- Nevada, USA. 7/10. General: the only state that does not prohibit corporate bearer shares (+), no income tax information exchange agreement with the IRS (+), highest IRS corporate audit rate of all the States (-).
- Nevis, BWI. 6/10. APT: has enacted APT legislation, affords protection to "immigrant" type of trusts that resettle there (+). (See full paragraph in text.)
- New Brunswick, Canada. NR. Currently developing regulations to compete in the captive insurance market.
- New Zealand. 7/10.

- Niue, South Pacific. 5/10. APT: has enacted APT legislation. (See full paragraph above.)
- Palau. NR. A tax haven.
- Panama. 6/10. General: has the Stiftung type of private foundation, hasn't fully recovered from the U.S. "invasion" to capture General Manuel Noriega, no tax on foreign-source income, special tax benefits granted, strict banking privacy laws but consequently suffers from a reputation for bank money laundering for drug money. IBC: low incorporation fees, (thus it has more registered corporations than any other offshore centre), it is more complex for an IBC than other jurisdictions in some respects, no required minimal capitalization, bearer shares permitted, minimum of three directors required (may be any nationality), natural persons are required as officers, and a President, Secretary and Treasurer are required, a registered Panamanian Agent domiciled in Panama is required, can have perpetual life or be a company that is limited in duration. APT: has recently enacted "Liechtenstein" type of trust laws (+).
- St. Kitts (St. Christopher) and Nevis, BWI. 6/10. General: no recognition of foreign judgments, see Nevis, above. St. Kitts is a source of second passports.
- St. Vincent. NR. A tax haven.
- The Seychelles. 4/10. General: no treaties with the U.S. (+). High profile for money laundering, attracting "suspect" money for eventual bank laundering. IBC: have a company act (+), require only one shareholder and one director and you may use an IBC for these roles, no public record of officers and directors (names and addresses) (+), no annual meeting requirement (+). APT: have enacted APT legislation.
- Singapore. 7/10.
- Sri Lanka. NR. A tax haven.
- Switzerland. NR. APT: although an IFC, the law of trusts is not recognized as a legal concept in this jurisdiction. It doesn't have trust laws but uses civil jurisdiction.

- Turks and Caicos Islands, BWI. 6/10. General: Although its ranking is on the rise, still far to go as a "first tier" jurisdiction, Eastern standard time zone, British Dependent Territory, English Common Law system, very popular with Canadians, no direct tax on income, companies, capital gains, or profits, no gift taxes or death taxes, infrastructure still not fully developed, financial services regulated by Financial Services Commission, no exchange controls, daily FedEx and DHL service, emerging as a captive insurance jurisdiction. APT: have enacted APT legislation (but still sketchy in the statute of limitations area) (-). IBC: excellent IBC jurisdiction (++).
- United Arab Emirates. NR. A tax haven.
- Vanuatu. 5/10. (See full paragraph in text.)
- Western Samoa. 5/10.

Note: By coupling or combining the above tax havens in series (sometimes referred to as "layering"[36]), further tax treaty or tax deferral benefits may be achieved and better asset protection afforded through greater privacy by utilizing geographic diversity. This is a complex topic best left to an international tax specialist.

📖 Legal Issues and Terminology

Without at least a cursory knowledge of legal terminology you will be at a disadvantage in the site selection process. For further elucidation on these terms, try the Glossary (Appendix B) or *Black's Law Dictionary* at your local library.

📖 Spendthrift Clause

Language in a will or trust provides, under good drafting practices, to protect the assets of the estate against the imprudent spending habits of a beneficiary. Distributions to the beneficiary will shift to

---

[36] *Layering* may be achieved with numerous combinations of entities. For example, 100 percent of the shares of an IBC being owned by the first trust, which has as its sole beneficiary a second trust.

the discretion of the trustee and may even cease if the beneficiary is insolvent.

📖 *The Statute of Limitations*

The statute of limitations (S/L) is the deadline date after which a party claiming to be injured by the settlor should (but still may) no longer file an action to recover his or her damages. For actual fraud, in California, the statute is one year from the discovery date and the discovery period can be as long as seven years. If the settlor would file a bankruptcy during that period, the bankruptcy trustee is granted an additional two-year period to file a recovery action extending the statute of limitations to nine years.

The statute of limitations prohibits creditor claims against the APT if brought too late (i.e., filed too late in the court of competent jurisdiction). Generally, the statute begins to run when the actual fraud was discovered or should have been discovered by the party who claims to have been damaged by the settlor. The Bahamas, Cayman Islands, Cook Islands and Mauritius for example have specific statutes of limitations on challenging an APT.

Most tax havens have abrogated the time period of the statute. The S/L clock can start to run when an APT is created or an asset is transferred to the APT. Most jurisdictions typically have a S/L of two years or greater; for example, the Bahamas have a two-year S/L, sometimes referred to as a Fraudulent Disposition Act, which limits the period in which a transfer or disposition of an asset can be attacked by a creditor.

The Cook Islands are unique in this area–it has by far the shortest S/L, being under one interpretation, only one year from the date of formation of the APT, whether the creditor has knowledge of the APT or not. Adding insult to injury, even when a creditor is successful in attacking the transfer, it is only beneficial on that creditor's behalf and *not for the benefit of all* the creditors.

📖 The Choice of Governing Law

A significant issue to ponder is the governing law for your structure or entity. For example, the Bahamas have in effect their Governing Law Act. Their act is quite clear in stating that if a trust is clearly governed by the laws of the Bahamas (in language to that effect contained in the trust deed), then the courts of the Bahamas have the exclusive jurisdiction with respect to any disputes arising with respect to the trust. A foreign judgment obtained in another jurisdiction with respect to assets or rights as contained within the trust would not be honored by the Bahamian courts. Nothing, though, precludes the party claiming to have been harmed by some language contained within the trust from filing an action in the Bahamas, but cost and geography are usually deterrents against the filing of an action or encourage prompt and reasonable onshore settlements of disputes.

Transferring Assets

The usual way to transfer funds is by cashier's check or wire transfer. Cashier's checks do not provide the instant cash equivalent in most of the world. In Nassau, for example, there is a 21-banking-day hold (that is, about a month) on a cashier's check– the bankers like to warm their hands on your cash, making money on the "float." Given the similarities of the Bahamian and U.S. banking systems, the high level of tourism and intercountry cooperation, I almost consider the Commonwealth of the Bahamas the 51st state.

  The wiring of U.S. dollars globally and electronically on the SWIFT banking system appears to be done by electronic book transfers among member banks in New York City. The transferring of USD then is done in the U.S. banking system, which appears to be vulnerable to snoops and not secure.

  Note the following e-mail message appearing on the "net-lawyer" mailing list (`net-lawyers@lawlib.wuacc.edu`) on the Internet:

```
From: "XXX XXXX" <XXXXXX@emh7.korea.army.mil>
To: Multiple recipients of list <net-
lawyers@lawlib.wuacc.edu>
Subject: Asset Locators

A while back, someone posted a listing of asset locator
services, but for
some reason I cannot find that particular post. Would
someone post the
names of some of these companies for me? I am
particularly interested in companies that can trace
electronic fund transfers. Thanks.
***********************************
XXXXXXXXXXX
Legal Assistance Attorney
Captain, U.S. Army
Yongsan Garrison
Seoul, Republic of Korea
```

What is surprising is that even if USD were to be wired from Zurich to the Cook Islands in the South Pacific, they would go through New York City. The process involves sophisticated encrypted electronics (the SWIFT System) without any actual exchange of paperwork by the correspondents. There must be a clear audit trail to protect member banks, but no actual cash exchanges hands except for final accounting. The expressed goal is to reduce banking errors to a minimum, but the end result is to provide little privacy to the parties involved. *The U.S. Federal Reserve wire transfer system is not a very private system.*

For privacy, clients have reported exchanging their currency to Yen or Deutsche marks for wire transfers with more privacy and then staying in those currencies.

For a sample of the jurisdiction selection process using case methodology (see Chapter 14).

APT Costs

For a turnkey APT with trustee and trust protector in place, the formation costs could be four to six times the cost of a U.S. trust.

5
What Structure Do I Use?

Once again, I must reiterate that there is no single response to the above question–each person's needs are unique. Steer away from offshore consultants who offer only one solution. Why are you going offshore? What are you trying to accomplish? Is it achievable? Does your OS structure have flexibility to accommodate future personal or business changes?

The following are the factors that lead up to the creation of the operating structure. Once again, they are not presented in any particular order of priority.

• Your age. If you are in your 40s, your prime earning years, you can take more risks, make some of your capital back if you lose it and consequently seek a higher return on your money. Do you have an imminent need for your money to provide for your family in the event of your premature death or disability? If you are close to your retirement age, you want safety because you don't have the time to earn it back again. You may also want to provide for your grandchildren or fund a family dynasty or private foundation.
• Your occupation and skills. The more removed you are from the day-to-day financial community, the more you should rely upon investment professionals. I don't think you can be the world's foremost cardiac surgeon and also know if and when to

sell Netscape[37] stock short. At least, I never met you–and if you can I certainly would like to.

• Nationality, citizenship, domicile and residency. All four are quite different and generally have tax implications that affect the operating structure. Those of you with active offshore relatives and trusted friends may be able to use them to assist in managing those offshore structures. Are you a resident alien or nonresident alien or married to a resident alien? Each has different major and subtle problem areas. As a resident alien, the IRS treats you as a U.S. person. As a nonresident alien (NRA, not the National Rifle Association), you have many tax breaks in the U.S.

• Investment philosophy. Are you conservative or aggressive? Do you want to give total discretion to your asset manager or retain investment decision powers?

• Pre-existing offshore entities and offshore funds. Do you already have an OS presence? Do you remember what it was for? Is it now obsolete because of major changes in your family (divorce, children, grandchildren) or because of changes or proposed change in the U.S. tax code?

Basic Offshore Entities

One of the most fundamental OS entities used as a building block for the OS structures is the international business company (IBC) (see Chapter 6), known in other jurisdictions as the *exempt company* (see Chapter 10). The typical IBC is used as an *operating* or *holding company*, as shown in Figure 5-1. Offshore it is referred to as a company because it is created under a "company act or ordinance." The IBC, like any corporation, has members (shareholders), officers and directors. In Figure 5-1 is a vertical line that I call the offshore line and designate "OS." Offshore would be defined as "foreign" under the Internal Revenue Code. (See Appendix B, Glossary, for the critical definitions of "foreign"

---

[37] Netscape stock hit highs of around $94 in December 1995 and a high of around $83 in February 1996. It was dropping through a price level of around $38 during March 1996.

FIGURE 5-1: Typical IBC

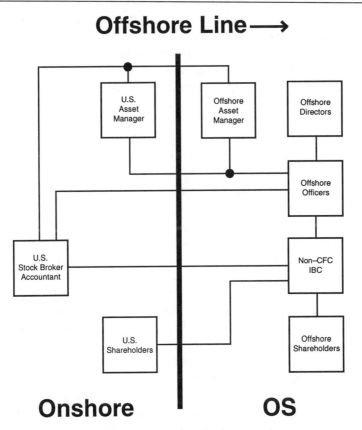

Offshore Line⟶

Onshore   OS

and "offshore.") Foreign would be any location other than the U.S., its territories and possessions. To the left is the U.S., in its broadest definition, and to the right, offshore. We see that the OS IBC has opened up a brokerage account with a U.S. stock brokerage firm. The assets can be managed and traded under a full discretionary account by the brokerage firm or by using an onshore portfolio manager. The IBC has entered into an engagement letter with the portfolio and asset managers to provide for his or her compensation—commissions, fixed fee or performance-based fee.

Under current U.S. tax laws, the IBC pays no capital gains taxes to the U.S. providing it is not a controlled foreign corporation[38] (CFC) (see Chapter 11). It may pay income taxes on U.S. source income or income effectively connected with the States (see Chapter 11). If the IBC is located in a zero- or low-tax regimen haven, it also pays no or little capital gains tax in the tax haven. (A withholding tax is assessed on any U.S. paid dividends on stock and withheld at the source.) This is not a tax windfall. Although the OS funds grow faster because of the compounding effects of utilizing untaxed resources, when the money is ultimately repatriated to America, the taxman gets his due. That's what makes it tax compliant. The distribution is the taxable event.

Figure 5-2 takes Figure 5-1 a major step further. It builds upon the concept of the holding company. Holding companies are generally created for a specific purpose; for example, to hold real property, to manage and trade stocks, bonds, etc., for currency or commodity trading or to own a U.S. business. The holding company may be an excellent vehicle for owning a company with high environmental risks or contaminated and polluted real property. It could be used to circumvent the prohibition against a trust owning or having an interest in restricted forms of investments (including real property).

Notice that we now have four IBCs (IBC1, IBC2, etc.), each being the shareholders or owners of the U.S. entities. I have intentionally made it quite complex to utilize as a teaching tool. IBC1 is the same operating company as in Figure 5-1, but now it is 100 percent owned by the holding IBC, IBC5. In our example, IBC2 is a shareholder of an American corporation.

IBC3 is involved with U.S. real estate. It could be the sole general partner of a U.S. limited partnership holding environmentally contaminated real property with an uncertain liability for clean-up. It could hold U.S. real property in its own name, but if it did it would subject itself to the Foreign Investor in Real Property

---

[38] 📖 IRC §951 and §957 collectively define the CFC as one in which a U.S. person owns 10 percent or more of a foreign corporation or in which 50 percent or more of the total voting stock is owned by U.S. shareholders collectively or 10 percent or more of the voting control is owned by U.S. persons.

FIGURE 5-2: Building on the Typical IBC

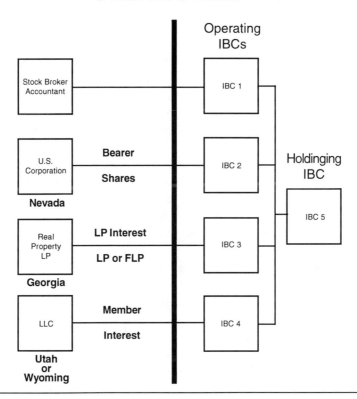

Offshore Line ⟶

Tax Act of 1980 (FIRPTA) and the Economic Recovery Act of 1981 and have U.S. capital gains taxes withheld in escrow upon sale of the property in the U.S. It could also be a limited partner in a limited partnership.

In Figure 5-2, IBC4 is a member (owner) of a U.S. limited liability company.

All four IBCs have central management through an OS holding company, IBC5. So long as it is not prohibited in the jurisdictions where established, there can be total commonality of management–the same directors and officers for all five IBCs. Further privacy could be achieved by placing the operating companies in the Bahamas and by establishing the holding company in the Netherlands Antilles. If money is no object and privacy is of utmost importance, or you are just plain paranoid, each IBC could be incorporated in a different tax haven. Further, each IBC could have different officers and directors. No one but you would know what was happening. If you arrange such a complex structure, make sure to leave good notes in case of your disability or premature death, or no one will be capable of running it. I suggest that you have a master book in any case, updated as necessary, held offshore, sealed and in escrow, for that ultimate day (see OAR in Appendix D).

Figure 5-3 is a variation of Figure 5-1. It is a simpler structure than Figure 5-2 in that the holding company is replaced by a family trust, called an asset protection trust (APT), where the APT provides insulation for the settlor and his or her family, see Chapter 7.

Note in Figure 5-3 that the prior roles of the IBCs' directors and officers have been taken over by a pair of administrators and fiduciaries called the trustee and the trust protector. The trustee and the protector manage the trust on behalf of the three beneficiaries identified as B1, B2 and B3. Figure 5-3 is a popular OS combination, combining the features of the IBC for asset management and the trust as an *inter vivos* and/or testamentary vehicle. The trustee could also act as the asset manager or hire an asset manager for the IBC.

A structure for handling the "problem" of excessive equity in U.S. real property is the *equity stripping* company (see Chapter 10). In Figure 5-4, the domestic real property is an attractive plum inviting litigation because you have assets (equity) that your prospective plaintiff and his or her contingent fee attorney want to take from you. In an "arrangement," for example, a loan is made by you and your real property is given as security, the collateral for the loan. This is not a taxable event in the year taken. A second mortgage or deed of trust is recorded against the real estate, reducing

FIGURE 5-3: A Popular OS IBC and Trust Combination

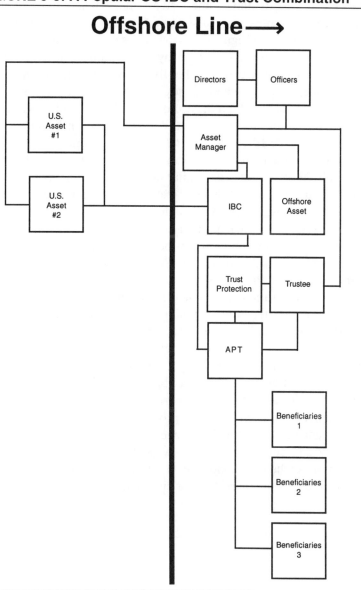

your equity. Perhaps, in the case of your residence, the equity is reduced down to the homestead[39] value, making the house unattractive as a means of satisfying a future judgment against you.

Referring to Figure 5-4, first, an escrow account is opened with an attorney or escrow company. A preliminary title search is performed and provided for the IBC. The officers of the IBC decide independently whether they wish to make a loan on your real estate. If so, they fund the escrow, which in turn distributes the money to you and records the second mortgage on behalf of the IBC. Because the IBC is a corporation, there generally is no usury limitation on the interest rate it can charge you, but it should be in line with the going rate for similar domestic loans so as not to be conspicuous. Proposed new laws may mandate a minimum interest rate. The new promissory note is due as a balloon in 5 or 10 years or upon sale of the real property. Or, for an administrative fee, perhaps one to five points, it can be rolled over for another term. What you do with the money received is only limited by the lack of imagination on the part of you and your OS consultant. Perhaps you buy a lump-sum, irrevocable offshore annuity due at age 65.

One of the few remaining tax shelters available to Americans is the *annuity* (see Chapter 9). With Congress' and the IRS's blessings, it is a method to defer capital gains and taxes until funds are actually received by you, the *annuitant*, hopefully at a time when you are in a lower tax bracket and have more need of the money. The annuity should be irrevocable and noncancelable if it is intended primarily for asset protection purposes. The RA can buy the annuity domestically or even go OS to a Swiss insurance company and convert his or her weak U.S. dollars into stronger Swiss francs when the annuity is purchased. It is not unpatriotic to hold your assets in other, stronger currencies.

---

[39] For a detailed explanation of the homestead allowance on your residence, see footnote 59.

FIGURE 5-4: The Equity Stripping Company

Offshore Line ⟶

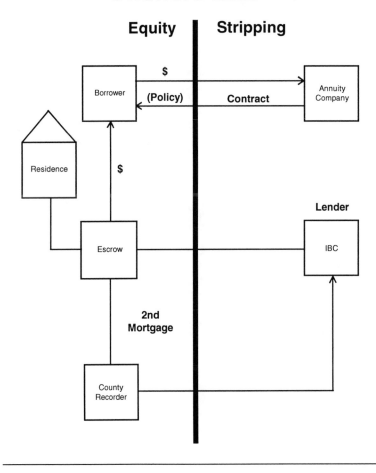

6
The Caribbean Style of an International Business Company: An Exempt Company

The international business company is an entity not customarily familiar to Americans, except perhaps for those living or operating in the U.S. Virgin Islands which permit a restricted form of an IBC. It is created under a Caribbean form of *company act*. The Caribbean style of company act has been adopted as a model throughout the world's tax havens but is not used universally. The alternative would be forming a company under an *exempt company* act in the tax haven, as is done in the European community, the Turks and Caicos Islands, etc., (see Chapter 10). This would not actually create an IBC, but the exempt company formed would have similar IBC characteristics.

A simplistic definition of the IBC is a corporation that is referred to as a company, generally created in a tax haven, that is authorized to do business worldwide *excluding the country of incorporation*. It can't directly hold title to real property (except for renting local office space) or even operate a local flower stand. Local banking is permitted (of course) as well as dealing with other, local IBCs. The IBC is an international operating company as opposed to a domestic company. It is readily accepted in the worldwide banking community as a proven structure to carry on financial or business interests. As such, many offshore trusts (see Chapter 7) carry on their financial and business transactions using one or more entities such as IBCs or limited liability companies (LLCs), where in each case it is totally owned by the underlying trusts and operated under the direction of the trustee. More complex and ambitious structures may even include a private foundation to pursue altruistic goals or permissive family interests worldwide. Under current U.S. tax laws, so long as the IBC is not a CFC, there are significant tax deferral features available from this structure because a foreign corporation pays no U.S. capital gains taxes as the incentive to invest money in the U.S. (see Chapter 11).

Since many of you are already familiar with American corporations, the following is presented in the form of a comparative discussion of the distinctive similarities and differences between them and IBCs.

What Can an IBC Do?

1.   *Engage in commerce.*
The IBC can promote and market goods and services worldwide except as may be restricted under the company act of the country of formation. Some of the types of services which are generally restricted or expressly prohibited in most havens include:

a. Banking services. The creation of a private bank is accomplished by a procedure separate and different than the formation of a company and is quite expensive and time consuming in the better tax havens.

b. Trust services. A separate license is required.

c. Re-insurance services. Formation of an insurance or captive insurance company (see Chapter 13 for this special type of company).

d. Act as an investment, stock or commodity trading company (see below).

2.   *Act as a holding company with ownership in other entities.*
This is one of the more complex topics and much beyond the scope of this book. Since it may encompass CFC treatment, investment companies, intercompany transfer pricing and

subsidiaries of CFCs, I refer you to your qualified tax consultant.

3.   *Act as a lender.*
An IBC can make its money work by providing loans. Conversely, it can borrow. It can pay finder's fees and commissions, as required.

4.   *Hold Real property.*
Other than where locally restricted, an IBC can take title (own) real estate and other interests in nonmobile assets worldwide, but not in the country of incorporation. However, many jurisdictions permit the IBC to lease or rent real property for local office space.

5.   *Enter into Leasing.*
An IBC may enter into leases for real property interests and personal property, such as vehicles and equipment, worldwide. My associates report that there are excellent vehicle leasing opportunities offshore for leasing companies.

6.   *Act as a trading company.*
As the level of worldwide exporting and importing skyrockets, the IBC can participate by performing the function of a trading company. The IBC can utilize a fulfillment company as well, to take orders from the customer, do invoicing, drop ship orders and collect on irrevocable letters of credit. Profits would then be captured offshore in a low- or no-tax regimen. The IBC could also license intellectual property. High-quality communications is essential for this type of function. Also, watch out for transfer pricing problems in this area.

7.   *Probate avoidance and privacy tool.*
An IBC can be utilized on behalf of an APT as a probate and privacy tool. Through the medium of a holding company, it could indirectly manage the APT's offshore assets, without it becoming part of the estate upon the settlor's death. This would

save on legal fees and probate (the same rationale for using a living trust) and provide greater privacy since the probate of a will in the U.S. makes it a public record.

8.   General.
As a general rule, it may participate in any lawful activity not restricted by the country of incorporation or the jurisdiction in which it desires to operate. This would include shipping companies, consulting companies, offshore manufacturing, shipping and air transportation companies and licensing and sublicensing companies.

Some of the more popular IBC jurisdictions are: the Bahamas, the British Virgin Islands (where the concept of the IBC was created), the Cayman Islands, the Isle of Man, Panama, the Channel Islands, Hong Kong and Gibraltar. Some desirable features of the IBC and factors that must be considered in selecting a location for the formation of the IBC are listed below.

IBC Features

General Considerations

As a fundamental proposition, an IBC that essentially runs almost automatically without the U.S. corporate formalities would be most desirable for the following reasons.

1.   No requirement for a formal annual meeting. All meetings can be informally fulfilled by telecommunications (telephone, e-mail, mail or fax), by proxy or even ratification after the fact.

2.   Multiple classes of stock may be issued, and there is an option for bearer or nonbearer types of stock.

3.   Permits a minimal number of directors, preferably only one, who may be a nominee. Please compare this with the

higher requirement of company formation for Panama in Chapter 4.

4.   No limitation or restrictions upon the nationality, citizenship or residency of its officers, shareholders or directors.

5.   No requirements that the officers or directors also be shareholders.

6.   Officers and/or directors may be other entities; for example, by utilizing a trust, another IBC, a LLC, a partnership, etc., act as an officer or director when permitted by law. Again, compare this with Panama.

7.   No requirement to publicly file the names of the directors and officers, as is required in all U.S. jurisdictions.

8.   Permits the books of the IBC to be maintained in another jurisdiction.

Tax Regimen

At first blush, a no-tax jurisdiction appears preferable to a low-tax one, but zero taxes is not the only factor that one must consider. It is essential to have a competent analysis performed of the dual tax treaty aspects (called "treaty shopping"). For more on taxes, see Chapter 11.

Simplicity and Flexibility of Operations

Select a haven that has no or minimal taxes on the capital account and no corporate income taxes.

Quality of Communications

This is an important area. Time means money, and poor quality communications can cause delays in transmitting essential instructions. I don't own AT&T stock so I can say (from personal experience, and without accusations of deriving insider benefits) that I consider AT&T the best for offshore communications. But don't overlook the lower cost (almost free) and privacy (using PGP encryption) that one can achieve using e-mail over the Internet.

Language

Unless you are fully conversant in another tongue, stick to an English speaking jurisdiction. Otherwise you will be adding a level of delay and complexity by requiring certified translations of each document.

Legal System

Again, unless you are fluent in its language and understand a given country's unique legal system, stick to those using the traditional English common law and the standard form of a company act. It appears that all the English speaking, British based jurisdictions are improving upon each other with their own form of an exempt company act. Minimal capitalization should be required. The level of capitalization effects the cost of the filing fee.

Costs: Registration Fees and Domicilliary and Management Fees

Low formation costs are not the only factor. Consider subsequent annual fees, as well. Also, get full disclosure on the costs for day-to-day transactional fees, further services available, the hourly rate and any other anticipated extraordinary fees or costs. Inquire as to their associates (chartered accountant, attorney, etc.) and their charges.

Privacy

One of the principal reasons other than asset protection the RA has for going offshore is the quest for enhanced privacy. Concerned with the monster computer databases in the United States and the apparent ease of eavesdropping the U.S. banking system and even the Federal Reserves wire transfer network, RAs seek confidentiality and privacy with respect to financial matters by selecting a jurisdiction that has no requirement to file public or private annual returns in the country of incorporation.

Choice of Name Restrictions

Because of various factors, a name you prefer or are currently utilizing in the U.S. may not be available offshore. For individuals seeking privacy and asset protection, it is strongly suggested that the name of the offshore company or entity be different than the one used onshore. In cases where a business name carries good will, using the same name offshore may outweigh using a different name.

I am aware of various restrictions on using the words trust, insurance, assurance, trustco, bank, bancor, sovereign, royal, imperial, financial, building society, chartered, chamber of commerce, co-operative and foundation, to name a few. Other jurisdictions limit names ending with S.A., Inc., Ltd., Corp., etc.

I strongly recommend against incorporating offshore using the same name as your onshore corporation. It ties the two together, destroying the very privacy you wish to achieve by using a common name.

Monetary Controls

Select a haven that has no or minimal exchange controls, one that affords the ability to transact business in any major world currency.

Applying for Company Formation and Agreement

A typical application submitted by you to form (create) and have managed a basic IBC structure is provided in Form 6-1 (see pages 80 and 81). Form 6-2 (see page 82) is for more a complex plan, a three-company structure being offered by offshore consultants. The Form 6-2 structure consists of three boxes, an IBC and two OS trusts. Initially, the IBC is formed. The IBC then is the settlor of an OS trust (a foreign grantor trust), called Trust 1; the IBC is the sole beneficiary (no U.S. beneficiaries) of Trust 1. Trust 1 (must be a foreign grantor trust) is the holder of more than a 50 percent equity position in the IBC. This avoids the IBC being characterized as a CFC by the IRS. Trust 1 (as a foreign grantor trust and using a U.S. NRA) creates, as the settlor, a second trust called Trust 2, while retaining the power to revoke Trust 2. Trust 2 (a foreign grantor trust created by an NRA) is then used as a vehicle for worldwide investing and gifting.[40]

The first trust has as its beneficiary the second trust. Where no tax or other link with the U.S. is mandated, U.S. persons who avoid holding a greater than 5 percent ownership interest in the IBC negate the IRS reporting requirement. The total U.S. ownership of the IBC is limited to less than 50 percent to prevent the IBC from becoming a U.S. controlled foreign corporation (CFC). A CFC must file a corporate U.S. income tax return. However, if the trusts have U.S. beneficiaries, there is a reporting requirement (see Chapter 11, IRS Form 3520).

An IBC Comparison Checklist

1.   Total out-of-pocket costs for incorporating a turnkey IBC, including all nominees' fees, registrar fees, agent's fees, share certificates and corporate seal, bank account establishment, banking services, re-mailing services, local presence, if required by you, etc.

2.   Subsequent years' costs, including company management and transaction costs.

3.   Availability of bearer shares.

---

[40] IRS Revenue Ruling 69-70 provides that a foreign trust make a gift to an American person free of U.S. taxes on the recipient.

4. Requirement to keep books in local jurisdiction.

5. Requirement for local directors.

6. Requirement for local meetings.

7. Public records of directors at Company Registrar.

8. Disclosure of beneficial owner(s).

9. Requirement of annual audit.

10. Tax imposed on offshore profits.

11. Company name restrictions.

12. British based common law legal system.

13. Total privacy of banking information.

14. Total privacy of records at Company Registrar.

15. Criminal penalties for the disclosure of banking records by bank personnel.

16. Criminal penalties for the disclosure of corporate records at registrar's office.

To illustrate this comparison, let's take a close look at a Bahamian IBC, which company formation people claim have major advantages:

1. Only one director is required.

2. A minimum of two subscribers for shares is required.

FORM 6-1: Company Formation Application Form

CONFIDENTIAL & PRIVATE
COMPANY FORMATION INFORMATION FORM
The Bahamas

1.   PROPOSED COMPANY NAME: (Give first choice and two alternatives)

(1)   _____

(2)   _____

(3)   _____

2.   TYPE OF COMPANY:
[ ] International Business Corporation   [ ] Regular Corporation

3.   CAPITAL & TYPES OF SHARES:
Capital - (1)   US$5,000 divided into 5000 shares of US$1.00 each

(2)   Other (Specify)

_____

Shares - [ ] Regular   [ ] Bearer   [ ] Other (Specify)

_____

4.   SHAREHOLDERS:
[ ] Nominees to be provided.

[ ] Issued to: (Provide a list, if necessary)

Name	Address	No. of Shares	Type of Shares

5.   BENEFICIAL OWNERS (For Internal Use Only):

Name	Addresses	Percentage of Capital

CONFIDENTIAL & PRIVATE

Page 1

FORM 6-1: Company Formation Application Form, *Cont'd*

CONFIDENTIAL & PRIVATE

6.   **REGISTERED OFFICE IN THE BAHAMAS:**
Unless otherwise specified, it will be a nominee. If otherwise, give specific name and address:

_____

7.   **REGISTERED AGENT IN THE BAHAMAS:**
Unless otherwise instructed, this will be a member of a legal firm in the Bahamas.

_____

8.   **DIRECTORS AND OFFICERS:**

[　] Nominees to be provided   [　] Other, please supply:

Name   Address   Position/Officer

_____

_____

9.   **PROPOSE TRADE OR BUSINESS:**

_____

_____

10.   **SPECIAL REQUIREMENTS FOR MEMORANDUM OR ARTICLES OF ASSOCIATION (Specify):**

_____

11.   **SPECIAL SERVICES (e.g., opening bank accounts, communications, etc.):**

_____

_____

12.   **OTHER SERVICES (e.g., reinvoicing, escrows, etc.):**

_____

_____

Signed: _____ **Dated:** _____

CONFIDENTIAL & PRIVATE

FORM 6-2: Company Information & Agreement Form

Company Formation Information and Agreement

By this agreement_____ ("Client")

of _____
      Street   **City**   **State**   **Zip**

do/does hereby agree to the creation of a company structure consisting of one Bahamian
International Business Company and two Bahamian Trusts.

Corporate Information

Name of Corporation: _____ (First Choice)

_____ (Second Choice)

Name(s) of Director(s):_____

_____

Name(s) of Officer(s): _____ (President)

_____ (Secretary)

Trust #1 Information
Name of Protector: Primary _____ Secondary _____

Trust #2 Information
Name of Protector: Primary _____ Secondary _____

Beneficiary of Trust:
       Primary Beneficiaries & %: _____

       Secondary Beneficiaries & %: _____

Banking Information

The Client should be prepared to make an initial bank deposit of $10,000 USD. In addition,
check what additional banking services you want. Additional services, such as debit cards,
may require additional deposits to this or a separate bank account.

_____ MasterCard or VISA Debit Cards   _____ Personal   _____Corporate

_____ U.S. check writing ability   _____ Securities trading   Other: _____

NO REPRESENTATIONS, WARRANTIES OR GUARANTEES ARE OFFERED OR
IMPLIED THAT ANY COMPANY OR COMPANY STRUCTURE WILL BE
SUCCESSFUL FOR ANY PURPOSE WHATSOEVER. NO REPRESENTATIONS,
WARRANTIES OR GUARANTEES ARE OFFERED OR IMPLIED REGARDING THE
TAX EFFECTS, BENEFITS OR IMPLICATIONS INVOLVING ANY COMPANY OR
COMPANY STRUCTURE. ALL PERSONS ARE ENCOURAGED TO SEEK
COMPETENT LEGAL AND TAX COUNSEL IN THE PARTICULAR JURISDICTION
WHERE THEY RESIDE.

AGREED TO BY UNDERSIGNED this _____ day of _____, 1994.

Client _____ Client _____

3.   A director may be another corporation.

4.   Board of directors' and shareholders' meetings may be conducted by electronic means such as telephone, fax and e-mail.

5.   The IBC may trade in its own shares.

6.   The IBC may hold treasury shares.

7.   There is no record of the names of the shareholders and directors in the public registry.

8.   There is no requirement for filing financial statements or annual tax returns.

9.   The government has guaranteed an exemption from taxes for 20 years.

10.   📖 No rule against *ultra vires* activities. The IBC may be established for any purpose not prohibited by Bahamian Laws.

11.   The IBC may transfer its domicile and conversely, an existing offshore (foreign) IBC may transfer to the Bahamas.

12.   No prohibition concerning transferring assets to a trust.

13.   Registration and annual governmental fees are considered low.

14.   The IBC may act as a guarantor of third-party obligations.

15.   The IBC is not subject to Bahamian Exchange Control Legislation.

16.   A foreign government may not nationalize the shares of a Bahamian IBC.

17.   A foreign government may not seize the shares of the IBC to satisfy a tax claim arising in the foreign country.

Bahamas does limit the IBC from the following activities:

1.   Cannot carry on business with residents of the Bahamas.

2.   Cannot own an interest in Bahamian real property other than leased office space.

3.   Cannot carry on a banking or trust business.

4.   Cannot carry on an insurance or re-insurance business.

5.   Cannot carry out the business of providing the registered office for companies in the Bahamas.

Other Forms of Companies

Although our major emphasis in this chapter is on the international business company, other forms of offshore companies are also available. These are discussed throughout this book and in summary are:

1.   Local companies.

2.   Exempt companies.

3.   Special companies.
        a. Banking.
        b. Insurance.
        c. Mutual Funds.
        d. Ship Ownership.
        e. Insurance.

7
The Offshore (Foreign) Asset Protection Trust

"Do APTs really provide "bullet proof" protection against lawsuits,
as one promoter claims?"
The Financial Privacy Report, Mike Ketcher, Editor

Trusts 101

In the offshore community, the buzzword for the 1990s is "APT."

The current OS Asset Protection Trust (APT) is a sophisticated, more modern mutation of the basic trust established principally for a specific purpose–asset protection. A basic trust is defined as a legal structure in which title to and right of possession of property (the trust "corpus") is in the hands of a "trustee." The trust is established by the settlor, creator or grantor. (The terms grantor and settlor are preferred by the author and are used synonymously[41] in this book. Creator is a term unique in the U.S. lexicography utilized in the areas of pure trusts and business trusts.) Surprisingly, *you* need not be the grantor in that some other entity or person may create a trust on behalf of your beneficiaries, more commonly known as a *nongrantor trust.*

The person or entity creating the trust and transferring assets to the APT by way of a testamentary disposition or gift is the settlor. When the APT is created and funded by will upon the death of the settlor, the APT will be a foreign nongrantor trust.

---

[41] 📖 A fine distinction arises in the case of a foreign nongrantor trust created by a third person who is a nonresident alien, the "nominee settlor." Although the nominee (third person) settlor is the "legal" settlor of the trust, he or it must be distinguished from the grantor or "true settlor," some other person.

Under proposed laws that will very likely go into effect (check with you tax advisor), the U.S. beneficiaries of this foreign nongrantor trust would become the grantors after the death of the settlor.

The APT should have minimal contact with the U.S. to avoid being characterized as a U.S. trust.

If the creator is a nonresident alien (NRA), if it is sited offshore, and if the assets are owned offshore, it will be characterized as a foreign nongrantor trust. This characterization is true even if all the beneficiaries are American persons.

Some purists suggest that the trust instrument actually be executed by the settlor offshore. The trust deed may be a grantor or a nongrantor trust. Note that nongrantor trusts create unique tax obligations, as discussed in Chapter 11.

The trustee has the right to manage, hold, and use and the duty to protect the asset on behalf of the beneficiary. A commercial trustee is usually required to be licensed by the jurisdiction. The trustee has an equitable obligation to deal with the trust assets fairly on behalf of the beneficiaries. A trust is a legal entity, having the ability to deal with banks in its own name and being required to file a trust tax return with the IRS and with the states in which it does business or has a nexus. It is an extremely flexible structure and may serve many functions, so long as they are not specifically prohibited by statute or law, illegal or in contravention of "public policy." (Public policy varies from country to country. Inquire of your counsel about specific prohibitions of trusts in your local jurisdiction.) Some of the powers of a trust (acting through its trustee) are:

• Take title to or acquire an interest in real property for any lawful purpose.
• Manage the real property owned by the trust.
• Take title to or acquire personal property, such as cash, stocks, bonds, art, antiques, businesses, promissory notes and other negotiable instruments.
• Manage the business interests of the trust.

- Provide better spendthrift provisions than are generally provided under U.S. laws.
- Use as a substitute for probate or to avoid probate.
- Provide the offshore role of a trust protector for better trust administration.

The trustee, as a fiduciary to the beneficiaries, has duties of professional competence imposed as well:

- The trust must be validly settled (created).
- The trustee must act as a reasonable, prudent businessperson would under the factual circumstances. He or she should know the nature and consequences of any trust transaction. The trustee must be properly equipped and qualified to take on the role and, failing that, can be deemed negligent. Further, the trustee could be held liable for the losses to the trust.
- The trustee must take control over the trust assets from the settlor. Failure to do so could result in the trust being deemed a sham transaction. How could there be a functional trust if the trustee does not have title to the trust assets?
- The offshore trust may not have been created for the primary purpose of hindering, delaying or frustrating existing creditors or claimants of the settlor, but it may be implemented to achieve estate planning. Many trustees require an affidavit or declaration of solvency of the settlor to that effect. The terms and significant representations generally required in this declaration are shown in Form 7-1.

The U.S. Living Trust

Most readers are aware of the attributes of the "living trust," a variation of the revocable *inter vivos trust*, but let's review its features for its applicability and contrast it with the APT:

- No estate tax advantages.

Form 7-1: Declaration or Affidavit of Solvency

1.   At the time of the transfer, you are not insolvent,[42] nor would transfers to the trust make you insolvent.

2.   You are not named as a defendant (cross-defendant) in any legal action, in a divorce or family law matter or any administrative proceeding.

3.   You are not using the APT to try to avoid any federal or state tax obligation.

4.   The assets being transferred are not more than _____ percent (settlor to insert an appropriate percentage here) of your total assets.

5.   The assets being transferred do not have as their origin any criminal activities under the laws of any country through which the assets passed, are not the product of or in violation of the bankruptcy laws of any connected country, do not violate the FDIC and RTC rules, are not the product of any fraud, drug trafficking, espionage, RICO violations, counterfeiting, kidnapping or hostage taking, or from smuggling, not in anticipation of an action for environmental pollution or copyright, patent or trademark violations. [*Author's comment:* In other words, it is "clean" or "white money," not black—or even gray—money.]

Date: _____, 199____

/S/
Sam Settlor

• Revocable by the settlor until the death of the settlor. (This defeats its efficacy as an AP tool since, during the lifetime of the settlor, a court can order the settlor to revoke the living trust under a threat of contempt of court.)

• Settlor can be a trustee of the trust. You manage your own trust. Although permitted, I believe it should *never* be done for the APT.

---

[42] During the peer review of the first draft of this book, I received an interesting comment from Mr. Jacobs to effect that the determination of an insolvency is extremely difficult, at best. Speaking as a CPA, he wrote: "I would doubt if more than a few CPAs could actually measure solvency in the way it is required for bankruptcy and fraudulent conveyance statutes, let alone a grantor. The rules appear to vary from state to state and solvency is *not* based on general accounting principles."

• Can provide for your dementia or other disabilities and avoid a costly conservatorship hearing in court. Can avoid the "public" conservator being appointed to manage the corpus of the trust.

• Created and effective while you are alive, not effective only upon your death, as in the case of the testamentary trust.

• The beneficiaries are "residual" beneficiaries in that they take what is left after the death of the settlor.

• The trustee has no duty to the creditors of the grantor, as would the executor of your will.

The Evolution of the Trust

The trust is of ancient and medieval origin. Legal historians report that within an Egyptian tomb, vestiges of a last will and testament dating 1805, BCE,[43] were discovered. Trusts were also utilized under Greek and Roman law. It is reported that the trust was so popular during the reign of August Caesar that Rome had a "trust" court for that purpose. Trust concepts continued to evolve under Islamic, Germanic and French laws, but the fundamental roots of primary interest to us derive from the English "common law." The law of trusts has been established since the Statute of Uses was adopted in England.

Naturally, through the process of evolution, the offshore islands of western Europe (Channel Islands, etc.) were at first utilized. To attract this type of business, they provided some of the following desirable characteristics.

• No taxes or low taxes.

• Tax exemptions.

• No tax status.

• Simpler regulatory requirements than the mainland.

• Active financial centres capable of providing the needed services.

---

[43] Before the Common Era.

Although the APT has its roots in the English common law, it is not to my knowledge being taught in U.S. law schools and is generally learned from attending special postgraduate seminars. The concept of going offshore for business is glamorous and romantic and also, from a practical standpoint, quite necessary for survival. Because of the globalization of institutions, I foresee a world soon to be managed (or very heavily influenced) by the multinational conglomerate more so than by the professional diplomat. World economics and individual needs break down and transcend Berlin walls, iron curtains and artificial political barriers. The world leaders of the future will be the "heads" of major multinational conglomerates. Will this global change be part of the "new world order?"

Perhaps what most precipitated the growth of the use of APTs in the U.S. is what is generally perceived as an exponential growth in litigation: You don't talk it over, you sue! Everyday one reads about the "runaway" jury awards for hot coffee spills (little old lady gets $2.7 million jury award from McDonald's[44]), teachers getting sued for giving a grade of C in mathematics, allegations of sexual harassment, recovered memories, US$9.7 million for a battery blast, New York City being sued by a firefighter for $5 million for a flea bite, landlord assessed $1 million in damages, $1,000,000 award for bee sting, and on and on. This environment of frivolous[45] litigation feeds upon itself and creates more and more copycat litigation, or even more "creative" litigation. When will *you* be sued? Notice, I didn't write "if," but "when." It may be only a matter of time; ask your friends! State

---

[44] Curiously, only the staggering initial jury awards make newspaper headlines. "If it bleeds, it leads!" What is given short shrift is the downward adjustments of these runaway verdicts by the appellate courts or the later, post-trial settlements between the parties for a more immediate resolution rather than the torturous and expensive appellate process. Parenthetically, after the so-called McDonald's hot coffee spill case appeal, the parties settled for a small fraction of the original amount.

[45] In December 1995, the U.S. Congress took initial steps against corporate frivolous litigation. Although limited to shareholder's types of suits, it is a first step towards capping runaway litigation in this area of shareholder claim fraud. Many states have followed suit in passing new laws.

Farm Mutual Automobile Insurance Company paid out $58.7 million for dog bite cases in 1994. One runaway jury returning a catastrophic judgment against you can wipe out your life's savings. Only the state and federal government can stop it by placing caps on the levels of the jury awards. I don't expect to see legislators (many of whom are attorneys) being able to do very much to protect defendants in the near future—*you must protect yourself.* As one attorney was reported to have said, "If people did to me what I do to them every day, I would be offshore with my assets."

The APT doesn't differ in many aspects from the traditional trust, except that it is traditionally offshore and irrevocable. However, the same litigious environment that encourages use of the APT may also create a higher risk of litigation because of your use of the APT. There still is a mentality that if you utilize an offshore APT you must be "guilty" and hiding something in the Caymans.

As a general proposition, your expectation should be that the APT is *a vehicle for protecting your assets by holding them offshore;* you should not be oversold that it is a guaranteed method for protecting assets in our litigious society. To avoid allegations of fraud with respect to current creditors or claimants, you must be solvent at the time you transfer the assets to the APT. I would conservatively measure solvency by two different tests, both of which you should meet.

1. Bookkeeping test. The value of your assets exceeds the level of your liabilities. For valuation purposes, assets are valued at liquidation values (FMV), *exempt assets are excluded,* and all contingent debts must be included. Assets to be transferred to the APT are excluded.

2. Bankruptcy insolvency test. You have the ability to pay your debts as they mature. Many offshore trustees require an affidavit or declaration of solvency to that effect (see Form 7-1).

The Asset Protection Trust is not necessarily utilized for tax considerations and privacy. It is primarily what the name suggests, to protect one's assets. It can be used by individuals or businesses and for alternative purposes, as well. Its uses are only limited by one's lack of imagination and creativity.

Who Needs an APT?

Some time back, the Oxford Club defined some yardsticks as to who needed asset protection. Paraphrasing and elaborating, here is their list. Their claim is that if you say yes to two or three questions, you need an APT.

• Are you in a profession with a high risk of litigation, such as physician/surgeon, manufacturer, commercial architect, CPA, or other? You know who you are by what is happening to your peers.
• Do you have a net equity of more than $500,000 free and clear in your residence?
• Do you have liquid personal property or assets with a value of more than $500,000?
• Are you a general partner in a real estate or other high-risk partnership?
• Are you an officer or director of a U.S. corporation?
• Are you a high net worth person contemplating marriage or remarriage?
• Do you have a teenager with a heavy foot on the gas pedal?
• Do you have a high financial profile or perception of high net worth that would attract litigation?
• Do you lease out equipment or rent out commercial property, or are you an apartment owner?
• Have you been underinsured or uninsured for a period of time?
• Some of the major reasons to consider a discretionary offshore APT:

• It responds to your reasonable suggestions (through "letters of wishes") while you are still alive and have your full faculties. Of course, this would be with the consent of the committee of advisors and trust protector.

• It provides for testamentary distributions offshore as an alternative to U.S. trusts. It generally insulates your provisions for future protection of your family from your current life. It can pass assets on to your beneficiaries. It could reduce or avoid probate costs and may save on estate taxes.[46]

• It enables asset managers or trustees to take positions in investment opportunities not available to U.S. persons. There is virtually an unlimited worldwide marketplace in which to invest (see Table E-2, in Appendix E, for a sampling of the varied exchanges in the world that could be utilized).

• It is a total substitute or supplement for a U.S. living trust or trust. It is an estate planning tool.

• It provides privacy–assets are not part of the U.S. banking or reporting system. (The IRS excluded–see Chapter 11.)

• It can discourage litigation (which may need to be offshore in a pro-settlor environment) and encourage earlier and hopefully less expensive settlements.

• It gives you an onshore advantage in negotiating claims against you.

• Coupled with insurance, it can be a powerful estate planning device.

• It provides for your children's and grandchildren's education.

• It can be structured to provide tax deferral, tax avoidance and minimize current tax liability (see Chapter 11).

• It provides private retirement income in anticipation of the demise of the Social Security System.

---

[46] Through skillful tax planning, the federal estate tax only applies to around 1 percent of the decedents' estates each year; approximately 25,000 returns are filed (as reported by the U.S. Treasury Department).

To protect assets, they must be *custodied* or *custodialized* (title held to, a British term) offshore. For APTs, all of the trusts' assets must either be transferred outside of the U.S. or invisible to any U.S. asset search. Table E-1 in Appendix E lists some of the diverse exchanges available for investing by the APT. If the assets are in the U.S., even though owned by an offshore entity, and if the U.S. courts can link it to you, they can still find some theory to assert jurisdiction over the assets. Even if some doubt exists in the mind of the court, they could still tie up the assets with a temporary restraining order (TRO) or a Mareva injunctive order[47] until the issue is ultimately resolved or you give up. Or a judge can issue an order that requires you to return assets to the U.S. and incarcerate you until it is done. And you thought there was no debtor's prison in the U.S.

Although known by different titles in different jurisdictions–for example, family settlement trust, family protective trust, trust deed, and trust indenture,–I believe that they all essentially serve the same purpose and treat them collectively in this book as APTs.

The Parties to the APT

The parties to the APT are the same parties as in the basic trust, except for 2, below.

1.   The creator, settlor or grantor, the person who created or settled the APT. The word "person" as used in this book is defined as an individual (including third party or "straw man"), business, company, partnership, corporation, IBC, LLC or any other entity with legal standing recognized in the jurisdiction of its creation. A sole proprietorship is not a person since it "speaks" through its owner. In this book we will use the term settlor. I believe that the settlor should not have the right to

---

[47] A Mareva order is usually sought by the creditor against the settlor. It enjoins the settlor from removing assets from the jurisdiction to frustrate the enforcement of a judgment against the settlor by a judgment creditor.

directly replace the trustee. The settlor could encourage the trustee to resign by expressing his or her dissatisfaction with the way in which the trust corpus is being managed in a private *letter of wishes*. If the trustee could not remedy the concerns, I believe that most reasonable trustees would cooperate and resign. They don't need or want adversarial scenarios with the settlor. The trust protector then could appoint a substitute trustee. Or, there may be a "standby trustee" previously appointed waiting in the "wings" to take over the role. Others use the technique of appointing three joint trustees at the onset, such that the resignation or temporary absence of a trustee fails to create a problem because the other two trustees are empowered to act.

Trust language may not provide for binding advice to the trustee and trust protector. It is advisory and not legally binding upon these parties. It can come from the settlor or the committee of advisors. When the settlor desires to provide an indication of his or her inclinations, it is traditionally done by delivering a letter of wishes to the Trustee as the means of exercising a permissible level of "trustee influence." The communications by letters of wishes may be an ongoing process with a discretionary APT as circumstances change. The following changed circumstances may precipitate a letter of wishes to the trustee: a birth, death, wedding, divorce, or separation; a provision for a disabled person; education and health care for the beneficiaries; and in response to changes in the U.S. tax laws or dual tax treaties.

The settlor may perform indirectly by being a director or officer of an offshore IBC that was created for the purpose of managing the assets of the trust. He or she could receive compensation, deferred compensation, perks, expense reimbursement, etc., some of which would be taxable upon receipt by a U.S. person. (See asset and portfolio manager, below.)

2.   The trust protector, the watchdog over the trust, oversees the trustee and the trust corpus to assure compliance of the trustee fulfilling the objectives of the APT. There may be more than one protector. The protector's duties could be defined as providing legally binding counsel and advice to the trustee on interpretation of the Trust Deed, construing the settlor's letter(s) of wishes and deciding upon the appropriate action after receiving advice from the committee of advisors, if one was authorized and in effect. The protector is not a trustee and does not manage the APT, but is an advisor to the trustee. The trustee recognizes the "veto" power of the protector. In an efficient APT, there is an ongoing dialogue between the two parties, both attempting to fulfill the wishes of the settlor but reserving the concern about all the beneficiaries being treated fairly and equally under the terms of the APT. Both act as reasonable and prudent businesspersons would under the factual circumstances so as to avoid future problems with one or more of the APT beneficiaries.

3.   The trustee is charged with the duty of capital conservation and income accumulation for the beneficiaries. A trustee is not generally recommended to be a U.S. resident or a citizen. Ideally the trustee should be a U.S. nonresident alien (NRA). This precludes the U.S. courts from issuing to the U.S. trustee court orders that are enforceable even though the assets may be located offshore. In larger estates (with a larger corpus) there could be multiple trustees, all with trust powers, and even a U.S. trustee among the group of joint trustees. Use of a U.S. trustee should be carefully researched by the service provider or planner because there may be express prohibitions in the tax haven. Many offshore trust companies may not want a U.S. based trustee. Some APT legislation specifically prohibits OS trustees. Furthermore, the Statute of Elizabeth override provisions may not apply with a U.S. co-trustee.

If there was a U.S. co-trustee, and the APT was under attack within the U.S., this U.S. trustee should intuitively resign. The trustee is usually given full discretion with respect to treatment of the beneficiaries and asset disposition with the consent of the trust protector. You need to know the trustee or have the utmost confidence in your consultant or planner who is selecting the trustee.

4.   The beneficiaries should not generally include the settlor. If the settlor is a beneficiary then there is little asset protection. However, it could serve alternatively as an offshore living trust or testamentary trust. Several classes of beneficiaries are generally created who receive in sequential order. Beneficiaries could include a family foundation, a favorite charity, children born or unborn of the marriage(s) or future marriage(s) of the settlor. A discretionary trust with full powers in the trustee grants the trustee the right to add new beneficiaries and substitute assets of equivalent value.

Although the beneficiaries can request distributions, they are at the sole discretion of the trustee and his or her interpretation of the trust.

5.   The jurisdiction's laws govern the APT. This power should be exclusive to the jurisdiction. The trust deed should unequivocally state that the trust is to be governed by offshore laws. The trust records should be maintained there or with the OS trustee, usually in the same jurisdiction.

6.   Behind-the-scenes service providers and offshore consultants may be known only to you, for your privacy. You may wish to pay by cashier's check to avoid having a permanent banking electronic record of a check drawn on your personal or business checking account. They "know" the U.S. and offshore technicalities and APT requirements. Further, they have the ingenuity to formulate a structure that won't become obsolete and fully takes into account your personal situation and present and future needs.

7.   Is the asset or portfolio manager for the trust's assets given full discretion as to investment decisions? If not, is there a committee of advisors to guide him?

8.   A committee of advisors to the trustee is optional. When one is established, the settlor can be its "chairman." The committee's opinion is not binding upon the trustee and is treated merely as advisory. It is not legally incumbent that the trustee honor the advice of the committee because the trustee must act in the best interests of the beneficiaries.

The APT is very private it is generally not a filed, registered or recorded instrument. There is no general requirement to register it with any regulatory bodies. Some jurisdictions, however, require a trust duty be paid (money-making technique) and even have a stamp affixed to the trust, but it has no local reporting requirements. Treat the APT as an unrecorded, written contract among persons. When sited in a tax free jurisdiction (the APT situs), there are no local tax filing forms, reports or other requirements. Of course, if the trustee is served with a valid court order from the local jurisdiction of competent jurisdiction, he or she would be compelled to disclose the content of the trust deed and the assets of the trust.

Other Trust Nomenclature

This final section of this chapter offers some optional legal and technical discussion.

📖 *The Rule Against Perpetuities (-)*

In English Common Law jurisdictions, equity abhors the vesting and distribution to the beneficiaries that are too distant in time. OS tax havens have adopted longer and therefore more favorable rules with respect to remote vesting than found domestically (+). For example, Bermuda, the BVIs and the Isle of Man have the

"Purpose Trust" or "Dynastic" settlements avoiding the rule against perpetuities.

This rule traditionally requires the vesting period to be generally not later than "lives in being plus 21 years." To become more attractive to you as a tax haven, some jurisdictions have extended this period, most typically the British Virgin Islands (BVI).

BVI now allows income accumulation by the trustee of the APT for any period *up to 100 years* (+). BVI has also abolished the concept that the trust is void if any beneficial vesting could occur beyond the 100-year vesting period. In addition, BVI has adopted a wait and see policy with respect to future beneficiaries. Because of these innovations and a lack of full trust legislation, some trust scholars in the offshore community are uncomfortable with BVI as an APT situs. This is a subjective position. I have referred clients there and I still am comfortable with the decisions.

📖 Rights of Settlement

Basically, the law of the trust governs. Any prohibitions against certain transfers at the settlor's domicile are inoperative with respect to the trust. The rules of inheritance and/or succession of the settlor's domicile do *not* govern the offshore APT and the assets transferred into the trust. Here again I raise the question regarding U.S. real estate. The situs remains the county in which it is located. Query: Can an onshore (U.S.) judge disregard the fact that it is owned by an offshore trust? Answer: Absolutely yes, and that is why real property is the most difficult asset to protect under asset protection strategies. I refer you again then to the concept of equity stripping discussed in Chapters 5 and 10.

📖 Different Types (Classes) of Creditors

Your alleged fraud (fraudulent transfer) with respect to your creditor or claimant falls into one of three classes based on *when* the factual situation occurred with respect to the asset transfer. These three classes are unique to the area of fraudulent transfers:

1.   present,

2.   subsequent, and

3.   future.

Item 3, future creditors, is the most difficult to address. The statutory laws of the tax haven determine the prescribed treatment for future creditors. Get professional help with this blurred issue. For example, what is the difference between a subsequent and future creditor? A tough issue to put in black and white.

Some tax havens have recognized the different classes of creditors: Bahamas, Bermuda, Cayman Islands, Cook Islands, Cyprus, Gibraltar, Mauritius, Nevis, Turks and Caicos Islands

The Statute of Elizabeth

In 1570, the English Common Law jurisdictions began to contend with the restrictions imposed by the Statute of Elizabeth, which was intended to defeat and set aside transfers of assets and property where the transferor's intended purpose was to frustrate, hinder or delay *future* but *unknown* creditors or claimants.[48] Tax havens that are more favorably inclined to court trust business have enacted legislation with provisions to override the Statute of Elizabeth. An old English case[49] started the confusion by blurring the distinction between subsequent and future creditors, establishing the principle that there was no difference between the two. The override statutes of the more progressive tax havens

---

[48] The laws of approximately 19 U.S. states have the equivalent restrictions as in the Statute of Elizabeth. California, for example, looks for "badges of fraud." The elements of badges of fraud include: Was the transfer to an insider? Did the transferor retain control over the assets transferred? Was the primary intent to "remove" or "conceal" the assets? Did the transferor receive adequate or fair consideration for the assets? Was the transferor being sued? The Statute of Elizabeth was first codified in the U.S. as the Uniform Fraudulent Conveyance Act and later replaced with the Uniform Fraudulent Transfer Action.

[49] Re: Butterworth, 1882, 19 Ch D 588.

remedy this problem. Clearly an immediate but subsequent creditor should be treated differently that a distant future creditor.

The following tax havens are known to have enacted override provisions (+): Bahamas, Cayman Islands, Cook Islands, Gibraltar, Mauritius and Nevis.

📖 *Forced Heirship*

You as a settlor cannot deprive the heirs to your estate (your wealth and assets) of their rights according to local law except where just circumstances may exist to disinherit them. For example, you can't bequeath or devise your spouse's community property interest in the community (the assets owned by the spouses). The APT circumvents the forced heirship laws of your local jurisdiction.

📖 *Choice of Law*

The trust deed may specify that the laws of a specific jurisdiction may govern the APT. I feel that this choice would be fine if there is some nexus to that jurisdiction. Where there are no contacts with the specified jurisdiction, problems may arise. At a late date, the court of the relevant jurisdiction may not believe it could carry out its equitable jurisdiction and the APT may not be recognized by the jurisdiction. Choice of law should have a basis in the local precedent of the jurisdiction and by general principles under international law.

Clearly, the following contacts should make for a sufficient nexus with the jurisdiction:

1.   A local trustee.

2.   A local grantor.

3.   Investment activity controlled locally.

4.   Local meeting between the trustee and trust protector.

📖 *In rem jurisdiction*

When the assets are physically located in the U.S., for example real property, the local court has jurisdiction over the property. The mere fact that the title of the real property is in the name of an offshore trustee does not negate the power of the U.S. court to affect the property. If the trustee objects to the court's proposed action, he or she is free to appear in the U.S. to object. Unfortunately, once appearing, the court then has jurisdiction over the trustee as well as the property.

What if the OS trustee is delivered a demand letter from a U.S. attorney, perhaps even one which includes a copy of a valid and enforceable U.S. court order with respect to the settlor? The trustee may ignore it (and usually does) because the foreign jurisdiction has no standing in the tax haven. The U.S. attorney is left with a difficult financial judgment call: Does he or she retain local counsel in the tax haven and file a new suit? If the statute has already "run," the attorney may be unable to effectively file. Does this give him or her the impetus to convince the judgment creditor to settle the matter?

Assuming we have a bulldog for counsel (in other words, on a contingent fee arrangement with the creditor) or a highly emotional plaintiff, money be damned, with a let's "sue the bastards" attitude, what do you do? You exhaust them emotionally and financially bankrupt them to a point where they will settle with you. How? By utilizing many of the following mechanisms: duress provisions, flight provisions, recandle provisions, "ransom" clauses, side letters of wishes and the "Cuba" clause, to name a few.

📖 *Actionable Fraud and the "Badges of Fraud"*

The APT and the settlor are attacked on the basis of transfers of assets made to the APT under circumstances alleged to be fraudulent. Fraud is considered under three different bodies of law:

1.   The state's laws.

2.   The Bankruptcy Code.

3.   The offshore fraud laws of the applicable jurisdiction.

The factual situation on the day of the transfer of the asset is to be considered. Was there an actual intent on the part of the settlor to hinder, defraud and delay the creditor by the asset transfer? Is there a *cloud of fraudulent conveyances*? Was the fraud hard or soft? *Hard fraud* is defined as a finding that the settlor actually intended to hinder, defraud and delay the creditor, whereas *soft fraud* is a constructive fraud ascertained by the facts.

The so-called *badges of fraud* are also referred to as the 11 commandments and the "indicia" of fraud. In nonlegalese they are summarized as follows:

1.   The settlor made a transfer of an asset before the APT was created to an insider such as a family member, friend, close professional, or employee.

2.   The settlor continued to assert control over the asset or retained possession of the "transferred" asset.

3.   The settlor made the transfer to remove the asset from his or her estate or to conceal its existence.

4.   The settlor failed to receive "fair" consideration for the transferred asset. It must be an equitable exchange or it fails the "smell test."

5.   The transferred asset was concealed from the creditor.

6.   The transfer was made while the settlor was being threatened with litigation or after actually being sued.

7.   The settlor transferred substantially all his or her assets to the trust.

8.   The settlor was insolvent or became insolvent at the time of the transfer or shortly thereafter.

9.   The settlor had absconded.

10.   The transfer was made just before or after the settlor accrued new debt.

11.   The settlor transferred all of his or her business assets to a secured creditor who in turn transferred them to an insider of the settlor.

How many badges of fraud give rise to a fraudulent conveyance? If they are major, only one or two are necessary.

📖 Duress Provisions

Your well drafted trust deed and/or letter of wishes provides direction and guidance to the trustee and protector. The condition of *duress* arises when a U.S. demand is made by a third party upon the OS trustee. A higher degree of duress would be when a copy of a U.S. court order is served upon the trustee OS or, even worse, served upon the OS trustee while present in the U.S. In the latter case, the U.S. court has acquired jurisdiction (power) over the trustee and the trust. We will ignore this unfortunate case and stick to the legal obligations of an OS trustee (or trust protector) to "foreign" demands or court orders.

Basic trust language and the side letter provides sufficient guidance to the trustee to automatically ignore any "foreign inquiry, demand or court order" creating a situation of duress. Some writers refer to this wryly as a ransom clause. Simply stated, the trustee and protector are bound and/or advised to disregard any demand for funds from any entity, including the settlor, in an environment of duress.

📖 *Settlor in Contempt of Court*

Once the settlor has irrevocably transferred assets to the APT, he or she has voluntarily yielded control over the assets. The question: Is the voluntary disposition of assets by a settlor with knowledge of the possibility of future claims against him an act of contempt?

One example of a condition of duress would be the settlor writing a letter to the trustee as shown in Form 7-2.

Form 7-2: Condition of Duress: An Example

123 Main Street
Anytown, USA
February 12, 1996

Re: The Smith Family Protective Trust

Dear Trustee:

Unfortunately, as a result of frivolous litigation and a runaway jury verdict, there was a large judgment entered against me in the Superior Court in California on February 1, 1995 on behalf of an undeserving litigant.

The appeal failed and the judgment has become final. The judgment creditor is seeking to collect on the judgment. I have been served with the attached court order. My attorney advises my that it is a valid court order and I must comply with it. It orders me to repatriate my assets and direct you to return funds in the amount of US$1,000,000, to satisfy the judgment. I have been ordered to satisfy this judgment with the assets offshore that are of a sufficient sum to do so.

I have no interest in being held in contempt of court with respect to this order and hereby direct you to liquidate any and all assets of the referenced trust to comply with this bona fide court order.

Your immediate and prompt attention to this order would be appreciated. Please advise when the funds will be wire transferred.

Sincerely yours,
/s/ A. Frustrated Settlor

What does the trustee do? With the appropriate clauses and language previously and unequivocally drafted in the trust deed and the letter(s) of wishes, nothing. Or even more to the point, what authority does a foreign person or court have in the

APT's jurisdiction or situs? Are you going to be found in contempt? Not likely, as you have done all you can do; you provided immediate and unequivocal instructions to the trustee. If the trustee fails to act, it was his or her judgment call. You did not obstruct the enforcement of the Order.

📖 Flight Provisions:
The "Fleet" Clause or the "Cuba" Clause

One could provide for political instability, major changes in APT or IBC laws (very unlikely) or onshore duress with *automatic* or *discretionary flight* language. The language providing for these events are sometimes referred to as "fleet" or "Cuba" clauses. Flight results from one or both of these specified events:

1. Major changes in the political environment of the tax haven affecting banking laws, privacy, the APT or the IBC, resulting in the trust being relocated or recandled in another IFC.

2. The occurrence of a condition of duress, the trustee and/or trust protector resigning and a standby trustee and/or trust protector assuming those duties.

📖 Enforcement of Foreign Judgments

Tax havens which don't recognize "foreign" judgments are preferred. They require that a new (*de novo*) action be filed. The settlor may benefit if the statute of limitations has run precluding the filing of a new lawsuit in the tax haven. The statute with respect to actual fraud begins to run when it is discovered by the damaged party or an asset is transfered to the trust.

📖 Costs

The APT and its companion entities comprising your offshore plan are complex to formulate. You must select a professional (or even multiple professionals) to assist you and be willing to pay reasonable fees. Don't forget the cost of maintenance services and annual reporting dictated by the IRC in the subsequent years.

Reasonable fees for setting up an APT are divided as between onshore and offshore and between the initial first-year set-up costs and the subsequent annual fees. Setting up your offshore structure properly will not be "inexpensive." But one must also consider the extrinsic benefits. The larger the estate going offshore, the more cost effective it becomes. The question is, "How much will ultimately go into the structure?" Measure costs in terms of value added as well as the subjective benefits–you *can* get ripped-off.

Some typical ranges of offshore fees you may encounter for an APT are:

• First year acceptance fee for setting-up the trust. $1,000 to $5,000.
• Annual trustee's fees in addition to the set-up fees. $1,500 to $3,000.

What should you get for your money?

1. A professional acting in the capacity of the trustee for the year.

2. A brokerage account opened for investing by the trustee or asset manager on behalf of the trust, if required.

3. A trust bank account opened.

4. Extraordinary services charged at flat rate negotiated with the trustee or at an hourly rate of $100 to $200 per hour.

5. Out of pocket expenses, for example, FedEx, DHL, UPS, banking fees, or wire transfer fees, charged as incurred.

📖 Technicalities

The following items are very complex technical issues. It is suggested that they be addressed with your OS planner and service provider–this subject matter is not suited for "do-it-yourselfers." All of these issues should be pondered and answered when applicable. Although directed towards APTs, they may apply equally to other OS entities.

1.   Settlor being a beneficiary of the APT.

2.   Level of "control" of settlor over the APT or IBC.

3.   When the APT is under attack by a creditor:
a. Degree of recognition by the tax haven of "foreign" judgments.
b. Local standards of law for the blocking or freezing the assets located there.
c. Standard of proof required in the local jurisdiction.
d. Upon whom rests the initial burden of proof? Does the burden shift and if so, when?
e. If the creditor is successful in setting aside the fraudulent transfer, does the APT remain valid?

4.   Efficacy of the "choice of law" selection in the APT. Generally factors to consider in the choice of law analysis would be: English common law, Statute of Elizabeth abrogated, stable economy and experienced professionals.

5.   Where flight of the APT has resulted in a new jurisdiction, what level of protection will be afforded by the immigrant APT in the redomiciled jurisdiction?

In summary, you need a trust you can trust, a proven structure and shield and a base for operating other investment interests. It may be for asset protection, estate planning or business planning purposes.

8
Offshore Banks and Banking Services

Offshore Credit or Debit Cards

Offshore bankers are competing with American bankers for your profitable credit card business and I believe the offshore credit card, having more advantages, is the winner. There is nothing illegal about possessing and using an offshore credit card.

If you crave privacy, avoid using your onshore credit cards. They provide an ongoing, permanent, electronic diary of where you have been, what you buy, how much you spend, where you shop, who you telephoned, what telephone companies you use, where you entertain and vacation, travel agents and airlines you use, etc. Charge your discrete expenses offshore!

U.S. credit card companies (card issuers) analyze this data and market the data for profit to any firm interested in demographics, consumer profiles and psychographics. Buyers consist of telemarketing firms, insurance salespeople, mail order houses, the IRS, private detectives, and even competitors of your credit card issuer. I am not aware of any laws prohibiting selling this data. Your assumption of the privacy of your domestic credit card transactions is a fallacy.

Recognizing this trend, more and more people are acquiring offshore credit cards for privacy. Be certain that the OS issuing bank is in a jurisdiction that has strong banking privacy laws;–not all OS credit cards are equal in this respect. (For a confidential issuer, see Offshore Assets Reconciliation Limited in Appendix D.) Credit reporting bureaus do not legally have access to the OS card system.

Most offshore credit cards are in reality "secured credit cards." Your card line of credit is generally between 50 percent and 66.66 percent of the amount on deposit in an interest bearing savings account with the offshore bank. It is wise from the privacy standpoint to use banks which do not have a branch office in the States. This prevents a *subpoena* or a *subpoena duces tecum*[50] from being served upon the U.S. branch to provide credit card sales records, or for that matter any kind of onshore court order from being effective.

General Banking Rules

The rule that one should bank with an offshore bank that has no U.S. branches applies to your other offshore banking needs. Although not having a branch in New York City, an affiliate bank is required to access the Federal Reserve Bank's wire transfer system for USD transfers. Using an affiliate does not give the OS bank a legal presence[51] in the U.S.

Unless you are suspected of being involved in money laundering or drug trafficking, offshore banks will not honor a request for information or an order from a court that is outside of their jurisdiction. There is much more banking privacy offshore in the tax havens than in the States.

---

[50] A subpoena duces tecum is an order to provide the demanded records without the necessity of a personal appearance, in contrast to a subpoena to produce the person.

[51] Familiarity breeds comfort. On first inclination, a Californian would probably be more comfortable with the Bank of America. The BofA is the largest California bank and the third largest in the U.S. with offshore banking in 37 countries. However, based on what has been seen before in the U.S. legal system, service of a subpoena upon the U.S. office of Barclays bank in New York was deemed sufficient service to compel disclosure of account information on an offshore account in an offshore bank. Thereafter, Barclays Bank closed its New York office.

In the U.S., if you can afford the price, you can do an asset search and identify the banks that a person uses as well as the account numbers and balances. Legal? I think not, but it is done regularly by commercial asset locators–for a fee of course. Every month the official State Bar of California magazine carries advertisements of this nature, and no one seems to be concerned about the privacy issues. I have yet to see or hear of banking privacy being so easily invaded in the tax havens. Such an action would cause a rapid flight of capital to another jurisdiction the country would be put out of the tax haven business. If you appreciate that in many jurisdictions the income generated by the financial community exceeds the income from tourism you can appreciate why banking privacy is so preciously guarded. The reputation for banking privacy is ultimate, and once lost it can never be fully regained. Those of us in the offshore industry still speak of scandals that occurred many years ago as if they were only yesterday. What happened to all the funds held in the Swiss Trust, operating in Brazil? "They" never found it! (Obviously, we have little to gossip about!)

Private and Numbered Accounts

The day of private Swiss banking[52] is *passé*. It is Swiss cheese! There is no longer such a thing as a secret Swiss numbered bank account. *C'est fini*! I no longer characterize Switzerland as a banking haven for privacy because the Swiss have "sharing arrangements" with other countries, including Germany and the U.S.; if Swiss deposits are found to be of a "criminal nature," the Swiss will share them with the country demanding their return– quite a profit center!

Swiss greed may tend to make their banking records too open to outsiders. Further, because of the Iran Contra scandal, BCCI money laundering and fraud, the American Express Bank's activities and other banking scandals, responsible offshore banks

---

[52] Jones, Michael Arthur, *Swiss Bank Accounts, A Personal Guide to Ownership, Benefits and Use*, 1990, Liberty Hall Press, an imprint of McGraw-Hill, Inc.

now are mandated to follow the philosophy of knowing their customers. Western European banks take accounts from people and companies from the CIS[53] with guarded reluctance. Caribbean banks generally require from new customers a passport or other photo ID, social security number or driver's license number (always give the latter), a personal visit, a reference letter from your present bank and perhaps even sponsors. Some even correspond with the bank issuing the reference letter to verify it. Unfortunately, this erodes your privacy, as the inquiry letter from the offshore bank becomes a permanent part of your file with your onshore bank.

Many banks now require their offshore customers to execute a consent form (see Figure 8-1 for a sample from Canadian Imperial Bank of Commerce, in Nassau). The release enables the bank to provide banking information to the *government (read IRS here) of other jurisdictions.* This overrides the banking privacy laws and obligations of confidentiality of the Bahamas.

The European Commission would like to standardize banking among its member countries, and numbered banking is not compatible with its agenda. But the glamour of the *chop block account*, Austrian *Sparbuch account,* and the *numbered account* remain, suggesting that we take a moment to discuss them for historical purposes.

The Chop Block Account

In an effort to provide banking services to their wealthy but illiterate customers, Hong Kong's British banks developed and accepted (some still do to a limited degree) a hand-printing device called the chop block. They were used just as one utilizes the rubber stamp. The adult population was largely illiterate, so this was essential to conduct commerce. As an alternative to the signature, Chinese would "chop" instructions to their bank. The chop originally was carved from ivory but now is carved on wood or stone or cast in metal. Because it was hand-carved, each stamp

---

[53] The new abbreviation for the former Soviet Union, the Congress of Independent States.

FIGURE 8-1: Consent Form—An Example

FROM: ───────────────   ───────────────
       NAME   SOCIAL SECURITY NUMBER

───────────────   (hereinafter referred to as "the Customer")
       ADDRESS

───────────────

───────────────

TO: CANADIAN BANK OF COMMERCE (hereinafter referred to as "the Bank")

1.   The Customer, being neither a citizen or a resident of the Bahamas, acknowledges that the Governments of other jurisdictions may have valid powers under their Laws to require the Bank under certain circumstances and after specified procedures have been accomplished, to produce information and records of the Bank to the specified Governmental and/or judicial authorities of those jurisdictions.

2.   The Customer has been advised and so acknowledges that the Bank's operations in the Bahamas and its obligations of confidentiality are governed by Laws of the Bahamas, which may not permit the production of information and records referred to in Paragraph 1 above, unless the Customer has specifically authorized the Bank to do so.

3.   The Customer hereby instructs the Bank upon the happening of an event in Paragraph 1 hereof to give information and to produce records pertaining to all transactions of the nature referred to in Paragraph 4 hereof where and to extent the Bank is of the opinion that the Law of those other jurisdictions requires the Bank to do so, to those Governmental and judicial authorities of those other jurisdictions.

4.   The forgoing instructions extend to information and records relating to transactions between the Customer and the Bank and to all accounts of the company and/or its principals.

───────────────   ───────────────
PLACE   DATE

───────────────
SIGNATURE OF CUSTOMER

was unique, perhaps as unique as one's fingerprints. The chop seal was fully accepted by the bank. However, one must distinguish how it was treated. The chop was like a bearer instrument; whoever had possession of the chop effectively controlled the assets.

It is suggested that if some foreign national would open a chop account for you and then turn over the chop to you, you would have an anonymous account. Currently, fewer and fewer Hong Kong banks accept the block, some limiting its use only to passbook savings accounts.

The Sparbuch (Savings) Account

Carrying the full name of the Austrian Ueberbringer Sparbuch, this form of private numbered savings bank account is exclusively Austrian. It is a "bearer" savings account book. The European Commission (the former European Union), under the "Doctrine of Euro-compatible" (author's language), had initially appeared to compel Austria to discontinue issuing this type of account effective July 1, 1996.[54] But it has apparently survived. The Sparbuch is intended to be a means of creating an anonymous bearer account for complete personal privacy. Although appearing suspicious to the outside world, they are completely legal in Austria. One could open the Sparbuch account in any name so long as it wasn't obscene. They are usually opened through "agents" who charge an administrative fee (from US$50.00-280.00) for doing so. I wonder how many John Smith accounts they have from the U.S.? The account is further protected by a personal password. Walk in with the passbook and the password and all the money is yours. Forget the password and say good-bye to your money. (See Appendixes C and D for contact names in Austria and the United Kingdom. If you speak German, you can probably open up a Sparbuch   yourself).

---

[54] As far as can be determined at this date, existing accounts will remain private under Austrian banking secrecy laws, but new trading and activities will be curtailed.

The *Wertpapierbuch* account, a securities book account, is similar in certain respects to the Sparbuch. It allows you to purchase and sell stocks and bonds with comparable privacy. Effective July 1, 1996, Austria will ban this form of anonymous security trading account to comply with EC initiatives. Only new trading will be prohibited; standing accounts will be permitted so long as there is no new trading.

Monetary Policies and Exchange Controls

This can be formal and expressed or de facto. Many countries have expressed laws regarding exchange control. These laws generally limit the amount of money one may move outside of that country without a license to do so. As a practical matter in the normal course of business, there should be no problems. The problem being addressed by exchange controls is that of limiting flight capital. Since flight capital rarely returns to that country, the loss results in permanent economic damage to the economy.

Private Banking

Private banking is not merely banking in privacy: It is the utilization of an offshore private bank for your onshore and international personal and/or business needs. If you can justify the economics, an OS private bank can be created just for you, issuing Visa cards carrying your portrait. Process that thought for a moment!

Generally, a private bank offers its services only to high net worth (HNW) individuals. Estimates are that such private banks currently manage more than US$2.5 trillion in OS funds, comprising significant flight capital. An international OS bank may create a private banking department for their HNW customers. The definition of a HNW customer generally is one having *liquid assets* to manage in excess of half a million dollars. HNW individuals seek protection, total service and flexibility; they need their personal wealth to fund business ventures as required without undue complications. While the funds are awaiting utilization, the private bankers are expected to provide fund or asset management, and they are more than happy to do so in that they generate management fees of around 0.5 to 1.5 percent per year on the assets under management. Asset management services can range from a fully discretionary account to a customer directed one.

For example, HSBC Investment Bank Asia Holding, the former Wardley, has a private banking unit called HSBC Investment Bank Asia. They report that they need a staff of over 100 people to serve more than 2,000 HNW customers holding more than US$9 billion. That is a ratio of only 20 HNW customers per employee and a US$4.5 million average for each client!

Switzerland continues to be the global kingpin of private banking with approximately a 40 percent market share.

Your Personal Private Bank

Weekly, I see for sale advertisements in *The Wall Street Journal* for private OS banks. Before rushing off to create your own bank, consider some of the following questions that need to be first analyzed and ultimately answered, presented in no special order of priority.

1.   Why bother? A custom-created IBC can perform most of the functions.

2.   Who do you utilize for a feasibility study?

3.   Where should you establish it?

4.   What can it do/not do?

5.   What should you expect of it?

6.   What will it cost?

7.   How long will it take?

8. Who can utilize it?

9. Who manages it?

10. Who will be the fund or asset manager?

11. Who should you use to create it?

If after digesting the 11 points above, if you still have a strong interest in acquiring your own private Swiss bank, take a look at a typical offering as shown in Figure 8-2 on page 118.

Privacy

As the Internet becomes more ubiquitous, more and more financial and encrypted transactions will occur by secure electronics. Many banks are seeking a proprietary global position by their affiliations. What is still lacking at the time this book was written is a secure way of handling financial and credit card transactions over the Internet. Too many systems are vulnerable to hacking and the theft of credit card account numbers. The Netscape™ secured system is limited by the U.S. government to a low level of encryption for export purposes, which puts their global system in jeopardy.

Mark Twain Bank in St. Louis, Missouri (phone number (800) 684-5623) is the only U.S. member of the DigiCash™ system, enabling its members to transfer money, called electronic cash or e-cash,[55] among themselves. In 1995 it began accepting account applications over the Internet that enabled customers to deposit and withdraw "e-cash," real money. Their initial test was conducted with a cap of 10,000 customers.

---

[55] The U.S. Treasury department is quite concerned about the opportunities for tax avoidance or evasion over the Internet, advised Joseph Guttentag, Treasury's international tax counsel. He is quite concerned over electronic payment systems that provide for anonymous Internet fund transfers outside of the "conventional banking channels." He is quoted as saying the Treasury will ". . . maintain tax toll booths on the information superhighway. . . ."

FIGURE 8-2: Swiss Bank Offer–An Example

Switzerland

A Tradition of Integrity & Trust

<u>Private Investment Bank available for Acquisition / Urgent attention required</u>

Gain the **edge** and **prestige** reserved for the **Swiss Investment Banker**
Profit from investment banking activities in Switzerland
Profit from investment banking activities internationally
Pristine offices in **Geneva** for meeting clients
Rare opportunity offers tremendous resale potential
Perfect vehicle for family trust investments
Financial privacy as an **offshore depository**
Cyber banking & brokerage capabilities for **"cutting edge"** trading
Gateway to **European markets** to enhance your corporate profile
Strength of license provides easy access to corresponding relationships
Stability & history of Switzerland provides **peace of mind**
Accounts with **major European banks**
Virtually **no tax** form host country on offshore activities
Expertise of local representatives offers competitive advantages
Benefit from placing international **IPO's**
Multicurrency Facility for arbitrage and hedge positions

Only one of a kind and . . .

Simply the best offshore opportunity ever . . .

<u>**Swiss Investment Bank & Brokerage**</u> *The distinction of being acknowledged as the world's greatest financial haven has been handed down by the Swiss from generation to generation. Today still, Swiss banking law is legendary, with every tax haven using the embodiment of their creditability as a benchmark. Through the offices of Worldwide Business Consultants, Inc. a fully chartered Investment Bank & Brokerage is immediately available for acquisition. One reward to business success is the ability to take advantage of unique opportunities that require substance, and yet offer considerable upside potential. This is one such opportunity. Full merchant banking authority, trust authority, brokerage authority, escrow accounts and much more are applicable. No liabilities exist. Call for an extensive report. Price: US$176,500*

This is neither an offer to sell nor a solicitation of an offer to buy either domestic or foreign securities

⌨ Mark Twain Bank at http://www.marktwain.com
⌨ DigiCash at http://www.digicash.com

Private companies, such as Offshore eAsset Reconciliation (OAR) in Nassau, capitalized on the current inherent privacy weaknesses of some existing systems by using a higher level of encryption than, for example, Netscape. A technology called Pretty Good Privacy (PGP™ for short) is utilized by OAR for their worldwide clients to exercise secured financial transactions.
⌨ Offshore eAssets Reconciliation Limited at
http://www.dnai.com/offshore/offshore.html

9
Annuities

General Background

The annuity appears to be one of the fastest growing new products offered by the U.S. insurance industry and now banks. Banks have discovered a new profit center in annuity products, and they now account for approximately 25 percent of the annuity sales in the U.S. Annuities are popular because of tax deferral and, because they encourage savings, they are endorsed by the U.S. government. American insurance companies finally noticed what the Swiss were doing and wanted a piece of the action.

It is obvious why annuities have become so popular providing tax deferral on earnings. They can also be used to supplement an IRA or 401(k) without any annual limit upon purchases by you. Annuities are intended to provide for long-term tax deferral. The annuity affords an opportunity to let capital grow and compound with an accumulation of interest and dividends, free of ongoing annual taxes. There are no taxes until distribution to the RA, the *annuitant*. As a caveat, the distributions are taxed at the ordinary income tax rates, not at the long-term capital gains rates. No federal, state or local taxes are assessed during the compounding period. It affords an excellent opportunity of providing for your retirement years, when you'll appreciate the security of receiving regular monthly or quarterly payments.

Much has been written about the various types of annuities, and I will leave that subject to other writers. Study and learn the new, strange vocabulary and the cost factors, for the initial purchase and ongoing expenses. For instance, can you define immediate annuity, deferred annuity, variable annuity, fixed annuity, single premium, lump sum or periodic fixed premiums, and two-life gift annuity? Your annuity is burdened with annual administrative expenses (and profits). These annual costs can vary from 1.4 to 2.25 percent, as a reasonable range. I have also seen 4 percent (ugh!). I highly recommend some background reading at your library before proceeding with the remainder of this chapter.

Going Offshore–The Swiss Annuity

Now that you have done some studying about the basics of an annuity and its unique vocabulary, let's continue. Many of these annuity offerings to the consumer come directly from and are actively solicited from offshore annuity companies. The Swiss are famous in this industry. I will use the term "company" hereafter for simplicity. Curiously, the annuity is *not* considered by the U.S. Supreme Court as an insurance policy but as a written unsecured contract (promise) to pay the annuitant (that's you) at a certain rate by the company, commencing upon the effective date you have selected, until your death. The terms depend upon your age, health, type of investment selected, last to die provisions and other factors. The annuity is treated as an offering of an investment in some dividend formats under many jurisdictions. The annuity may or may not have residual value that flows into your estate upon your death.

The U.S. government monitors this OS capital outflow by their imposition of a 1 percent excise tax upon the annuitant for the principal payment to some OS annuity issuers. Check with your OS consultant.

An annuity is one of the few remaining forms of a tax shelter. After sending your tax-neutral funds offshore to the company, they can grow free of annual capital gains and other U.S.

taxes until they are distributed.[56] Upon annuity distributions, certain tax rules apply. The return of your own funds is not a taxable event. Only the capital gains and interest (dividends) paid by the company are taxable in the tax year distributed. Not all offshore companies issue a U.S. form 1099R at year end, so it is important to keep your tax records.

A Swiss annuity[57] offers excellent asset protection. Under Swiss law, an annuity cannot be seized by any court-ordered collection procedure instigated by creditors. Thus, even though you might become the victim of a frivolous lawsuit, the judgment could not be enforced in Switzerland. Swiss annuities are exempt from reporting to the IRS even though the amount may be over $10,000. Most Swiss annuities allow you to designate a choice of three currencies, the Swiss franc (SFR), the Deutsche mark or the ECU. In 1995, the Swiss franc outperformed the USD. The profits earned by the annuity is free of Swiss taxes. Swiss insurance companies are extremely stable. In 130 years, no Swiss insurance company has failed to meet its financial obligations or ceased operations. They provide trust, stability, discretion and reliability.

The Private Annuity

The private annuity is derived from the scenario where an elderly person transferred a highly appreciated business interest to a child or younger employee. It resulted in a stream of payments and was a substitute for insurance. The value of the private annuity must be at least the value of the asset transferred.

An offshore private annuity is a further refinement. A private annuity is defined as an *unsecured contract* between the issuing company (the offshore IBC) and the annuitant and is based upon the age and health of the annuitant at the time of contracting

---

[56] Distributions create a tax liability whether or not the funds are expatriated—returned to the U.S.

[57] 🖳 For information on the advantages and features of a Swiss Annuity plus many other topics which should be of interest to the readers of this book, surf to Switzerland: http://www.jml.ch/jml/

(life expectancy), the maturity date and the stream of payments. The life expectancy tables can't be used where the death of the annuitant is certain within 12 months.

Under one of the last Internal Revenue Code's more popular loopholes, intended to encourage the future financial security of the RA and reduce the need for governmental old-age assistance, we find a variation of the traditional annuity. The *offshore private annuity contract* is becoming a more popular variation of the basic annuity as an advanced international tax planning and asset protection strategy. The private annuity (PA) is generally issued by or through an OS IBC created specifically for that purpose. By issuing the PA offshore, it can afford better asset protection to the annuitants in that the principal cannot be reached by an onshore creditor. If the PA is irrevocable and issued from offshore, no creditor or domestic court order can affect its OS sanctity. The exception would be for the income stream received by the annuitant, which could be attached by creditors, but only as it is received.

Continuing on with the scenario, the RA, as the annuitant, purchases a lump-sum private annuity from the IBC. The annuitant pays money or transfers assets (for example, some highly appreciated stock) as the consideration for the PA, or perhaps that money which was borrowed under an equity stripping arrangement (see Figure 5-4). Alternatively, he or she can transfer highly appreciated liquid assets at current market value for the PA. The IBC takes and gives equal value for value and neither has a capital gains obligation upon the transfer; it is not a sale if structured correctly. The capital gains tax problem has been shifted to the offshore IBC. The annuitant pays capital gains and income taxes later as the annuity payment stream begins. After the death of the annuitant the private annuity may be part of the decedents estate unless other provisions are made in structuring the PA. This way you have frozen the market value of the asset in return for the face value of the PA. The capital gains and income taxes are deferred until receipt.

The IBC usually obtains the annuity contract from another entity, usually another offshore IBC2. Upon maturity of the PA, the IBC acts as the fulfillment organization and makes the appropriate payments.

10
Other Structures and Strategies

Offshore Exempt Companies

In those jurisdictions that don't approve of the concept of a Caribbean style company act (most of the European jurisdictions don't) but do want to attract and encourage international company business, we find local variations of exempt company acts. Some jurisdictions may believe that the IBC is a tainted form of company structure used by some for tax evasion or at least for "sharp practices."

Some legal scholars even go so far as to postulate that the IBC may create a unique, untested legal problem: actual recognition of the IBC in the international courts. The interesting legal issue is that if a jurisdiction has two types of companies, one for locals that requires complete disclosure and a second type of company (the IBC) to be used only by foreigners requiring no disclosure and providing complete privacy, should this "pirate" company be given international recognition? There has not yet been a case addressing this issue.

An OS Company Limited by Guaranty

This form of company (corporation) has different characteristics than traditional in America. It is more comparable to the limited liability company. It is generally authorized under the English type of company laws, as found in the Bahamas, the British Virgin Islands, Hong Kong, Gibraltar, Cyprus, the Republic of Ireland and the Isle of Man, among others. With drafting skills, for example, a company can be formed with the characteristics of a partnership.

A Company with a Limited Lifetime

This type of company includes provisions for limiting the duration or lifetime of the company. Under traditional U.S. corporate laws, a corporation has an infinite lifetime. Limiting the lifetime of the company provides for automatic liquidation of the company upon the expiration of its established lifetime or a resignation of a member. Further provisions could also be made that would restrict the transferability of interests in the company, which is more difficult to do with an IBC.

The Contract Hybrid Company

This is a newer form of exempt company originally developed in the Isle of Man. It was first presented at the American Bar Association meeting in London in 1996. The Contract Hybrid Company (CHC) was developed in anticipation of the ultimate passage of the Revenue Reconciliation Bill of 1995 sometime in 1996. The CHC provides for U.S. persons to take and hold assets offshore without giving rise to any tax liability to the U.S. or any U.S. reporting requirements. A U.S. tax will arise when the assets are repatriated to the U.S., but so long as assets remain in the Contract Hybrid Company taxes are indefinitely deferred. Because the CHC is new and without mass competition, they are quite dearly priced, starting at a minimum of US$16,000 to setup and $8,000 minimum to annually maintain.

Demystifying Residence:
Domicile, Citizenship and Passports

For a number of decades, Europeans have been using the elements of residence, domicile, citizenship and passports to implement very successful tax avoidance and asset protection strategies. In recent years, a number of reluctant Americans have also been following this strategy. The exponential growth of this trend has become so pronounced that it has been the subject of a *Fortune* magazine cover story (see "The New Refugees," November 1994). Unfortunately, it has also drawn the attention of the U.S. government.

The good news is that there is still an opportunity to limit or avoid U.S. estate taxes; the bad news is that the elimination or reduction of income, capital gain and gift taxes may become curtailed in the next year or so by the proposed Revenue Reconciliation Bill of 1995.

People interested in the question of residence have various personal agendas as to why it is of interest. It might be a combination of one or more of the following factors:

• Fear that holding a specific nationality's passport puts you in high peril from terrorists. For example, Americans are very popular with terrorists who take hostages for ransom.

• Fears of eventual political instability in the United States, government overregulation, policies and taxes construed as confiscatory; concerns over lack of personal privacy, perceived weaknesses in the American banking system; preparation for an OS retirement and a quest for financial security.

• Concern that certain countries may unexpectedly confiscate one's principal passport because it contains a visa or entry stamp from a prohibited country. Or a concern that while visiting offshore civil disobedience or war may cause a confiscation of one's passport.[58]

• Need to open an offshore bank account or brokerage account more privately.

• Limitation of some real estate acquisitions, employment opportunities or business ventures to only those with passports.

• Need to legally preserve or salvage some of your assets if you are a party to a very hostile divorce or partnership dissolution. You can legally open an OS bank account using tax-neutral money with the second passport in a second name, as an a.k.a. (also known as) so long as it is not for any fraudulent intent.

• Need for a temporary refuge after a bankruptcy or if you are a victim of a runaway jury verdict.

• Ability to travel without creating a permanent record of where you have been on your U.S. passport.

To begin to develop strategies in this area, you must first understand the vocabulary.

1.   *Residency*

Residency generally has both a tax and an immigration element. Tax residency is usually based upon a count of the number of days in a jurisdiction or a review of various indicia of residency indicating centralization of living in the jurisdiction. Immigration residency is usually granted on a temporary or permanent basis by a country. It may allow physical presence, re-entry, employment or study rights and land ownership.

---

[58] During World War II, an American, Varian Fry, led a mission to France in 1940 to save Jewish artists and intellectuals from certain death. With 200 American visas from first lady Eleanor Roosevelt as a start, he is reported to have "purchased " 50 passports from the Czechoslovakian Consulate in Marseilles and travel documents from the Chinese Consulate. The Jewish refugees he saved between 1940 and 1941 (when he was deported to Spain) included painter Marc Chagall, German-born philosopher Hannah Arendt, sculptor Jacques Lifschitz and writer Leon Feuchtwanger. Fry was not acknowledged for his lifesaving mission until almost 30 years after his death.

2. *Domicile*

This is an estate tax concept that looks at a person's "ultimate home." All persons, even "perpetual tourists," are deemed under law to have a domicile. A person acquires a "domicile of origin" at birth. They may then acquire a "domicile of choice" by changing their residence and acquiring long-term indicia of domicile, such as gravesites and new wills. They then can acquire a subsequent "domicile of choice" by severing these ties and reacquiring the same in a new jurisdiction. If a person abandons their last domicile of choice without acquiring a new one, then their domicile either reverts back to their last domicile under the U.S. rule or their domicile of origin under the British rule.

3. *Citizenship*

This is a status granted by a country and may include various rights, such as travel documents (passports), voting, land ownership, and ability to hold public office, etc. A country may choose to grant citizenship through various methods, including:

a. Birth in the jurisdiction.

b. Lineage (through parents or grandparents).

c. Marriage.

d. Naturalization.

e. Religious affiliation (for example, the law of return to Israel).

f. Meritorious service.

g. Economic benefit to the country.

4. *Passports*

Passports are generally thought of as travel documents issued by a country to its citizens. However, entrepreneurs have created new "passportlike documents" which have values ranging from minimal to worthless and even to dangerous. This genre includes the following variations:

a. *Camouflage passports.* The so-called camouflage passport is a nonofficial document of a nonexistent country. It can be of extremely high quality and have a very genuine appearance. It is generally created using the name of a former country, for example the Republic of Ceylon or British Honduras, now called Belize. It is a novelty item not issued by any government, and is legal to possess in most countries if not utilized for fraudulent purposes. It is never to be used for entry into a country (border crossings) or for any custom purposes. To do so would be fraudulent and generally carries a heavy criminal sentence.

Further supportive evidence of your purported citizenship is also provided in the form of a driver's license and supplementary identification. Camouflage passports are relatively inexpensive to acquire. They may be useful to those persons that do have the expectation of protection against terrorists or hijackers, angry foreign mobs, surly hotel clerks, "weirdoes" or those opposed to the "wealthy American." The user hopes that the passport will protect them against acts of terrorism directed towards Americans by presenting the passport in lieu of their true American passport.

b. *Bogus passports.* Beware of bogus or fraudulent passports, which can be fakes or real documents illegally obtained. For example, recently Venezuelan passports were being sold on the black market. Apparently disgruntled and displaced governmental employees took official documents when they left or were discharged. They in turn sold these genuine but illegal documents underground to obtain additional income.

Also avoid passports which are fraudulently obtained. I have heard of "love child" passports obtained from Italy and Brazil claiming that you are the illegitimate love child of one of their citizens.

c. *Noncitizenship passports.* Several countries (notably Panama and Uruguay) issue passports for "noncitizens." These documents are not useful for travel purposes because visa requirements or exceptions are based on citizenship. Many countries you will visit will seize these "passports" immediately, leaving you with just an expensive memory and failed expectations.

Obtain a passport through *legal* means, not by answering an advertisement in *The Economist.* Be certain it is being issued by the government *au current* to avoid wasting your money, being embarrassed or being arrested. (Canada may sentence you up to 14 years for obtaining a passport illegally.)

Renouncing U.S. Citizenship

Now that you are familiar with the terminology, let's discuss the strategy for the reluctant American: locate and obtain a new residence, domicile and/or citizenship to reduce or eliminate U.S. tax liability. You may immediately recoil at the suggestion that you give up (renounce) your U.S. citizenship. However, since only two other countries (the Philippines and Eritrea) other than the U.S. are tax-based on citizenship, and millions of Brits, Canadians, Aussies and other nationals seem to get along quite nicely without U.S. citizenship, Americans who stop and think begin to warm up to the concept.

It could make sense for you if it would *also* [59]result in substantial tax savings. This political agenda of soaking the rich businessperson who is "running" offshore and "hiding" with his or her millions has resulted in many proposed changes to our tax code. If you are entertaining the thought of renunciation, *your plan may take years to mature fully.* For example, obtaining a Canadian citizenship requires a three-year residency.

---

[59] 📖 If your *principal purpose* of renouncing your citizenship is *for tax purposes,* you will still owe them for a period of *up to 10 years,* as far as the IRS is concerned.

For guidance, I refer you to an expert Canadian attorney, David Lesperance, specializing in this field (see Appendix D). For U.S. tax advice on the ramifications of renunciation, I refer you to CPA Vern Jacobs (also Appendix D). For general information on the different tax havens, see the Internet Resources list of Web sites in Appendix C.

Implementing an "exit" strategy involves careful planning to ensure a clean exit from the United States. It is necessary to avoid the 10-year attribution rule on expatriation. It is also necessary to avoid unwanted tax liabilities in the jurisdiction of your new citizenship, domicile and residence. Note that all three elements may be in the same country or may be in three different countries. By now you should realize that this is clearly a complicated process. Your advisor should address the following issues:

• An American *may* legally acquire a second passport or citizenship without the risk of automatically loosing U.S. citizenship. In fact, the renunciation of one's U.S. citizenship is quite a formal, complex and lengthy process and does not include, as a basis, the mere acquisition of a second passport by a U.S. person.

• One must also distinguish between the acquisition of a passport and the acquisition of citizenship and voting rights in a second country. They are mutually exclusive. One can obtain an "economic" passport without ever becoming a citizen. As a practical matter of economics, many tax havens are seeking capital for development. As an incentive for economic participation, these countries may reward the investor with a passport but not necessarily citizenship or voting rights. Typical programs require placing funds in a "local" bank for a specified term, establishing a new business enterprise and/or purchasing real estate in a governmentally approved development.

• Secure a second passport that is functional. An example of one that initially appears not too beneficial would be one from the

Republic of Cape Verde.[60] The Cape Verde Islands, of Portuguese derivation, a country located around 300 miles west of the coast line of Senegal, Africa. It would only provide visa-free traveling to Portugal. However, by adding visas to the EC, for example, it becomes quite functional.

• A further disclaimer is required because the political instability of a country can result in rapid and major changes in passport and citizenship requirements and nullify your status. For those of you who can surf the Internet, I recommend a Web site with extensive general information on the acquisition of other citizenships:

     🖳 http://www.aztec.co.za/exinet/fb/index.html, and other sites as shown in Appendix A.

     For those of you interested in some of the tax ramifications of second citizenships and renunciation of U.S. citizenship, see Chapter 11.

     The analytical process described in Chapter 4 applies here, as well. How do you select the best jurisdiction for you or you *and* your family? Some of the factors to consider in selecting the best jurisdiction for a second passport or citizenship follow:

• Political stability of the country. Would your want to live there or retire there? Is it still O.K. to visit the U.S.?

• Proximity to the U.S., to family or friends and perhaps to the business interest that you turned-over to your son, daughter or younger partner.

• Your association with the jurisdiction, its principal language, culture, your ancestors, its principal religion, etc. Are you prepared to take a two- to three-year period to learn a new language so that you can enjoy the new country, speak with the locals, make new friends and enjoy the cultural aspects in the native tongue?

---

[60] For futher information or a visa to Cape Verde, contact the Embassy of the Republic of Cape Verde, in Washington, D.C., phone: (202) 965-6820, fax: (202) 965-1207.

- Banking stability and privacy. The security of the U.S. banking system is provided to the individual through the Federal Deposit Insurance Corporation (FDIC). Only the U.S. and Canada have government account insurance; there is no counterpart in the entire world. Consequently, the choice of your bank requires a new factor not generally considered by the reluctant American; that is, "How strong is the bank and how safe are my funds on deposit?" Lest you forget, the strongest banks in the world are not U.S. banks! (For banking privacy issues, see Chapter 8.)
- Visa-free traveling. The ability to travel, free of the need for a visa, to as many countries as possible, especially the EC countries, should be an essential requirement.
- Duration (lifetime) of and renewability.
- Initial and future costs.

Typical Second Citizenship Acquisition Programs

The Caribbean Jurisdiction of Nevis affords a good example of the second citizenship mechanism. The Federation of St. Kitts and Nevis is characterized as a socially stable country. Its population is primarily of African descent but friendly towards other races and respectful of the law.

Nevis, a British commonwealth, needs foreign investment to bolster its economy, elevate its banking system and become recognized as a leading tax haven. Nevis rewards participants with a nonvoting citizenship and passport: You invest US$250,000 in a government-approved investment or government bond that generally pays a return competitive with alternative investments. Also, you pay the required governmental and professional fees to qualify. For an additional fee, your family members can be added to the program as well.

With your new citizenship, you can reside on an exceptionally beautiful Caribbean island. When bored, you can use your new passport and visit over 50 countries without the need for a visa, including the British commonwealth and the EU.

In a nutshell, here is a list of some second passport jurisdictions:

Please note:

1.   **(-)** = avoid unless you have family or cultural ties with these countries.

2.   **(--)** = avoid because of bogus, illegal passports on the black market or fraudulent passports, which are common.

- African Continent (--)
- Argentina (-)
- "Banking" Passports (-)
- Belgium (-)
- Belize (-)
- Brazil (--)
- Cape Verde (+); need EC visas (-)
- Chad (-)
- Chile (--)
- "Diplomatic" (+ or -); when purchased, use with caution.
- Dominica (++)
- Dominican Republic (--)
- Guatemala (--)
- Honduras (--)
- Ireland economic contribution citizenship program. (+); qualifying ancestor necessary, grandparent or parent, or substantial investment or purchase in Ireland. Long processing time.
- Israel (+ or -); available for Jews only; may be dangerous to possess in a terrorist hijacking situation.
- Mexico. (--)
- Nigeria (--); not generally honored in the diplomatic community.
- "Non-United Nations" Countries (--); to be avoided.
- Panama (--)
- Paraguay (--)

- Peru (+); economic passport granted for financial participation in the country.
- Portugal (-)
- Sierra Leone (-)
- St. Kitts (St. Christophers) and Nevis (+); three-pronged economic citizenship program.
- South Africa (-)
- Spain (-)
- Uruguay (-); limited in scope to non-nationals; not a citizenship program.
- Venezuela (--)
- "World Citizenships" (--); bogus.

The Living Trust

This form of "non-APT" trust was discussed in Chapter 7. Of principal importance here is that you recognize that it is *not* intended as an asset protection tool. The living trust is tax neutral. Its primary purpose is as an estate planning tool created for its inherent expediency in the disposition of assets upon death or disability of the settlor, for avoiding some types of probate delays and for reducing overall probate costs. Since it is a revocable trust, it easily fails when under attack by a judgment creditor.

The Family Limited Partnership (FLP)

The parties to the FLP are the same as in a traditional limited partnership; that is, the general partners (GPs) and the limited partners (LPs). The primary difference is that the LPs are generally family members (usually children) to whom the GPs, usually the parents, are conveying their interest in an asset to the FLP. For news about FLPs:

  🖳 http://www.haledorf.com/trust_news.html

Initially, the FLP was thought to have many favorable attributes including being used for the asset protection of the "jewel of the crown" real property, a stock portfolio or the family business. Don't mix assets into the same FLP. The fragmenting of the ownership interest among many LPs resulted in a valuation discounting of the fair market value (over a range of 20 to 40 percent)[61] of the property. One needs an expert appraiser though to support the discounted value. Costs for a competent appraisal may be in the thousands of dollars. I have seen legal fees for the FLP run between $5,000 and $50,000.

I often see FLPs being used by practitioners principally because of the reluctance of their clients to go directly offshore with their personal property assets. FLP asset protection was thought to be achieved by the following rationale and sequence:

1.   The claimant would first sue a limited partner and get a judgment.

2.   Then, he or she would seek a charging order from that court against the limited partner's respective interest in the partnership. Although the judgment creditor would prefer to dissolve the LP, he or she is limited to this remedy.

3.   Although the judgment creditor could obtain a lien against the LP's interest, it would be relatively useless because LPs have no power to get to the assets of the FLP without the consent of the GP.

4.   The effect would be to create a taxable event in the eyes of the IRS—so-called *phantom income*[62] was received and is subject to taxes by the judgment creditor.

---

[61] The greater the discount taken, the more IRS "chokes" on it. While a 20 percent discount is generally IRS acceptable, 30 percent pushes the IRS envelope of tolerance, 40 percent will most assuredly involve a dispute.

[62] While this book was being drafted, Federal legislation was pending that gave judgment creditors relief from the phenomena of phantom income tax recapture. Consult with your tax advisor for the current status and proper treatment of this tax relief measure.

5.   The further effect then should be to initially discourage litigation against the limited partner. This would be even more so if the LP was an offshore company or other person.

6.   The judgment creditor could also foreclose on the charging order if permitted under state laws.[63]

Well, it hasn't necessarily worked out exactly that way. Some believe that the FLP is shaky as an asset protection tool.

On the positive side, the FLP continues to be an excellent estate planning tool for reducing the value of an estate but only in the correct factual situation. Where there is a highly appreciated asset–for example, real property or the family business–the owner can transfer the asset to the FLP and remain in control as the general partner with a 1 to 2 percent interest. Since the remaining interest has been divided up among many LPs and the owner has no control, the LP interest now has a discounted value; a reduced fair market value.[64] The sum of the LP interests is highly discounted from the original fair market value, reducing the exposure to estate taxes. See a qualified appraiser about obtaining the necessary appraisal or discount valuation for the new FLP partnership interests. It should be documented at the time of the transaction for possible later use in an IRS audit. The lower the valuation discount, the less likely it will precipitate an IRS audit, so don't be overly aggressive! If you are, the IRS may assess a penalty tax as high as 40 percent.

A further positive aspect is the ability to shift income to family members who may be in a lower income tax bracket than the GP.

---

[63] The Georgia Uniform Partnership Act (UPA) does not provide for foreclosures of limited partnership interests. Many planners thus make Georgia the state of choice for FLPs.

[64] The *valuation discount* is based on two factors: 1. a lack of transferability due to those restrictions contained in the FLP agreement; and 2. the creation of minority ownership (even where the LPs own 98 percent) of the FLP. Minority ownership means a lack of control.

The Weakness of the FLP as an AP Tool

The first problem arises when the general partner elects to withhold distributions to the limited partners. Does the creditor with the charging order have any recourse? What if the general partner selectively withholds dividends from the limited partner who has the charging order by complying with the limiting language in the partnership agreement that distributions may be made only to family members? This is similar to the so called "spendthrift" provisions in a trust. Would this be characterized as a fraud on the future creditor or a preference problem under bankruptcy law in a later bankruptcy? Could the creditor outwait the partnership? Could this force a settlement between the creditor and the limited partner for an earlier resolution? All are interesting complications of the FLP. Your author has more questions than answers.

What if the creditor is successful in placing the partnership into an involuntary bankruptcy? Are the bankruptcy trustee's interests the same as the judgment creditor with the charging order? Not very likely.

Onshore real estate creates further problems. If the FLP involves real property as the principal asset, you can't move it offshore. No matter what you do on paper, the court of the country in which the real property is located continues to have exclusive jurisdiction over the real estate. If the judge doesn't like the factual situation surrounding the FLP, he or she can make any order he or she wishes affecting the real property. If the offshore LP is unhappy about what the U.S. court has done, they can always submit themselves to the jurisdiction of that court and try to oppose the court's action. That would be counterproductive to maintaining the privacy of the offshore LP.

Liquid assets and mobile personal property are the best suited for asset protection treatment, as they can actually be moved offshore.

Also, the FLP is not a structure that you create and forget. It requires that you follow the formalities of being an ongoing limited partnership. You need to function as an FLP and not revert to the casual, informal ways of operating as commonly practiced among family members.

A partnership is traditionally business motivated and oriented. It must have a stated business purpose and, as such, it uses a business checking account, pays real and personal taxes, charges family members the going market rate for use of the FLP's assets, files the necessary tax returns, acquires the necessary insurance at reasonable levels, and utilizes the partnership bank account for partnership transactions. Paying the LPs personally and then seeking reimbursement from the partnership is *not* encouraged.

Each time the partners fail to operate as a true partnership, it weakens the protection claimed by the FLP. Where the LP agreement provides that, upon a creditor demand being made upon an LP, the partnership will be dissolved, then the security of the FLP begins to unravel.

The attack brought upon the FLP to avoid the above charging order problem is under a theory of fraud, and further, it seeks a dissolution of the partnership and a disposition of its assets. The legal argument is raised that since the FLP *was created primarily for asset protection,* as demonstrated by the lack of compliance with the formalities of operating as a true business partnership and also there not being a primary for-profit business, it is a fraud upon the judgment creditor of a limited partner.

In two cases where partners took steps to frustrate the charging order, in California and New York, the courts *allowed foreclosure on the real property.*

Upon review of the above, a conservative position would be that, if all of the above problems were sufficiently addressed, the FLP could provide some degree of asset protection. However, never let the legal problems of one limited partner destroy the entire FLP structure and cause the loss of the property to foreclosure. See item ten in the following checklist.

📖 *An FLP Checklist*

1.   The FLP should be a *limited* partnership. The asset being transferred should have a value not less than $1 million. Don't mix types of assets.

2.   Provide for successor general partners.

3.   Restrict dissolution of the FLP by using antiliquidation clauses.

4.   Provide restrictive language in the FLP agreement to the effect that a creditor who acquires a limited partnership interest does not become a partner.

5.   Provide for assessment powers on all parties holding an interest in the FLP whether or not they are partners.

6.   Consider including optional buyout language by other partners with extended provisions for payments.

7.   Provide in the agreement for assessment powers over the judgment creditor for the cost of becoming an owner.

8.   Have guaranteed payments to partners thus having a devaluating effect on the FLP market value since they are an encumbrance.

9.   Provide for full indemnification of the general partner for legal exposure. For example, costs of toxic contamination removal, underinsured court judgment, underinsured acts of God etc.

10.   Final caveat: Creating an FLP and transferring assets for asset protection must be done *before* a liability arises.

Real Property Equity Stripping:
An Asset Protection Tool

The high-profile person attracts litigation. It is a fact of modern U.S. life in this highly litigious society. Very few contingent fee attorneys would pursue an expensive case and advance extraordinary costs for investigators, depositions and experts without there being a perceived pot of gold at the end of the rainbow. Logically then, they are pursuing the malpractice insurance policy limit, a regulatory or licensing agency's recovery fund or the defendant's deep pockets (assets).

Determining whether an individual has deep pockets is relatively easy. Since tradition, naiveté, ego and the need for a favorable financial statement keep major assets such as real property (real estate) highly visible, with an asset search being relatively inexpensive and easy to obtain from the public records, plaintiff's counsel can make this determination fairly cheaply.

The obvious answer is balance, moderation and a change of lifestyle. You can be a litigation target at any time; you needn't be in a high-profile industry (neurosurgeon, real estate developer, entrepreneur soliciting funds, etc.) to become a victim of an overzealous plaintiff's counsel. As a safeguard, consider following our 70:30, 60:40 or 50:50 rules. Reserve a substantial percentage of your estate as the sacrificial lamb, willingly and begrudgingly given up for litigation reserves and the balance (50 to 70 percent) being placed out of the reach of creditors as your "nest egg." Placing only one quarter or one third of your estate into an APT would even be better from a fraud defense perspective. Remember all the while that one cannot legally totally strip themselves of all assets. To do so would clearly be fraud against future claimants and judgment creditors.

A solution that I greatly advocate for highly appreciated real estate (other than the FLP solution) has acquired the label of "equity stripping" (see Figure 5-4). Through a special arrangement with offshore lenders, significant equity can be stripped from your real property. The residence, for example, can be stripped to the homestead level and thus discourage litigation, encourage earlier and cheaper settlements and/or become fully protected from a runaway jury verdict. The corresponding funds received then would need to be placed in an exempt asset, be gifted, used to purchase an annuity and/or be transferred to irrevocable instruments.

The Unincorporated Organization or Unincorporated Business Organization

The unincorporated organization (UO) or unincorporated business organization (UBO) (-) is an archaic form of business structure presumably used for asset protection and miraculous tax avoidance benefits (see Figure 10-1). Highly touted in the past by promoters in the classified advertisement pages of *The Wall Street Journal,* but now gone the way of the dodo bird, thankfully. Figure 10-1 remains, however, as a useful teaching tool.

Proprietary Triple Trust Structure

For several years, until he withdrew from the trust business, Mr. Karl Loren proposed and marketed a layered structure consisting of three trusts in series (-) (see Figure 10-2). The first trust was a domestic trust identified as an unincorporated business organization doing business as a trust (UO). The beneficiary of the domestic trust was the first OS trust (FT1). The beneficiary of FT1 was the second OS trust, FT2. Each trust had a trustee and trust protector and possibly a committee of advisors.

The assets to be protected were transferred to the UO in return for a *certificate of beneficial interest* (CBI) that was alleged to be a tax free exchange of equal value. The asset then was gone, deleted from the balance sheet and records of the settlor. The certificate was of contingent value and thus not very marketable, so it would not be an attractive asset for attachment by a judgment creditor. (*Comment:* Nothing I could locate in my research supported the proposition of a tax-free transfer for a CBI.)

FIGURE 10-1: Use of the UO–Domestic & Offshore

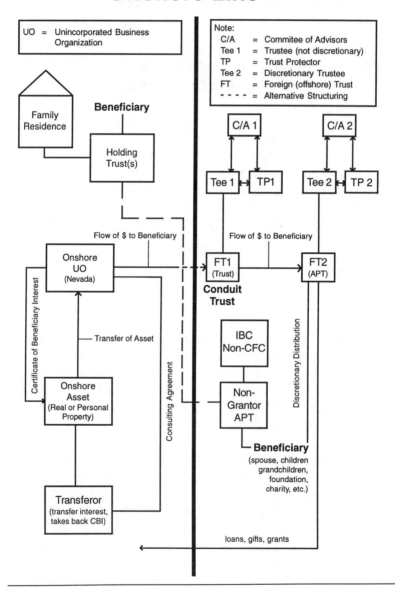

FIGURE 10-2: Proprietary Triple Trust Tier Structure

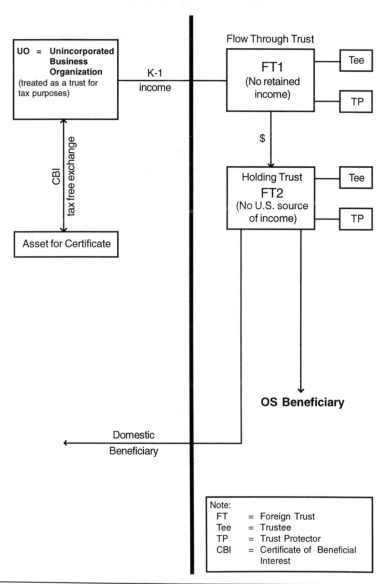

Offshore Line ⟶

UO = **Unincorporated Business Organization** (treated as a trust for tax purposes)

CBI tax free exchange

Asset for Certificate

K-1 income

Flow Through Trust

FT1 (No retained income)

Tee

TP

$

Holding Trust **FT2** (No U.S. source of income)

Tee

TP

OS Beneficiary

Domestic Beneficiary

Note:
FT = Foreign Trust
Tee = Trustee
TP = Trust Protector
CBI = Certificate of Beneficial Interest

It was suggested that money could flow from the UO to FT1 and then to FT2 free of U.S. taxes. The tax argument was that since FT2 received no U.S. source of income and was not doing business effectively connected with the U.S., then FT2 had no obligation to file a U.S. tax return or to pay U.S. taxes. Your author never was able to accept that premise comfortably.

Contemporary Three-Tier Structure

Capitalizing on a more modern variation of the proprietary triple trust structure, current tax savings promoters are marketing a variation of the three-box structure (-) (see Figure 10-2) and are still claiming total tax avoidance. A call to me in January 1996 from a Las Vegas chiropractor confirmed that it was indeed true. The first box of the structure was changed to an LLC from a domestic UO filing as a trust (see Figure 10-3). The same tax avoidance claims were now made for this newer, modified structure as were previously postulated by Mr. Loren.

See if you follow this logic. Box 1, the LLC, distributes income to Box 2, the first offshore entity, an APT called FT1. LLC issues a form K-1 to FT1. The sole beneficiary of FT1 is FT2, another OS APT. FT1 distributes all of this income to FT2, OS APT to OS APT, from one zero-tax regimen jurisdiction to another zero-tax jurisdiction. Now, if you are still with me, follow further: because FT2 did not receive any U.S. source income or money effectively connected with the States, it need not pay U.S. income taxes on the money received.[65] Is this tax avoidance scheme U.S. tax compliant or is it in the "gray" area or even clearly "black" area? The consensus of my reviewers of this book was that it fell into the black area and was tax noncompliant. If you are using this structure you need to see an international tax expert immediately and implement corrective action, see Appendix D.

---

[65] At the time of drafting this book, the tax rate for income effectively connected with the U.S. was 34 percent.

FIGURE 10-3: Contemporary Variation of the Triple Trust

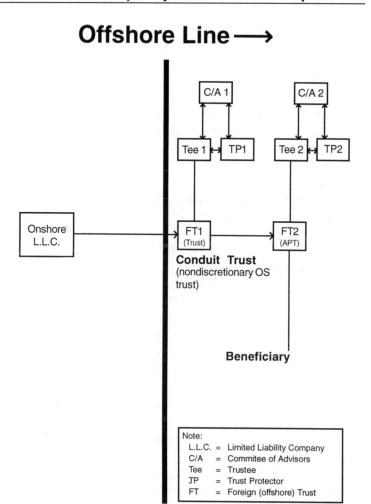

The Pure Trust

The following paragraphs actually contain some materials posted on the Internet by the pure trust (-) advocates.

Defined

A pure trust is one in which there are three parties, the creator or settlor (never grantor), the trustee and the beneficiary, and each is a separate entity. A pure trust is claimed to be a lawful, irrevocable, separate legal entity. There *must* be a minimum of the three entities (parties).

Its advocates (promoters, in some instances) quote case language supporting this definition, such as "It is established by legal precedent that pure trusts are lawful, valid business organizations,"[66] or ". . . a trust or trust estate is a legal entity for most all purposes as are common law trusts."[67]

Unfortunately, some promoters advocate the use of trusts in a noncompliant tax manner. Their pure trust package is a scam *structured primarily to evade taxes* based on legitimate trust laws. The pure trust has been tested in the courts in a series of cases called the "Family Trust" cases. The cases hold that the taxpayer/creator of a pure trust is to be responsible for the taxes that he or she so carefully tried to evade. Not surprisingly, the promoters of the scam have long since disappeared. Due diligence will prevent your getting drawn into this quagmire.

Some promotional literature and advocates state that the procedure for establishing a pure trust is under "contract" law—a "Common Law" contract rather than a "statutory" law contract. As a consequence, you isolate yourself from being a taxable entity, protect yourself from exposure of any liabilities and also shelter yourself from government intervention.

The trust is sometimes called a "Pure Contractual Trust." It is created by an instrument (document) entitled a "Declaration of Trust" written under Common Law with no reference to the

---

[66] Baker v. Stern, 58 A.L.R. 462.
[67] Burnett v. Smith, 240 S.W. 1007 (1922).

jurisdiction of a state or federal statutory law. The pure trust is set up by the settlor and the first trustee for the benefit of the beneficiary. Be aware that if you retain ownership or are still in control of any trust assets, creditors could pierce the protective veil supposedly provided by the pure trust vehicle.

Assets are usually transferred to the pure trust by way of donations or gifting to the trust, for example, from a third party (see Chapter 11, Form 709). Promoters claim that if the pure trust has a situs in a state that recognizes its legality (for example, in the state of Florida[68]), the trust can function under the control of "U.S. common law" which will recognize and acknowledge the state's laws and statutes. They further claim that if you wish to establish a situs in any other state, province or country, that you simply change the situs or jurisdiction address by passing appropriate "Trust Minutes," as would be the case under typical contract law.

There are further refinements to the pure trust. It may be structured as a *business trust*, so it can operate an existing business for profit, or as a *management trust*. Being an entity a person under the IRC–the trust must obtain a tax ID to function. It is permitted to operate an existing business that has been transferred to the trust, but only for the purpose of sale or liquidation and subsequent distribution of the assets to the beneficiaries at a later date as defined in the trust or under the discretion of the trustee.

Promoters also market the pure trust as an asset protection device. They claim that using such a trust isolates your personal assets from the separate conduct of the pure trust. They allege that trust assets belong to the trust, not you. If there is a judgment entered against you, your creditor cannot seize what is owned by the pure trust, a separate person. If you had previously transferred title to your assets to the trust, without knowledge of any claim against you, then the assets are protected from your creditors. Conversely, as a person, the trust can be sued or can sue others.

It is further claimed that the creator's filing bankruptcy will not affect the trust, nor will a subsequent divorce. Others have used the pure trust as an alternative to a prenuptial agreement.

---

[68] Florida has a unique Statute (F.S. 609) that promoters claim does recognize and acknowledge that a Common Law instrument is allowed.

At this point, you may be shouting, "If a pure trust is so wonderful, why the heck doesn't everyone use it?" The trust promoters are pretty slick in this regard. The following examples are typical of their approach; see if you can pick up on the psychology being utilized to capture you. These examples are provided without endorsement or rejection, though I have already given trusts a (-) rating. You must make your own independent decision as to suitability for your purposes.

Truth is, not everybody can operate a pure trust. It takes a small degree of finesse and business savvy to understand and remain under the protection of a TRUST. The average person will not want to devote the time or the patience to grasp the knowledge and understanding they need in order to work through a TRUST. Sometimes, there are no clear-cut rules concerning trusts. It may involve legal matters and rulings, etc. at times. It's clear, though, that those people who take more chances, end up with more in the end. It's like anything else worth having; the average people won't do it. Now, obviously, you're not average or you wouldn't be reading this information. You've gone through considerable time and research to get this far in your understanding of a pure trust and I know you're serious about wanting to understand all you can.

Were you sold on this product? The hype continues:

You should be the First Trustee, the one who contracts initially with the Settlor to donate assets to the trust organization for the benefit of the beneficiary(ies). The Settlor should be someone neutral, whether it be a friend, associate or partner. Someone, obviously, you trust considerably. Even though they won't have any day-to-day duties of maintaining the trust, they help with the initial input of naming the beneficiaries. I would set up your children as beneficiaries. If you don't have children, use a brother, sister, niece or nephew, etc. with whom you can work directly to support the credibility of the trust.

Unfortunately, the promoter discourages the use of a will if you have a pure trust without regard to what happens if a court strikes down a pure trust in total. Read this promotional material with that concern in mind.

The pure trust is all an estate one needs to direct the proper distribution of present and future assets. You've already transferred ownership of your assets to the trust. Now, it's just a matter of who controls those assets. . . . Upon your death, if your heirs are the beneficiaries of the trust, there are no changes required. The heirs appoint a new First Trustee (if that was your title) and conduct business as usual. If your heirs were not the beneficiaries at the time of your death, and would like to be afterwards, the present beneficiaries need to relinquish their position and have it cleared by the trustees. If your heirs simply want to control the assets like you did before your death, you need to make sure their names are established as "Successor Trustees' in appropriate minutes. That way, in the event of your death, they automatically take over your position as First Trustee.

The promoters further claim that "Everything you need to know" is in their "simple pure trust kit." Just follow the format of the promotional materials and sample formats that are included and you'll do just fine.

FINAL NOTE: The procedure of operating a TRUST is always an ongoing learning situation. You will always be learning new ways in which to maneuver yourself or your assets to be most favorable for your tax situation or financial well-being. Although we can't be your legal or tax advisor,[69] we will tell you everything we know about the position of running a TRUST. If you ever need to talk to us or have any questions, we will be glad to talk. Drop us a line or pick up the phone and call. We'll do everything we can to help you.

---

[69] *Author's comment:* If the above is *not* legal advice, I have difficulty in establishing what level of legal counseling *is.*

If you have any further questions on the pure trust, you might surf the Web.[70]

The Business Trust

The "business trust" (BT) (+ or -, it depends) remains with us to this date. The IRS recognizes four general classifications of trusts: the ordinary trust, the investment trust, the liquidating trust and the business trust. You probably are most familiar with the ordinary trust usually created by a will or an *inter vivos* declaration.

The business trust is either an evolution of the "Massachusetts" business trust or an entity unto itself. Its advocates claim that is it an excellent asset protection tool. Some even claim it results in tax reduction. Well, that depends . . .

Some structures include two trusts in series: an operating trust held by its beneficiary, the holding trust. Initially, the business or real property is transferred to the trust or operating trust. While the original owner remains on as an asset manager, he or she is receiving Form 1099 income for his or her services. The trust is "insured" in its own name and defends any lawsuits against it and the asset manager. But, the original owner of the asset claims no interest in it any longer and therefore he or she shouldn't be a defendant in any lawsuit against the business trust.

The business trust is not a traditional entity, so few CPAs or business attorneys will recognize or encourage utilizing it. To find out more about it, you need to get with the "cult" that perpetuates it.

The Pure Equity Trust

The pure equity trust (-) is marketed by promoters as a specially designed trust claiming attributes consisting of the "greatest possible advantages" for asset protection, tax savings, simplicity of trust management and flexibility. The creator, who creates or sets up the trust, exchanges assets with the trust. In return, the creator

---

[70] One source of information can be found at:
🖳 http://www.catalog.com/corneer/diykit.htm

receives a certificate of beneficial interest (CBI) in units of beneficial interest (UBI) in the trust. Generally one unit equals 1 percent. The beneficiaries hold (own) the CBIs.

The creator is not a beneficiary but is usually retained by the trustees to "manage" the assets. The trustees are of two types, independent or "adverse." Independent is defined as not being related by blood, marriage, adoption or by an employer/employee relationship with the creator. The adverse trustee is defined as one who has a substantial beneficial interest in the trust assets as well as the income or benefits derived from the trust.

Fraudulent Trust Characteristics

1.   Intuition tells you it is an "abusive" trust.

2.   Suggests that the trust is guaranteed to eliminate all taxes.

3.   Suggests that the trust will permit personal grants for school scholarships, medical expenses, special loans, etc.

4.   You become a "caretaker" of your own residence.

5.   You receive a "pre-filing" notice from the IRS (see Glossary for definition).

Providing for a Child in a High-Risk Profession

High net worth parents wanting to gift earlier in their lives to their child who is working in an industry fraught with the risks of litigation have to be concerned that what they gift could be lost to a successful litigant.

To satisfy this concern, parents could gift to an irrevocable domestic trust, a family limited partnership or an offshore trust for the benefit of that child and the children of that child (their grandchildren) in a form of an educational trust or a fully discretionary trust, containing spendthrift clauses which would provide for the child's well-being (+++). Such a trust could not be invaded by the child's creditors. In this form of trust, the child is only a discretionary beneficiary and never can be construed as a settlor.

Offshore Charitable or Private Foundations

The offshore charitable foundation (+, or +++ with tax reform) is no longer just for the very wealthy families. The Ford Foundation and the Rockefeller Foundation are clearly the pioneers, but now many foundations may be formed by less wealthy Americans to implement their altruistic and charitable philosophies. OS charitable foundations are less costly to form and administer than their American counterparts. Further, they are free of overly restrictive U.S. laws that limit, overcontrol and monitor.

The Liechtenstein form of private foundation, the *Stiftung,* can be also found in other countries such as Panama. The private foundation is a legal entity. It is utilized for religious, charitable, public or family objectives. It is not intended to be profit oriented, so it may not generally engage in commercial activities on a regular basis. It may engage in commercial transactions to the extent necessary to accomplish its charter. For example, if the foundation holds stock in a company, it may exercise its rights as a shareholder of a corporation.

However, one negative aspect is a loss of U.S. tax deductibility for U.S. source gifts or donations to a foreign charity or foundation. Private-interest foundations are used as asset protection vehicles for high net worth persons.

Bankruptcy, with an Asset Preservation Plan

If regrettably, as the last recourse, one must file a bankruptcy, one should consider the following:

1.   Make a complete disclosure of your offshore transfers and interests on the schedules which accompany your petition, as filed with the Bankruptcy Court.

2. Assume that disgruntled former employees, a vexatious former spouse, dissatisfied partners, parasitic relatives or others in your personal and/or business life are now adversarial towards you because of the losses they sustained in the filing of your bankruptcy. They will blab their heads off to the trustee.

3. If the bankruptcy trustee for your case detects a fraud upon the court, omissions in the schedules filed with the court or evidence that you're concealing assets and lying, he or she is compelled to pursue you and your former assets wherever situated. A U.S. bankruptcy trustee has been known to go the Isle of Man seeking recovery of concealed assets, and as he was able to make out a case for fraud, the Man courts took jurisdiction over the funds hidden there.

4. The trustee specializes in locating and detecting concealed assets and does so on an ongoing basis. It is his or her full-time occupation, he or she has the expertise and experience (i.e., is smarter than you as a mere dabbler) to locate them. The trustee earns fees based on the recovery of assets. This is a very motivating factor. The trustee's attorneys work on a form of contingent fee–if they recover assets, they are paid for their services at a court-approved hourly rate plus all reasonable costs. No recovery, no attorney fees.

5. A failure to list one's interest in an APT may be the basis for a bankruptcy judge denying your bankruptcy discharge *and* prohibiting you from filing bankruptcy again for six years.

6. If your conduct is found abusive enough to be characterized as having made fraudulent transfers and your conduct violates the Bankruptcy Code, you may be referred by the court to the U.S. Attorney for investigation and prosecution for bankruptcy crimes. This would be in addition to item 5 above. You could go to jail!

7.   The "look back" period for examining the fraudulent transfers of assets depends upon several factors.

a. The relationship of the transferee to you.

b. Was the transfer during the 90 days prior to filing the bankruptcy petition, the so-called *preference transfer*?

c. Was the transfer to an insider during the one-year period preceding the filing?

d. What is the statute of limitations period for fraud under your state laws?

8.   Don't forget that it is legal to convert nonexempt assets to exempt assets (called "transmogrifying") before you file your bankruptcy. Your bankruptcy attorney, being an officer of the court, is limited as to how far he or she may go in "advising" you to transmogrify, but he or she can certainly tell you what the legal exemptions are in each of the 50 states of the U.S. If a relocation is viable, ask about the preferred States. If your bankruptcy attorney doesn't know, get a better attorney. Texas and Florida,[71] for example, are most generous with their homestead allowance.

9.   The U.S. Bankruptcy Code has not abrogated the Statute of Elizabeth with respect to future known and unknown claimants (creditors).

---

[71] 📖 Texas and Florida homestead laws are based on physical size, location (city or suburb) and realty improvements of the residence without regard to the fair market value of the homestead. For example, a financially troubled debtor could file a bankruptcy in these two states and retain a ranch without limit with respect to its value. California law places a limit on the homestead allowance of $50,000, $75,000 or $100,000, depending upon such factors as marital status, age, health and income.

11
Tax Treatment, Ramifications and Deferral

"No man in this country is under the smallest obligation, moral or otherwise, to arrange his legal relation to his business or to his property as to enable the Inland Revenue to put the largest possible shovel into his stores."
British Judge Lord Clyde

"You can have a lord, you can have a king, but the man to fear is the tax collector."
Found in the Tigris and Euphrates Valley, circa 4,000 BCE

Offshore Taxes 101

This is a difficult topic to write on because the discussion may become outdated [72] while being written or before publication because of tax bills pending in Congress[73] and on Mr. Clinton's desk that affect offshore foreign trusts. There are proposals for enlarged IRS reporting requirements on foreign trusts. Further, the quantity of incorrect information and the promulgation of misinformation by tax scheme hucksters is staggering. Your offshore planner needs to update you before you can proceed. If you don't use offshore planners who understand the relevant U.S. tax laws you will very likely be in noncompliance with those tax laws.

I use the word "foreign" in this chapter to be consistent with the IRC. The U.S. Congress has become notorious for changing the tax code retroactively, making OS tax planning extremely difficult. Accordingly, the appropriate disclaimer would be to treat this section as reference and historic material for academic discussions. Review any of the materials, especially the

---

[72] *The Offshore Money Book* will have an update service. If you are interested in keeping currrent on the subject, please sign up using the form in the back of the book.

[73] For example, the Revenue Reconciliation Bill of 1995.

tax materials in this book, with your informed consultant before proceeding.

Your possible participation in foreign accounts and foreign trusts is disclosed to the IRS on Schedule B of the IRS 1040 tax form. That pertinent portion of Schedule B, page 2, Part III, is shown in Form 11-1.

Offshore jurisdictions with their low tax rates, tax exemptions and in some cases no taxes, occupy a vital and growing role in international tax deferral or possible avoidance. The tax regimen of the jurisdiction being considered is a most important consideration.

For privacy, it should be axiomatic that offshore funds remain offshore, out of the U.S. banking system, which lacks the element of privacy.

As a general proposition, no U.S. tax savings should be anticipated unless one uses tax deferral devices such as offshore annuities or invests in stocks for future capital gains rather than current dividends[74] or income.

📖 The U.S. is unusual in that it taxes its citizens and foreign residents on the basis of their worldwide income; only citizens from the Philippines and Eritrea suffer from this same problem. If a UK citizen works in the Cayman Islands, he or she pays no income tax, since the Caymans have none and the UK doesn't tax offshore income. But a U.S. person working in the Caymans would, after an initial offshore exemption, pay taxes to the U.S. The price for the privilege of U.S. citizenship is high– maybe even inequitable!

Paradoxically, the U.S. is a safe tax haven for around 90 percent of the world's population and foreign central banks.[75] To

---

[74] Cash dividends from stock: At the time of drafting this book, the current tax rate on dividends paid on stock to an offshore, NRA person was 30 percent. It is by a withholding tax and is withheld at the U.S. source, either the paying corporation or by the broker with street stock. The dividend is considered non-exempt U.S. source income.

[75] In February, 1996, the U.S. Federal Reserve Bank reported that foreign central banks increased their holding of U.S. government securities to a record US$515.332 billion.

FORM 11-1: IRS 1040 Tax Form, Schedule B, Part III

Schedules A&B (Form 1040) 1995	OMB No. 1545-0074	Page **2**

Name(s) shown on Form 1040. Do not enter name and social security number if shown on other side.	Your social security number

Schedule B—Interest and Dividend Income

Attachment Sequence No. **08**

Part I
Interest Income

(See pages 15 and B-1.)

Note: If you received a Form 1099-INT, Form 1099-OID, or substitute statement from a brokerage firm, list the firm's name as the payer and enter the total interest shown on that form.

Note: *If you had over $400 in taxable interest income, you must also complete Part III.*

1   List name of payer. If any interest is from a seller-financed mortgage and the buyer used the property as a personal residence, see page B-1 and list this interest first. Also, show that buyer's social security number and address ▶

	Amount

2   Add the amounts on line 1 . . . . | **2** |

3   Excludable interest on series EE U.S. savings bonds issued after 1989 from Form 8815, line 14. You MUST attach Form 8815 to Form 1040 . . . . | **3** |

4   Subtract line 3 from line 2. Enter the result here and on Form 1040, line 8a ▶ | **4** |

Part II
Dividend Income

(See pages 15 and B-1.)

Note: If you received a Form 1099-DIV or substitute statement from a brokerage firm, list the firm's name as the payer and enter the total dividends shown on that form.

Note: *If you had over $400 in gross dividends and/or other distributions on stock, you must also complete Part III.*

5   List name of payer. Include gross dividends and/or other distributions on stock here. Any capital gain distributions and nontaxable distributions will be deducted on lines 7 and 8 ▶

	Amount

6   Add the amounts on line 5 . . . . | **6** |

7   Capital gain distributions. Enter here and on Schedule D* . | **7** |

8   Nontaxable distributions. (See the inst. for Form 1040, line 9.) | **8** |

9   Add lines 7 and 8 . . . . | **9** |

10   Subtract line 9 from line 6. Enter the result here and on Form 1040, line 9 . ▶ | **10** |

If you do not need Schedule D to report any other gains or losses, see the instructions for Form 1040, line 13, on page 16.

Part III
Foreign Accounts and Trusts

(See page B-2.)

If you had over $400 of interest or dividends **or** had a foreign account or were a grantor of, or a transferor to, a foreign trust, you must complete this part.

		Yes	No

11a At any time during 1995, did you have an interest in or a signature or other authority over a financial account in a foreign country, such as a bank account, securities account, or other financial account? See page B-2 for exceptions and filing requirements for Form TD F 90-22.1 . . . .

b If "Yes," enter the name of the foreign country ▶ ....

12   Were you the grantor of, or transferor to, a foreign trust that existed during 1995, whether or not you have any beneficial interest in it? If "Yes," you may have to file Form 3520, 3520-A, or 926 .

For Paperwork Reduction Act Notice, see Form 1040 instructions.   ⊛ *Printed on recycled paper*   **Schedule B (Form 1040) 1995**

☆ U.S. Government Printing Office: 1995 - 389 - 540

encourage investment in the U.S. stock market, the offshore investor pays no long-term capital gains on U.S. securities. To encourage deposits in the U.S. banking system, there are no U.S. taxes on interest earned.

Tax Implications for U.S. Persons

The IRS presumes that most American-owned OS entities are tax neutral flow-through vehicles where the tax liabilities are attributed to U.S. persons. When using an offshore IBC, great care must be used to not trigger the U.S. attribution rules limiting ownership of that entity. The primary factor is the threshold level *of ownership or control* by U.S. persons. At the time of drafting this book, the threshold levels were:

1.   Ownership or control of less than a 5 percent interest need not be reported to the IRS.

2.   A 10 percent or more ownership or control by a U.S. person creates a controlled foreign corporation (CFC) or foreign personal holding company (FPHC).

3.   Or, a 50 percent or more of ownership or control by a U.S. persons in aggregate triggers the same problem.

    This is essentially the definition of the controlled OS company. By avoiding these thresholds, you avoid the CFC or FPHC characterization by the IRS. Those with OS family, friends and/or business associates may find legal means of structuring to prevent the CFC or FPHC attribution. If the OS company is characterized as either a CFC or FPHC, U.S. investors are taxed each tax year by the U.S. on their prorata OS income even if it is not distributed; there would be no tax deferral. Further, a U.S. investor may have another U.S. tax issue if the income received is designated as being from a passive foreign investment.

Tax on the U.S. Trustee

I don't recommend using a U.S. trustee for your APT since the IRS can then tax the trust on a worldwide basis because a U.S. trustee is permanently (a resident) based in the U.S.

Special Tax Concession by Local Jurisdictions

Some jurisdictions are characterized as providing special tax laws that make them ideal for special applications. Some that have been identified include Andorra and Cyprus for the EC community, BVI in the Caribbean, Macao on the South China coast and Nauru in the Pacific. A detailed discussion of each jurisdictions is beyond the scope of this book; however, your offshore consultant should steer you to the site most beneficial to you.

Excise Tax

The IRS levies an excise tax upon the transfer of appreciated assets to an OS APT. It is a "heavy" tax, a flat 35 percent of the unrealized gain. It is imposed when property *that has appreciated in value* is transferred to a foreign trust by a U.S. citizen or resident alien, U.S. corporation, LLC, LLP or partnership, or a U.S. trust or estate. The tax is based on the fair market value of the assets transferred to the extent it exceeds the adjusted basis of the transferor, or the amount of gain recognized by the transferor when the asset is transferred.

Taxes on Annuity Proceeds

📖 IRS §72 defines the tax treatment of annuities. Offshore annuities are generally (author's recognition of exceptions) taxed the same as onshore annuities. There is one distinguishing factor, the gains or losses of principal due to fluctuations in currency exchange rates can affect annuity performance when not in U.S. dollars. The IRS uses an allocation formula based on the life expectancy of the annuitant. The formula factors in the return of capital and the annuity income under an allocation formula.

Non-annuity withdrawals are taxed as income until *all* of the deferred income is distributed. The balance remaining in the annuity is then treated as a return of capital.

There are no tax deductions on money put into an annuity such as with an IRA, 401(k) or Keogh plan. There may be an excise tax of 1 percent levied upon the purchase of an offshore annuity. It is advisable to inquire about this tax with your OS service provider and planner. With respect to income taxes on the earnings of the annuity, they are tax deferred until received by the annuitant. Being tax deferred, the money compounds and grows faster. Income taxes are paid at the ordinary income tax rates by the annuitant for the year in which distributions are actually paid. Only the earnings and capital gains are taxed; there are no taxes upon receipt of that portion of the distribution consisting of the return of your own money.

U.S. Taxes on the IBC Investing in the U.S. Stock Market

As an incentive for offshore companies to invest in the U.S. business economy, IBCs are not required to pay any long-term capital gains taxes on profits made in the stock market. They do, however, pay a 30 percent tax on dividends. The 30 percent withholding tax is generally withheld at the payor or by the stock brokerage firm and not distributed offshore.

The High Tax on Renouncing U.S. Citizenship

A U.S. person has a constitutional right to renounce his or her U.S. citizenship; the problem is that the renouncement in itself does not terminate future tax obligations to the U.S. The determination of whether the expatriation by the U.S. person was clearly an intention to avoid taxes is pivotal. For further reading, see the various anti-expatriation rules in the IRC.[76]

---

[76] ⬚ See §§ 877, 2107 and 2501(a)(3) of the IRC of 1986, as amended.

IRS Requirements for an Offshore Principal Office

A U.S. person that maintains an OS office as its principal office would not be engaged in trade or business in the U.S.[77] if all or a substantial (the definition is again subjective) number of the following items are performed OS. These are the RA's 10 commandments:

1. Financial reports were provided OS.

2. Communications with the members was done OS.

3. Marketing and solicitation for sales of the IBC's stock was OS.

4. New member's subscription for stock was OS.

5. General public communication was OS.

6. The principal corporate books and records were maintained OS.

7. Payments and cash disbursements were made from OS.

8. Shareholders' and board of directors' meetings were conducted OS.

9. The company's books were audited OS.

10. Corporate management is conducted from the OS "principal office."

---

[77] 📖 See IRC §864.

Applicable IRS Forms

When the RA's APT is structured as a foreign grantor trust, the trust income, credits and deductions are attributable to the U.S. grantor. To be in compliance with the tax laws of the U.S. and the grantor's state, certain forms must be filed.[78] These are presented below in numerical order. There are a total of 13 forms discussed that may need to be filed. There are different filing dates for some of them, and unless you have determined whether or not any one of the 13 need be filed, you may not be in full IRS tax compliance. In 1995, I heard that the IRS believed that there were billions of U.S. dollars offshore and not in compliance. I don't agree with their high numbers, but don't *you* be their first test case!

Whether or not you need to file some of these forms depends upon whether you have a *tax neutral* APT structure as a U.S. trust or a foreign trust or whether you are reporting on a *genuine* nongrantor foreign trust.

1.   IRS Form SS-4, an "Application for Taxpayer Identification Number" for the APT or the IBC. Obtained by telephone by the trustee or company officer from the IRS in Philadelphia upon the creation of the APT or IBC. The easiest way to obtain this form is from any CPA or Enrolled Agent (EA), or call the IRS and request that form SS-4 be sent to you. This will allow you to apply for an Employer Identification Number (EIN). The completed SS-4 is then faxed or mailed to the IRS, just follow the instructions. If you are in a hurry, with a copy of the SS-4 completed and available, the OS trustee or IBC officer may call the IRS in the U.S. and get an EIN over the phone. He or she then is instructed to fax the form to the IRS.

2.   IRS Form 56, a "Notice Concerning Fiduciary Relationship," usually prepared by the trustee advising of the creation of a fiduciary relationship. Form 56 requires evidence of the trustee's authority, usually a copy of the trust declaration.

---

[78] All of the forms described may be ordered by telephone from the IRS by telephoning 1-800-829-1040.

It's filed with the first form 1041 filing or may be filed earlier when the fiduciary relationship is created and accepted by the trustee.

3.   Treasury Form TD 90-22.1, a "Report of Foreign Bank and Financial Account," generally prepared by that person having certain authority of foreign accounts. By June 30th of each year following the preceding reporting year, this form must be filed by each person who possesses:
    a. Any financial interest.
    b. Signatory authority.
    c. Other authority over any bank, securities or other financial account in any foreign country, if *at any time during the reporting year* the account(s), singly or in combination had a value of more than $10,000.

4. IRS Form 709, the "U.S. Gift (and Generation-Skipping) Tax Return," to report gifting. Must be filed by April 15th for the preceding year in which the gifting was made; this is a disclosure type of tax return, filed by the settlor even for an "incompleted" gift. A copy of the trust is attached to the form 709.

5. IRS Form 926, a "Return by a Transferor of Property to a Foreign Corporation, Foreign Estate or Trust, or Foreign Partnership," is filed by the grantor. This may result in an imposition of an excise tax.[79] The tax is imposed only if one transfers assets that have appreciated in value. This form should be filed on the day of the transfer to the APT, though in reality, is rarely done on time.

---

[79] IRC §1491 provides for a tax upon transfers of assets to the OS APT. Currently, the tax is a whopping 35 percent of the fair market value of the assets transferred less the adjusted basis. The exception is for a grantor APT.

The Treasury Department wants to tax the gain that has accrued before the transfer. If this law did not exist, it would be very easy to avoid a built-in capital gain tax by simply transferring the asset to a foreign entity and then having the foreign entity sell the asset offshore.

6.   IRS Form 1040, and a state income tax return, to report APT income on the settlor's individual tax returns. Filed on April 15th for the prior year.

Your special attention is called to the Schedule B attachment to Form 1040. More specifically, at page 2, part III, questions 11 and 12 (see Form 11-1). Over the years, this Part III has slowly evolved to more and more comprehensive questioning as to your offshore financial transactions. In Form 1040 for the tax year 1995, let's analyze the two questions, 11 and 12.

Question 11 regards your degree of control or ownership in foreign accounts. Check the Yes box if the answer to any of the following is appropriate:

a. At any time during tax year 1995 (even if for a fleeting second of time),

b. You had an "interest" (whatever that means),

c. Or, in the disjunctive, you had signatory authority,

d. Or you had "authority" (again whatever that means),

e. Over a "financial" account in a foreign country. "Account" is defined to include bank account, security account or other—whatever that encompasses—accounts.

f. Where, in what foreign country? You must list them all.

If you had during the prior year a combined foreign account value that never exceeded $10,000 offshore, you may check the No box.

Question 12 regards your involvement in foreign trusts:

a. If a foreign trust existed at any time during tax year 1995, (even for a fleeting moment),

b. Were you the grantor (creator or settlor) of that trust, or,

c. Did you transfer (as transferor) any assets to any foreign trust,

d. Whether or not you personally were the beneficiary of that trust or had any beneficial interest in that trust,

In addition, the grantor of a grantor trust must report the interest and dividends received by checking the Yes box at the bottom of Schedule B.

7.   IRS Form 1041, the "U.S. Fiduciary Income Tax Return," is filed by the grantor of a grantor trust.[80]

8.   IRS Form 3520, advising the IRS of the "Creation of or Transfers to Certain Foreign Trusts," is to be filed by the 90th day after the creation of the APT. This form *requires the disclosure of the names of the trust beneficiaries*, their addresses, their dates of birth and their "identifying numbers" (social security number or other U.S. tax I.D. number). File with the IRS in Philadelphia.

9.   IRS Form 3520-A is an ongoing report of the "Annual Return of Foreign Trust with U.S. Beneficiaries," *required of APTs with one or more U.S. beneficiaries at any time during the preceding year* (-). Filed on the 15th day of the fourth month following the end of the grantor's or settlor's tax year. Filed with the IRS in Philadelphia.

10.   Customs Form 4790 is for advising with a "Report of International Transportation of Currency or Money Instruments" of the importing or exporting of $10,000 or more of currency or other monetary instruments. Filing is done by the shippers or mailers and by the recipients.

---

[80] 📖 IRC §679 provides that where there is a foreign grantor trust, the grantor of that foreign trust is taxed on all the income of the trust whether or not there is a distribution, if the trust had or could have a U.S. beneficiary.

a. The recipient files the form within 30 days after receipt, not with the IRS but with the U.S. Customs Officer in charge at any port of entry or departure. It may also be made to the Commissioner of Customs, Attention: Currency Transportation Reports, Washington, DC 20229.

b. Shippers or mailers may file by mail if the currency or monetary instruments did not accompany a person while departing or entering the U.S.

c. Travelers carrying money or instruments must file Form 4790 with the Custom Officer in charge at any Customs port when departing or entering the U.S. Curiously, tourists leaving the Bahamas for the U.S. are cleared by U.S. customs in the Bahamas. At that time they are asked if they are carrying more than $10,000 in currency (note that I didn't specify U.S. currency here) or monetary instruments.

11.   IRS Form 5471, an "Informational Return on U.S. Persons with Respect to Certain Foreign Corporations," requires U.S. citizens or residents to disclose a 5 percent or greater interest in a foreign corporation or partnership. This interest can be attributed through a trust, as well. This form is filed with your income tax return for the year of acquisition of said interest.

12.and 13.   IRS Forms 8288/8288-A, disclosing transfers of real property by a foreign APT, filed within 20 days of the transfer of the U.S. real property and accompanied by any taxes withheld. U.S. escrow companies or attorneys handling sales of real property transactions may withhold the taxes and forward them to the IRS or be personally held liable to the IRS for the uncollected taxes.

Classifying Tax Havens Based on Tax Attributes

From a tax viewpoint, an IFC falls into one of three tax regimens.

1.   Token tax or zero tax. This is a true tax haven in that there are no or token taxes assessed. Some zero-tax jurisdictions are

the Bahamas, Bermuda, the Caymans and the Turks and Caicos Islands.

2. Low tax. The definition of a low tax rate is subjective; however, the British Virgin Islands, the Channel Islands and Hong Kong are representative of low-tax jurisdictions.

3. Special exemptions, credits or privileges. Tax havens such as Ireland, Madeira, Panama and the Netherlands Antilles provide special tax concessions to encourage the establishment of certain types of business in their countries.

12
Offshore Communications and Privacy

"A country's ability to assert its sovereignty without the interference of outside forces (the U.S.A.) is a major deciding factor in choosing a place to invest and protect personal property."
Attorney Oscar Sabido, 1995, Belize[81]

Privacy

The best laid plans for offshore privacy are often compromised by a simple thing, such as a telephone bill. The telephone can not only reach out and touch someone, it can reach back and bite you in the derriere. Your long-distance telephone service provider creates permanent electronic records of every offshore call you make, when and where. Upon service of a subpoena, the phone company is compelled to provide your telephone records in essence, your daily telephone diary. Many privacy aficionados make their sensitive calls using a telephone calling (debit) card from public telephones. Only you can decide your comfortable level of privacy.

If you do decide to use the calling card, buy it anonymously, for cash and not as a charge on your U.S. credit card. You will receive a personal identification number (PIN) to use, consisting of 10 to 12 digits long enough to ward off hackers. Write it down in your address book in code. Memorize or scramble the 800 number as well and then shred the calling card. *Never recharge the card again, especially by using a domestic credit card.* It is best to get a new card each time your card has expired.

---

[81] In re the case of *SEC vs. Swiss Trade and Commerce Trust, Ltd.*

For frequent callers to the 809 area code of the Caribbean, you can purchase a local prepaid calling card. As an example, with the Batelco (Bahamas Telephone Company) calling card sold in Nassau you can call the Bahamas from the U.S., Canada, or the UK using their 800 number in those countries. You can actually get a Batelco dial tone from Nassau in the U.S. and complete your call through their system with no records on your local telephone bill or in the U.S. linking the call to you. (You can purchase the card by mail order from a Nassau company called OAR (see Appendix D).

By the time you are reading this book, it may be possible to engage in full duplex (simultaneous two-way) encrypted voice communications over the World Wide Web. Things are moving so fast in the communications field that you could be talking to your asset manager in the Isle of Man in an encrypted mode over the Web using your cable company's Internet services and not pay telephone toll charges.[82]

Following are some of the more common ways your assets are traced other than the traditional credit report, DMV public records, your checking account and a real property title search or personal property search at the Secretary of State's office. Who will be searching? Your former (vindictive) spouse, an adversarial former partner or business associate, a plaintiff or potential plaintiff or heaven forbid, the IRS.

1.   *Passport Review and Travel Agent Records.*
Visits to high-profile banking destinations are red flags, giving snoops a place to start looking for hidden assets. Obviously, multiple visits to some of the following countries clearly will raise suspicion: Switzerland, the Cayman Islands, the Bahamas, Isle of Man, Netherlands Antilles and other jurisdictions

---

[82] In April, 1996, Netscape Communication announced "CoolTalk," a software addition to their Netscape Navigator Web browser. CoolTalk enables more than 20 million current users of Netscape to hold long-distance conversations over the Internet avoiding long distance telephone toll charges. Look out Ma Bell! The next logical step would be to add voice encryption to CoolTalk.

characterized as tax havens. The IRS has characterized approximately 30 jurisdictions as tax havens.

2. *Telephone Records.*

By examining your telephone bills for calls made from home, work, hotels and your cellular phone, as well as your fax bills, telex records, saved e-mail on your computer or other documents, one can identify undisclosed business associates and professionals. An examination of the telephone directories in any geographic region where you live, work or have a presence may be revealing. With the new CD technology inexpensively providing millions of names and phone numbers, such searches become routine. For example, after I had a "cameo" appearance as a participant on PBS's *Frontline*, for a TV program that was an exposé of former corrupt banking practices in the Caribbean, a prospective client located me by using his national CD business phone directory. He was quite proud of his feat!

3. *Frequent Flyer Programs.*

A review of your various airline frequent flyer mileage statements reveals scuba diving trips to Virgin Gorda. Isn't that in the British Virgin Islands where they "hide" money, too? Also, an emotional plaintiff who can't afford to travel might be most upset by those jaunts of yours to vacation destinations.

4. *Wastebaskets and Garbage Cans.*

Get a cross-cut shredder[83] and use it! If it's not cross-cut it's not shredded–you read it here. If one takes the time, effort and money, one can easily glue 1/4-inch strips back together again. It may be a very boring "jig saw" puzzle but it can be accomplished. Don't let a cheap shredder lull you into a false sense of security. You can buy a lightweight cross-cut shredder for around $279-700, depending on the number of sheets you want to shred on each pass through the machine (4-10,

---

[83] I have seen cross-cut shredders priced from as low as $179 to $320 for the one we use, to $700 for a Fellowes brand machine from Reliable Office Supply (1-800-735-4000).

respectively). The peace of mind it affords even makes shredding therapeutic. I affectionately named mine "Janet Reno." Also don't forget to shred your carbon paper, typewriter ribbons, telephone messages, phone bills, frequent flyer statements and printer ribbons.

5.   *Computer Files.*
Save sensitive materials on an encrypted segment of your hard disk on your computer only. Work only in the secured mode. Don't make back-ups on floppies nor on an unsecured back-up tape. Turn off your computer when not in use. Stop using paper records except as a back-up master located offshore. Communicate by encrypted e-mail using PGP. Anything else is an open postcard. You'll be surprised how much cleaner your desk will be, also.

To ensure privacy, you must be aware of some computer basics. For example, deleting a sensitive letter or file on your computer does *not* erase it. The delete function merely makes the file invisible to the directory by disabling the first segment of the file, but it is still there and it can be resurrected with very simple, low-cost utility programs.

6.   *Business Associates.*
The people with whom you do business may be associated with offshore involvement. Keep that list for your eyes only.

Your intentional or inadvertent disclosure of the offshore IBC or APT in the wrong hands may lead to unique problems. A disgruntled worker or spouse may be tempted to blackmail you with respect to their perception of there being unreported income from the offshore entities. They may alert the IRS or other taxing agencies if they want to be vindictive. In fact, the IRS even offers rewards for reporting tax fraud.

Companies and private investigators may specialize in this type of asset search. There should be no difficulty in finding your assets onshore but the difficulty is in their ability to search offshore, as well. The abilities of their offshore associates are critical. For a sample listing of onshore asset recovery specialists, take a look at the following New York World Wide Web site, "Legal Classifieds," 🖥 http://www/ljx.com/cgi-bin/class_wais

Encryption

Attacks against encryption techniques are succeeding at a frightening rate. This effort is being accomplished by governments and through industrial espionage. In the U.S., computer secrecy experts warn that encryption "locks" proposed by the U.S. government are far too susceptible to attack. Government intelligence and industrial spying poses more of a threat than do "hackers."

Illicit decryption has become economically feasible for industry. It is reported that a codebreaking computer system could be devised for as little as US$30,000. Secrecy experts claim that this computer could break an encryption key of 40 bits in under 20 seconds. The current U.S. standard in a 56-bit key, which the experts claim could be broken in three hours. A cost estimate for illicit decryption is around $38 per key. With faster computers, the 56-bit key could be broken in as little as six minutes.

For security, computer experts now suggest a 90-bit system. A 70-bit system will only be adequate through 1996.

13
The Captive
Insurance Company

Captive Insurance Defined

American entrepreneurs have always sought to improve the company's bottom line. A major expense of running a business may be their mandated or defensive insurance costs. That cost element is always under scrutiny. Whether insurance is dictated by law or carried at levels constituting good business practices, it still costs money. What is particularly frustrating to a businessperson is the ratio of the substantial dollars expended for insurance premiums as compared to the dollars returned for claims and litigation defense. The comfort derived by being insured doesn't necessarily compensate for the cost element of the insurance. Consequently, the concept of becoming self-insured, to some extent, can look more and more attractive in low-risk but high-premium industries.

Creating an onshore company for self-insurance can be so costly and time consuming that it is, for all practical considerations, not feasible. Voilà, the concept of the offshore insurance company, or technically the *captive insurance company* (captive), is born. Forty percent of the U.S. insurance market is offshore. For example, under the Caymans Islands insurance laws, there are three types of insurance businesses characterized as follow:

1.   One which insures a person against liability for loss due to a risk.

2.   One which, upon the occurrence of a defined event, pays money to the insured or beneficiary.

3.   One which carries out the function of reinsurance among other insurers.

Initially, the captive protects itself against exposure by reinsuring with other companies, through underwriters or buying insurance from wholesalers. As reserves accumulate due to a low level of claims, the necessary level of reinsurance diminishes.

Nothing stated above is intended to limit captive coverage merely to companies. A captive could also insure other entities such as persons, hospitals, professional practices, partnerships, LLCs, foundations, officers, directors, etc. Several tax havens favor and court such business—Bermuda, the Caymans and Guernsey, to name a few. Bermuda is considered the leading international insurance domicile but the Caymans remain quite popular in this specialty as well. Combine a favorable government environment with a level of regulation to assure the ability of the insurer to respond with qualified professionals, and this industry attracts the world's insurance business. Recently the Canadian province of New Brunswick announced it was developing regulations on classes of businesses and fees in order to compete in the world's captive market place.

There are two types of captive ownership:

1.   Where a *Fortune* 500 company wishes to create an offshore captive to insure the risks of its own parent.

2.   Where a group or association (trade or professional), having a common interest, creates a captive to respond to the needs of the smaller to medium size companies or professional associations.

Why would you form a captive insurance company offshore?

1.   Unavailability of coverage. Your inability to get insurance or obtain sufficient insurance at a reasonable price in order to have the protection against claims for your business may be a problem. You may be forced into the captive insurance business because of this problem.

2.   Cost efficiency. If the loss history of the parent is considerably better than the industry, there may be a premium saving by self-insuring.

3.   Cash flow. There is control of the cash flow offshore from the premium payments while waiting for a future claim.

4.   Taxation. There may be certain tax deferral and invest-ment build-up benefits of the offshore captive from the reserves.

Some jurisdictions offer captives "off the shelf." Although tempting at first blush, do explore the comparative features of such a product and inquire as to which is the better jurisdiction for you in terms of set-up costs, maintenance costs and capital reserve requirements.

Let's explore the following scenario. Widget, Inc., is one of the most conservative, low-risk companies operating in a field that traditionally has high insurance premiums because of a general perception affecting them or a history of high claims by other companies in the field. For every dollar they pay as premiums, an audit shows that they get back only 25 cents of benefits. Widget has an exceptional year and is flush with cash. As a closely held company it doesn't have to account to outside shareholders, so the officers decide to form an offshore captive insurance company and become self-insured, in a small way.

What type of licensing should they apply for initially? Using the Caymans again as an example, there are three classifications of insurers. The three categories are local, exempt or external. In addition, there are three types of licenses granted.

After meeting with professionals in Georgetown (not to be confused with George-Town, Bahamas) and introducing themselves to the necessary governmental officials, they create the Paradigm Insurco, a Cayman Island captive insurance company. Most jurisdictions restrict the use of company names such that any word suggesting the business of insurance or assurance is limited only to those companies licensed as such by the jurisdiction. Some other restricted words are indemnity, guaranty, insurance, reinsurance and underwriting.

The surplus cash of Widget capitalizes Paradigm, and they then start to reduce their onshore insurance coverage and premiums. This is not without some concern—what if they are hit with a "killer" lawsuit, a runaway plaintiff's judgment? But, from a philosophical point of view, business and life itself is a risk. Fortunately, providence shines upon them, and after several years of continuing low claims, Insurco is now a fully funded captive insurer with more than adequate reserves. Little by little, more and more of their insurance in handled by Paradigm. By this time, Paradigm may be able to share the risk with other[84] insurance companies and re-insure or co-insure the risk through them. In general, they ultimately would be Class A, which permits a local or OS insurer to carry on business on the Islands. More likely, they would start as a Class B restricted licensee permitting Paradigm, as an exempt insurer, to operate OS but not locally. A Class B unrestricted license allows Paradigm to carry out its insurance business on the Islands but not for domestic (local) business, it is their next level before going to Class A status.

As this scenario unfolds, Paradigm amasses surplus funds after claims are paid in a tax free and favorable jurisdiction. The offshore assets of Paradigm are put to work and earn tax free dividends, interest and capital gains, all professionally managed OS by an asset manager. As an insurance company it can operate anywhere in the world.

---

[84] This is a pivotal point. IRC §162 prohibits a current deduction for premiums paid to a wholly owned (captive) insurer. If the captive provides insurance to *other* companies or is not wholly owned, a deduction may be allowed.

Some time in the future, Paradigm may retain one or more officers of Widget as consultants and pay them for their services. Unfortunately, they may have to travel to Georgetown for many meetings.

I have seen the above concept work very well. A former environmental engineering consultant teamed up with his friend, who was already an insurance broker, and formed a captive in the Caymans (joining around 400 other insurance companies). The broker "cherry-picked" from his better, low-risk, low-claims companies. They offered these companies lower premiums and made tons of money. All were satisfied.

Is a captive insurance company right for your company? Perhaps not now, but keep it in mind.

Costs

The minimum share capitalization of the Bermuda captive wishing to write property and casualty business is $125,000; to write life insurance as well, the capitalization increases to $250,000.

Typical Statutory Requirements

1. Maintaining certain financial ratios and margins.

2. Annual audits.

3. Acceptable loss reserve practices.

4. Restrictions on certain types of assets.

5. Annual statutory filings.

6. Audited financial statements.

Global Insurance Resource on the Web

InsureWeb is one insurance resource available through the Web. InsureWeb is a computer on the Internet where registered brokers– agents, brokers, and reinsurance brokers–can offer risks to carriers–registered insurers, wholesalers, MGAs and reinsurers.

InsureWeb is in its final testing stage. It *serves the worldwide community* and can be used to serve any particular geographical area (e.g., Europe, U.S., etc.). In addition, a search-key procedure allows any carrier to accept business from a designated group of brokers.

The site can be reached at ⌨ http://insureweb.com

14
Conclusion:
Applying What You Have Learned

"Success in your venture was the journey and is not the destination."
Anonymous

A Case Study: Putting the Pieces Together

Let's take a journey to an IFC and apply the materials you have
mastered so far to a case study. I have selected the British Virgin
Islands as a proposed site for your APT and have given them my
subjective rating on a scale of 1 to 10 in each of the following
areas. In another exercise, for an IBC, a different final numerical
score for the BVI as a proposed site could result.

1.   Geographic considerations.
Only about three miles from the U.S. Virgin Islands (St. John).
Why don't you take a ferry ride from St. Thomas for a day? The
BVI are a mere 60 miles south of Puerto Rico. A short hop on
American Eagle gets you to Beef Island, the site of their airport.
Rating: Easy to get there, so let's say 9.

2.   Political and fiscal independence.
The defense of the BVI is provided by the UK, which also
handles its external affairs. Banking is monitored and regulated
by the Bank of England. Status of the BVI is similar to the IFC
of Jersey.
Rating: 8

3.   *Language.*
English is the official language.
Rating: For Americans, 10

4.   *Currency.*
The official currency is the USD. There are minimal exchange
costs for financial transactions.
Rating: 10

5.   *Economy.*
Tourism is number one. The financial industry is behind the
times. Has one of the highest per capita incomes in the
Caribbean basin.
Rating: 7

6.   *Political stability.*
A conservative population provides for a very stable
community.
Rating: 9

7.   *International relations.*
Very linked to the UK, a British Dependent Territory, not an
independent country. Not part of the European Economic
Community, the EC.
Rating: 6

8.   *Political stability.*
Quite stable.
Rating: 9

9.   *Transportation and communications.*
Regularly scheduled air transportation to San Juan and Antigua
(another tax haven). Communications are quite good.
Rating: 8

10.   *Time zone.*
In Greenwich Mean Time +4 zone. Good for the Eastern

seaboard, poorer for the West coast with a four-hour differential.
Rating: 8

11. *Banking secrecy.*
Almost excellent.
Rating: 9

12. *Double tax treaties.*
None with the U.S.
Rating: 9

13. *Statute of Elizabeth/rule against perpetuities.*
Ignored in this case study.
Rating: Not included in scoring.

14. *Proposed changes in U.S. and tax haven laws.*
Ignored in this case study–surprisingly, the BVI still doesn't have an APT Act.
Rating: Note included in scoring.

My total rating score is 102/120, considered very good. Using the above rating parameters, a rating of 110 is considered excellent and 120 impossible to achieve. If the problem in item 14 above would be remedied, the score would be much higher.

Why don't you try this analysis on another jurisdiction; perhaps the Bahamas or the Cook Islands? You can expand the parameters to as many different elements as you wish. *You* determine what is important for you.

A Test for the Reader

If you would like to determine whether you now have a moderate level of understanding of the materials in this book, I have postulated some questions to challenge you.

1.   Can you name at least seven uses for the APT? I've put the answer in the footnote so don't refer to it until you're ready.[85]

2.   Why wouldn't you name the following as beneficiaries of your APT or a foreign grantor trust?
        a. Your U.S. estate.
        b. Your U.S. creditors.
        c. Creditors of your U.S. estate.
Answers:
        a. You shouldn't return the offshore assets to the U.S. and subject them to possible estate taxes unless necessary.
        b. You should not alert your U.S. creditors as to the existence of an OS APT.
        c. You should pay them with domestic money.

3.   Why would an individual trustee of an APT be preferential over a bank trustee?
Answer: I have seen a lack of permanence with bank personnel due to transfers and job relocation. Better continuity may be achieved with an individual trustee.

4.   What is the difference between an IBC and an exempt company?
Answer: See Chapters 6 and 10.

Avoiding Offshore Scams: "Greed-O-Nomics" 101

Since you're going OS, don't let down your traditional, protective safeguards. There are less than savory members of the financial community (in other words, con artists) and scams all over the world. It is not a uniquely U.S. problem. The U.S. doesn't have a

---

[85] Answer to question: For asset protection, for tax planning, for estate planning, as a substitution for a will, trust or living trust, for privacy and confidentiality, as a holding entity and to circumvent exchange controls and the restrictions on the holding of title to real or personal property and for possible tax deferral or other tax benefits.

monopoly on the pyramid and Ponzi schemes, either. Know the people with whom you are working. Don't be dazzled by figures; numbers do lie, and promoter's claims may run to hyperbole. Do a spot audit on some of the figures provided to see if they check out and *you* can verify them. If they won't provide the detailed figures, walk away. If you don't understand it and how it works, don't get involved.

What is best, you inquire? A referral by an OS professional can be treated as a personal guaranty by that person and is very selectively given. Their personal reputation in a small community is at stake. Even worse, their work permit could be subject to revocation by the regulatory body. Here is my basic scam alert list. Before you write that check, refresh yourself by re-reading my *touch of realism check list.*

1. *"Windfall" test.*
If it is so good, why are they sharing it with you? If it is a get rich "scheme," have you ever really seen one work? "Guaranteed" and "safe" high returns of 50 to 300 percent are suspect per se. Don't get seduced or you will be reduced in your wealth and never see the money again.

2. *"Guarantees" alert.*
The higher the return, the higher the risk. You can't get one without the other.

3. *"Safety" test.*
How credible is the person making the claim of safety for your funds? Who are they? Who is their company?

4. *"Issuer" test.*
Who is the original source of the offering? Check the offering out with state and federal regulators. If the offering is required to be registered with your state and isn't, that in itself is a scam alert to you. Why wasn't it registered? Get real references and check them out. Be cautious of shills being used as references.

5. *"Hype" marketing.*

Do your own independent research before investing in the offering.

The Nigerian Scam

Even though the Nigerian scam has whiskers that shame Rip Van Winkle's, it continues. The latest variation (May, 1996), is soliciting non-profit organizations, churches, etc. The Nigerian scam feeds on greed and naiveté with a get-rich-quick scheme. It offers millions of dollars for doing very little. You have a better chance of winning your state's lotto, and at least some of that is going to a good cause.

Trying to catch-up with my workload one Sunday at the office, the fax machine rang, startling me. As I read in amazement I realized they're still trying the same scam, whiskers and all. I have seen several variations of this fax and have added excerpts from similar requests in brackets ([ ]).

```
From: Panasonic FAX SYSTEM PHONE NO.:Sep. 03 1995 10:18PM P1
                                      52 Kinsway Road,
                                      Ikoyi, Lagos,
ATTN:    ARNOLD L. CORNEZ            Nigeria.
                                      Telephax:
                                      234-1-5850501
                                      234-1-5850503
Dear Sir,

STRICTLY CONFIDENTIAL
[REQUEST FOR URGENT BUSINESS TRANSACTION
TRANSFER OF $35M AMERICAN DOLLARS]

I am DR. LIPMAN DABUP, Assistant Director of Finance and
Supplies [I am the Financial Controller] at Nigeria National
Petroleum Corporation. Your esteemed address was give to me by
a business associate, who assure me in confidence to try your
ability and reliability to handle this pending Transaction.

[The money in question which want to remit into your account
is not related to arms (dealings) or drugs. It is money we got
from gratification on contracts we awarded to some foreign
firms towards technical assistance analysis, supervision of
the operation and behaviour of the components of the N.N.P.C.
Also supply, erection and optimisation for the computerised
remote control network.]

The business is, there is a floating fund of US$25m (TWENTY-
FIVE MILLION UNITED STATES DOLLARS ONLY). The fund is the
interest element of the extra gains made by Nigeria from Oil
```

Sales during the Gulf War. The actual Proceeds has since been turned over to Government. This fund being the interest element, has remained unaccounted for in the Account of the Nigerian National Petroleum Corporation.

As a result of changes in Nigeria, we the men in charge at the Nigerian National Petroleum Corporation (NNPC), the Federal Ministry of Finance and the Central Bank of Nigeria (CBN) have decided to wire this money to any trustworthy company or organisation who will at last share this money with us.

You are to have 30%, 5% for Local and International expenses incurred by both parties and 65% for us (the officials). You are therefore required to send to us as quickly as possible through Fax your Account number, Name, Address, Telephone, Telex and Fax Number of your bank.

[This money is now ready for wire transfer by the authorities of the Central Bank of Nigeria. Into an account that will be provided. We have finalised all arrangements for this project but our problem lies that we do not have a foreign account as such an account is against the civil service law of conduct Beurue (sic) in Nigeria. We have taken recognition of the foreign and ambassadorial nature of the contract and have made a perfect home work (?) for a hitch free transfer of this fund into an account you will provide.]

I would like to inform you that we have made every necessary arrangement to finish this transaction as soon as we receive your documents. This business must remain secret, because individuals involved are Senior Government Officials and any information leakage may harm them.

[We will invest part of our own share of funds in your Company by expanding its industrial scope. Finally, we will want this project to carried out on the following terms.
(1) That you will provide an account where there is a free banking policy and where toll will not be taxed much on this money.
(2) That you must maintain absolute sincerity and confidentiality.
(3) That our share of the funds be remitted into your account will be given to us.]
Please reply urgently stating your private telephone and fax number for faster* communication.

Best Regard,

/s/

DR. LIMAN DAPUP

[Yours Faithfully,

/s/

Mallam Jakubu Gowon]

Send the details in paragraph 4 by fax only.

NB. Do not discuss with your bank yet.

To report a fraudulent Nigerian business proposal contact:

U.S. Secret Service
Financial Crimes Division
1800 G Street, N.W., Room 942
Washington, DC 20223
fax: (202) 435-5031

For help in determining the legitimacy of a Nigerian business proposal contact:

Nigeria Desk Office
Office of African, Room 2037
U.S. Department of Commerce
Washington, DC 20230
fax: (202) 482-5198

There *is* a Central Bank of Nigeria but they disclaim any relationship with NNPC. There is no NNPC that I have been able to confirm.

U.S. TV's prestigious *60 Minutes* did an excellent exposé on Nigeria. They visited Nigeria and portrayed it as a very corrupt country with a political environment where bribery and payoffs were the rule. I saw the scam for the first time over 10 years ago. A prospective client came in to ask me to "participate" with him. I graciously declined. Yet, it continues to persist to this date.

In January 1996, I received a call for assistance from a desperate person in Marin County, California. One minute into the call, it became clear he had lost tens of thousands of dollars and was quite embarrassed about being conned by the Nigerians despite the fact that alerts have been all over the media—frequently showcased in *OFFSHORE* on the Internet. A Texas associate of mine told me how his clients ignored his warnings and took a chance with a US$17,000 advance for attorneys' fees and government charges to Nigeria. The money was lost, of course. The scam only works where it can pander to your greed—what I call "greed-o-nomics."

In the second fax, there is usually a request for an advance for governmental fees in the range of $10,000. Reponse to the second fax is followed by a further request for attorney fees, for duty for taxes, customs, etc.. Another $10,000 to $25,000 goes to Nigeria. Then comes the need for you to travel to Nigeria with more money. By this time you have so much money and time invested in the "deal" you might even go and visit Nigeria. Don't go, cut your losses! Save yourself money, time and avoid the aggravation and make a donation to your favorite charity instead and at least get a tax write-off.

The Prime Bank Note, Prime Bank Guaranty and Roll Program Scam

One of the major advantages of being the editor of *OFFSHORE, an eJournal*, is that it places me at a focal point of developments. Starting in 1985, I received numerous inquiries and requests for information on "roll programs." These programs essentially purported to buy prime bank guaranties from major world banks in need of money and rapidly resell them for a profit, each sale being called a "tranch." With multiple purchases and sales throughout the year, vast fortunes could be made.

The following roll program claims are the actual language used in various promotional materials:

1. "A risk-free means of investing."

2. "High returns that investmentwise [sic] sound too good to be true, yet are realistic."

3. "Arbitrage, utilizing unpublicized liquid and freely-transferable obligations, major international banks (J. P. Morgan, Barclays, Credit Suisse, Paribas, Deutsche Bank, etc.) as with securities."

4. "Offered to quickly raise tens to hundreds of millions without notice; features of issuers of structure, much higher

returns vs. publicly-available like investments, 1-10 year maturity selection and liquidity provide for continuous demand on resale."

5.   "Instruments, programs relatively unknown; due to fears of disintermediation by large depositors in lower-yielding obligations, existence vehemently denied by banks."

6.   "U.S. and foreign government referencing for verification, sanction available."

7.   "$1,000,000 to $10,000,000 minimums."

Don't ask me what it means! I'm still struggling with my fear of being "disintermediated." Would you give the roll program promoter who wrote the above promotional materials $1,000,000? Of course not, but many others did, resulting in substantial losses and frauds. Annualized returns of as high as 1,600 percent were promised in the literature and believed by gullible investors.

The infamous roll program is known by many other sophisticated and seductive names that also use obscure vocabulary. For example, ponder the following terms: the prime bank note by one of the 100 largest world banks; the prime bank guaranty; the self-liquidating loan; tranches; the irrevocable and transferable letter of credit etc. Once promoted by smooth, very persuasive marketers, it has gone from slick advertising in the sacrosanct *The Wall Street Journal* to word-of-mouth solicitations to finally being driven underground because it very likely violates federal and state security laws.

The fact that it continues to sell is because of investors' fantasies that they'll get a much higher "insider rate" of return on their money and because of a lapse of their normal investment safeguards, they fail to recognize the practical impossibility of what is being offered. Structured as a Catch-22 situation, it very rarely works except (according to some) in multimillion-dollar transactions with a stable world interest rate and using high-quality institutions and professionals. Usually, gullible investors forfeit their up-front fees because all the conditions precedent can't possibly be met.

An *OFFSHORE* subscriber reported reading an advertisement in a Florida newspaper by a person looking for this type of investment. By the nature of the "ad," the subscriber and I speculate that it was a "sting" by either a federal agency or the state because it was clearly marketing an unregistered security, a crime.

Others claim that the roll programs or *self-liquidating loans* are 99.9 percent scams. That doesn't leave much room–0.1 percent–for possibilities. Again, at the risk of repeating myself for your protection, I have never heard of anyone ever successfully closing one of these. One reader reported that he had personally spoken to officers of the Securities Exchange Commission, and they have a complete package of documents disclosing roll program scams all across the U.S. If I push hard, I can obtain information on all the deals that didn't materialize or didn't succeed and nothing from anyone who can document that they did succeed. Those who lose are reluctant to admit to their naiveté.

The "liquidating loan" ads have appeared in business magazines and other publications promoting these programs. They also have gone underground, but seem to appear on occasion. The promoters claim you can easily get a $500,000 or $50,000,000 loan without any credit check, but they can't document that they've obtained one for themselves; yet they claim to be the experts.

Obviously, anyone or any entity lending money wants to make a profit and minimize risk. "Everything must have a *make sense* characteristic to it. If it's too good to be true, boy, it probably isn't true, unless you're naive," writes an *OFFSHORE* subscriber.

Scam variations may also include the marketing of worthless books or reports. "Once again, people in their greed snatch up these books, making the promoter more money," continues the subscriber. "Now, I do a lot of research on investment and moneymaking ideas. My background being banking, a loan officer, mortgage officer, investment broker, etc., I have spent a considerable amount of time, like everyday, reading international newspapers, magazines, etc., looking for investment ideas that are real and sound. Through my research, I have composed a list of over 500 of the best (top) CTAs (commodity trading advisors) in the world. This kind of investment is about as close as you can get to "major" returns without using the roll program, which I said I don't think exists."

Readers comment further of commodities and futures trading, "that this is a legitimate legal business, which is registered with the FTC (Futures Trading Commission), the government, the SEC, requiring a business operating license, audited financials, something real that you can put your finger on and say, yes, this is real . . . no smoke, no mirrors, no Houdinis playing disappearing tricks with your last $10 million dollars (if you or I ever had that much!), none of that questionable stuff. The futures and commodities business is very risky, but that shouldn't scare away the roll program investors, since they already are in an even riskier *ghost investment* vehicle."

Another subscriber reports, "I have also personally spoken with the Comptroller of the Currency, and have been given the same information. I have also spoken to a top Letters of Credit officer, manager of the department at Sea-First Bank, formerly owned by BofA, and have received the same negative reply. He is German, and has traveled the world, and has never seen any of these work. As far as I am concerned, the roll programs do not exist. If they do, they are rarely successful, otherwise, the only way they exist is as a scam."

Some will always argue that the roll program is a secret method used only by the very elite banking community—most people and professionals aren't familiar with it, and that's why so many people get ripped-off and lose millions. These people believe they know something secret, possess insider information that not even the commercial bankers who do letters of credit everyday worldwide and the top people at the U.S. Comptroller of the Currency office have access to. They become so caught up in the scam and mesmerized with the euphoria over the possibility of making millions, that they lose all ability, if they ever had it, to use good judgment, logic, reason, and, especially to exercise "due diligence" before getting involved. Our subscriber summarizes quite well with this statement: "The promoters, white collar criminals, who market these scams know that the victims are greedy and they are masters at manipulation of this personal weakness of the victim."

Farewell to the Reluctant American

If you still are asking, "How do I get back *my* money from offshore?," I'm sorry, but apparently, I have failed you. It is not yours any longer! That is how you get asset protection. After studying this book, you will understand your offshore consultant better when he explains this concept to you.

The grantor of a trust could reserve the power in the trust to reacquire an asset by substituting other property of equal value.

A little bit of knowledge is a dangerous thing. After reading this book, if you think you have what it takes to play games offshore and outsmart the IRS, good luck to you. The U.S. Internal Revenue Service has a lot of smart people and unlimited resources which will wear you out, timewise and cashwise, using computer databases (their own or purchased from vendors) to trace your transactions. Tax "avaison" is a serious subject. The IRS may assess a taxpayer a 75 percent penalty for tax fraud.

Any time some promoter wants to "sell" you on a new strategy or concept for asset protection or tax avoidance using such pitches as "aggressively utilized by prominent families such as the Kennedys, Mellons, Rockefellers Fords and Hunts," or perhaps a variation of "formerly, only the rich could use these strategies," run, don't walk, to the nearest exit. You'll thank me later.

Tax neutral structures don't invite an IRS audit but can provide asset protection. Don't expect your structure to do everything. It can't!

Offshore tax deferral or avoidance is always encouraged. It is achieved by using arrangements such as deferred annuities, which are legal in the U.S.

Asset protection is not just for the wealthy. Early asset protection measures are imperative as part and parcel of your total estate planning. You are committing fraud if you implement AP structures after being sued or with knowledge of a bona fide claim against you. U.S. judges will not let you manipulate the legal system to your advantage to conceal assets from your legitimate claimants or judgment creditors. The judges will ignore the law and legal precedents to punish you. However, where there is bona fide intent to implement estate planning and that encompasses OS strategies as well, it should fare better in a fraudulent conveyance[86] attack within the U.S. legal system.

Local and competent professionals familiar with the OS financial and tax arena are difficult to find. You need someone who sees the big picture. This is not the place for unjustifiable loyalty to your domestic professionals, as much as you like them, even if they have been your best friends of many years. Practice global geographic and professional diversity.

Practice privacy. Go digital and save a tree. Better yet, go PGP and then thank Phil Zimmerman, its creator, with a donation to his legal defense fund. Although the U.S. government dropped their case (claiming he was instrumental in exporting PGP internationally over the Internet, a federal crime) against him in January 1996, he was forced to run up staggering legal fees in his defense.

After studying *The Offshore Money Book*, you will be better prepared to attend seminars on the subjects of asset protection and utilizing offshore structures for wealth conservation. You'll be surprised how much incorrect, noncompliant tax advice and outright illegal material and information is being propagated. And lastly, before you make the big plunge, why don't you visit the offshore people with whom you will entrust your money? A caveat: Be careful out there!

Lest you get the wrong notion after reading this book, for the record, I love my country, the U.S. of A. During my lifetime, I have visited over 23 countries and still believe that ours is the best

---

[86] See the discussion of the "badges of fraud" in Chapter 4.

on earth, even though the so-called American Dream is fading somewhat. Nevertheless, our American civilization is definitely *not* crumbling.

But I don't like the runaway growth of government; I don't like the gradual intrusion of government into my private life; I don't like the blur of distinction between the two major political parties in our country; I don't like it when the interest on our national debt eats up most of my federal income taxes; I don't like an income tax system that is incomprehensible and unfair, one that only a CPA can comprehend; I don't like confiscatory taxes and social engineering redistributing our hard-earned wealth; I don't like corporate America's lack of social responsibility; and, finally, I really don't like our present litigious society being driven by a surplus of very creative attorneys needing to pay their rent and meeting their office "nut" and judges callously disregarding legal precedent. *But, it still is a great country with the highest standard of living in the world!*

See you on Paradise Island or, even better, the Côte d'Azur—but only for a "visit."

Au revoir.
Arnie
e-mail: offshore@bahamas.net.bs

P.S.   Keep on surfing the Net! Let me know of any interesting offshore sites.

Appendix A
"CyberShore"™
Resources on the Internet

It is now possible to roll out of your bunk bed at noon on your yacht *The Tax Haven,* (formerly, *The Hedonist*), Panama registry, somewhere in the Caribbean, log on to a remote computer site in Abu Dhabi, Belize or Hong Kong and conduct your international business without leaving a scrap of physical evidence about the transaction. By using a highly secured level of encryption (for example, PGP), readily available worldwide, your communications would be completely private. Using financial systems such as OAR, Digi-Cash, Cybercash, or Mondex,[87] (see below), digital cash or money can also be moved privately, without any physical records linking the transaction back to you. And now the "smart" OS ATM cards are or will be available for moving cash external of the U.S. banking system. And it's all legal.

🖥 Offshore Related Sites on the Internet

The following World Wide Web sites were selected as being informative with respect to the RA's need for elusive offshore

---

[87] Mondex is a British joint venture among British Telecon, Midland Bank and National Westminister. They are developing a "smart" credit card that will be embedded with an electronic chip. With the card one may move money (cybercash) from an ATM to another ATM or over the phone and ultimately anywhere in the world. Your local bank and the taxman are worried!

materials. I don't claim that it is an exhaustive or even complete list; it is only a sampling of the vast resources available to the Net surfer. Note that site addresses occasionally change or even mysteriously disappear. If any Web site doesn't connect, try searching by subject or name using such search engines as Yahoo, Lycos, etc., as listed.

World Wide Web Search Engines

1.   All-in-one search page:
      http://www.albany.net/~wcross/all1search.html

2.   Directory of search engines available for public use:
      http://www.netins.net/showcase.nwc-iowa/

3.   InfoSeek:
      http://www2.infoseek.com/
      (This is not a free site–you pay as you search.)

4.   Lycos:
      http://www.lycoc.com/

5.   Savvy Search:
      http://www.cage.cs.colostate.edu:1969/

6.   The McKinley Internet Directory:
      http://www.mckinley.com

7.   WebCrawler:
      http://webcrawler.com/

8.   Yahoo:
      http://www.yahoo.com/search.html

⌨ In all, there are about 19 search engines available on the Internet. New ones, better and faster, continue to be announced.

Pretty Good Privacy (PGP)™

1.   Where to Get PGP:
        http://draco.centerline.com:8080/~franl/pgp/where-to-get-
pgp.html

2.   PGP Pretty Good Privacy:
        http://draco.centerline.com:8080/~franl/pgp/

3.   How to download PGP 2.6.2i:
        http://www.ifi.uio.no/~staalesc/PGP/download.html

4.   The International PGP Home Page:
        http://www.ifi.uio.no/~staalesc/PGP/home.html

5.   Mike Babcock, PGP:
        http://users.feldspar.com/~mbabcock/PGP/pIndex.html

6.   Using Microsoft Windows with PGP:
        http://www.lcs.com/winpgp.html

7.   AutoPGP:
        http://www.ifi.uio.no/~staalesc/AutoPGP/

8.   Quadralay Cryptography Archive:
        http://www.quadralay.com/www/Crypt/Crypt.html

9.   CryptoLog, The Internet Guide to Cryptography:
        http://www.enter.net/~chronos/cryptolog.html

Privacy Publications and Web Sites

1.   Full Disclosure Live. Privacy, surveillance and technology
publishers. Glen L. Roberts, Publisher. Host for radio show on
topics available on shortwave. See Web site for further details:
        http://pages.ripco.com:8080/~glr/glr.html

2.   Electronic Privacy Information Center Home Page:
        http://www.epic.org/

3.   Bacard's Privacy Page:
        http://www.well.com/user/abacard/

4.   Cypherpunks 15th Archive by thread:
        http://www.hks.net/cpunks/cpunks-13/index.html#382

5.   Scope International:
        http://www.britnet.co.uk/Scope/

6.   The Offshore Entrepreneur:
        http://www.au.com/offshore

7.   Asset Protection & Becoming Judgment Proof:
        http://www.catalog.com/corner/taxhaven

8.   TaxBombers Privacy Site:
        Http://www.taxbomber.com

General Offshore Materials

1.   The Global Group:
        http://www.dnai.com/offshore/offshore.html

2.   Scope International:
        http://www.britnet.co.uk/Scope/

3.   The Offshore Entrepreneur:
        http://www/au.com/offshore

4.   Offshore Tax Haven, Trust and Banking Reference Page:
        http://www.cadvision.com/nolimits/offshore.html

5.   Antigua, the Perfect Tax Haven:
        http://www.eub.com/eub2.htm

6.   The Freebooter Newsletter:
        http://www.aztec.co.za/exinet/fb/index/htm

7.   Why Costa Rica?:
        http:/www.shore.net/~icorporate/netman/parad_2.htm

8.   Burke's Offshore Tax Haven:
        http://www.inforamp.net:80/~nuyen/index.html

9.   Aruba Travel Information:
        http://www.interknowledge.com/aruba/
        e-mail: atanj@ix.netcom.com

10.   Currency and Currency-Exchange Rates:
        http://www.wiso.gwdg.de/ifbg/currency.html

11.   Taxbomber's Home Page:
        http://www.geopages.com/WallStreet/2087/

12.   How Not to Be a Money Launderer:
        http://ourworld.compuserve.com/homepages/how_to_not_
be_a_money_launderer

13.   A Guide to Living Abroad:
        http://www.livingabroad.com

14.   Offshore Tax Help:
        http://www.rpifs.com/ostax

15.   Koblas Currency Converter:
        http://www.ora.com/cgi-bin/ora/currency

16.   Bloomberg Exchange Rates:
        http://www.bloomberg.com

17.   Islands on the Net:
       http://www.law.vill.edu
       ~mquarles/caribbean.html

Tax Information

1.   TAXFAX World Wide Web site:
      http://www.pix.za/taxfax/ghaven-in.html

2.   U.S. Tax Code Online:
      http://www.fourmilab.ch/ustax/ustax.html
      The complete Internal Revenue Code, 2.8 million words,
21 megabytes of data. Cross-references for the user throughout the
tax code.

3.   TaxSites:
      http://www.best.com/~ftmexpat/html/taxsites.html
      Provides links to tax related sites, including U.S. federal
and state tax forms, tax software, U.S. tax law and archives for
newsgroups.

4.   Villanova Tax Law Compendium:
      http://www.law.vill.edu/vill.tax.1.compen/

5.   International Tax Resources:
      http://omer.cba.neu.edu/othersites/international.html

6.   Irish Tax Site by the Institute of Chartered Accountants:
      http://www.icai.ie/

7.   Internal Revenue Service:
      http://www.irs.ustreasury.gov
      Hint: Select shortcut to IRS tax forms to go directly to the
IRS and instructions.

8.   The IRS Tax Forms:
        http://www.ustreas.gov/treasury/bureaus/irs/taxforms.html

9.   State Tax Forms:
        http://inept.scubed.com:8001/tax/state/state_index.html

10.   Adobe Acrobat Reader (for reading IRS forms):
        http://www.ustreas.gov/treasury/bureaus/irs/acroread.html

11.   AM & G-Accountants and Consultants:
        http://www.amgnet.com

12.   More Tax Forms & Tax Code Information:
        http://www.scubed.com/tax/tax.html

13.   Tax Bullets:
        http://www.arentfox.com/newslett/taxbul.htm

14.   Tax Discussion Groups:
        http://205.177.50.2/groups.htm

15.   Recent Tax Developments:
        http://www.halcyon.com/lesourd/recent.html

16.   Tax Notes NewsWire:
        http://205.177.50.2/news.htm

17.   KPMG Tax Online Australia:
        http://www.kpmg.com.au/tax.html

18.   US Income Tax Law–GPO Access:
        http://ssdc.ucsd.edu/gpo/

19.   Italian Taxation System: A Primer for Foreigners:
        http://www.icenet.it/cosver/html/primer_uk.html

20.   Tax Planning for Business and Individuals:

http://www.hooked.net/users/mshbcpa/plan/index.html

21.   Professor Doernberg's Tax Law Web Site:
        http://www.law.emory.edu/~lawrld/

22.   Offshore Tax Help:
        http://www.rpifs.com/ostax

23.   Internet Income Tax Information:
        http://www2.best.com/ftmexpa/html/taxsites.html

24.   Tax Resources:
        http://www.biz.uiowa.edu/acct/tax.html

25.   Tax News Groups on UseNet:
        misc.taxes
        misc.taxes.moderated

26.   Offshore and International Taxation Page:
        http://www.law.vill.edu/~mquarles/int_tax.htm/

Asset Protection

1.   Asset Protection and Becoming Judgment Proof:
        http://www.catalog.com/corner/taxhaven

2.   Financial $olution On-Line:
        http://www.rpifs/ap

Offshore Banking and Credit Cards

1.   Banks and Tax Havens:
        http://www.hks.net/cpunks/cpunks-5/0935.html

2.   European Union Bank:
        http://www.eub.com/eub7.htm

3.   Offshore Accounts and Credit Cards:
       http://www.cashmoney.com

4.   Prosper International League Ltd. (PILL).[88]
       http://www.flinet.com/~islandsun/belize1.html
       e-mail: lp-global@ix.entrepreneurs.net

5.   The World Bank:
       http://www.worldbank.org/

6.   The Excelsior Bank, Bridgetown, Barbados:
       http://www.village.com/excelsior/

7.   Mark Twain Bank, St. Louis, Missouri, U.S.A.:
       http://www.marktwain.com

8.   Offshore Banking and Financial Privacy Frequently Asked
Questions:
       http://apollo.co.uk/a/Offshore/Privacy/fpn-faw.html

9.   Offshore Banking:
       http://www.wiso.gwdg.de/ifbg/bank_off.html

10.   International Money Fund:
       Gopher://imfaix3s.imf.org/
       Provides offshore banking information and currency
exchange rates.

11.   Federal Reserve Board statistical files from NY University
School of Business:
       ftp://town.hall.org/other/fed

12.   Offshore Visa Card:
       e-mail to ucs@bahamas.net.bs

---

[88] A worldwide MLM marketing program (-) of APTs coupled Visa cards, a program with numerous U.S. domestic resellers who earn a fee for each PILL program they sell, and on their buyer's sales, etc.

E-cash Companies

1.   Cybercash, Inc.:
      http://www.cybercash.com

2.   Digicash BV:
      http://www.digicash.com

3.   First Virtual Holding, Inc.:
      http://www.fv.com

4.   Mark Twain Bank, St. Louis, Missouri, U.S.A.:
      http://www.marktwain.com
      Creates digital e-cash, a form of currency.

5.   Netscape Communications Corp.:
      http://www.netscape.com

6.   Offshore eAssets Reconciliation Limited:
      http://www.dnai.com/offshore/offshore/offshore.html
      e-mail: ucs@bahamas.net.bs

Global Business, General

1.   Financial Resource Guide:
      http://www.libertynet.org/~beausang/
      Provides information on currencies, stocks, exchanges, etc.

2.   Doing Business in Mexico:
      http://daisy.uwaterloo.ca/~alopez-o/busfaq.html

3.   Pacific Rim Job Opportunities:
      http://www.Internet-is.com/tko/index.html

4.   Malaysian Business Pages:
      http://www.beta.com.my/biz

5.   U.S. Council for International Business:
      http://www.uscid.org/

6.   Canadian Business InfoWorld:
      http://www.csclub.uwaterloo.ca/u/nckman/index.html

7.   World Currency Converter:
      http://www.dna.lth.se/cgi-bin/rates

8.   World Stock and Commodity Exchanges:
      http://www.lpac.ac.uk/ifr/

9.   Offshore Insurance, Re-insurance, Captive Insurance:
      http://www.webcom.com/~wrsl/

10.   International Trade Administration:
      http://www.ita.doc.gov

11.   Library Map Collection, Perry-Castaneda:
      http://www.lib.utexas.edu/Libs/PCL/Map_collection

12.   Jersey and Guernsey, offshore.net, The Offshore Finance
Industries of:
      http://www.offshore.net/home.htm

13.   The World Fact Book from the CIA:
      http://www.odci.gov/cia/publications/95fact/index.html

14.   Travel Advisories from the State Department:
      ftp://ftp/stolaf.edu/pub/travel-advisories/advisories

15.   International Air Mail Service from the U.S. Post Office:
      http://www.usps.gov/

16.   Connected Traveller:
      http://www.well.com/user/wldtravlr/

17.   *Export Today* Magazine:
        http://www.exporttoday.com

18.   National Trade Databank:
        http://www.sta-usa/BEN/Services/ntdbhome.html

19.   Global Risk Management Network:
        http://www.emap.com/grmn/

20.   Links to Numerous Foreign Embassies:
        http://www.llr.com/

21.   CubaWeb, a business clearinghouse of information:
        http://www.cubaweb.com/

Media

1.   *The Wall Street Journal*:
        http://www.adnet.wsj.com/

2.   *The Economist*:
        http://www.economist.com

3.   *Fortune*:
        http://www.pathfinder.com/@@N7PYjHCh0QAAQHoY/fortune/fortune.html
4.   *Time* Magazine:
        http://www.pathfinder.com/@@wNe9a9B20QAAQHwY/time/magazine/magazine.html

5.   *The Bermuda Sun*:
        http://www.bermudasun.org/
        This site, updated every Friday, contains full versions of all print stories, including business, investment, and legal listings.

The *Sun* is beginning to accept advertising on its site, including job postings and page sponsorship. Advertising department: 441-295-2102.

6.   *Reuters Newsmedia:*
       http://beta.yahoo.com/headlines/current/business/summary
.html

7.   *The Daily Record* and *SundayMail,* Glasgow, Scottland:
       http://www.record-mail.co.uk/rm/

8.   *Barron's Online:*
       http://www.barrons.com
       To be launched on June, 1996. Estimated price: US$99/year.

Couriers

1.   Federal Express:
       http://www.fedex.com/
       For tracking your onshore and international air bills over the Net.

2.   United Parcel Service:
       http://www.ups.com

Estate Planning

1.   National Network of Estate Planning :
       http://www.netplanning.com/

Appendix B
Glossary of Terms and Abbreviations

ADR. American Depositary Receipt. Also, an Advance Determination Ruling obtained upon application to the IRS. Used, for example, to determine if a multinational policy decision is tax compliant.

Adverse trustee. One who has a substantial, beneficial interest in the trust assets as well as the income or benefits derived from the trust. A trustee that is related to the creator by birth, marriage or in an employer/employee relationship. The term is generally found in the "business" trust or dual trust program.

Annuitant. The beneficiary or beneficiaries (in a last-to-die arrangement) of an annuity who receives a stream of payments pursuant to the terms of the annuity contract.

Annuity. A tax sheltering vehicle. An unsecured contract between the company and the annuitant(s) that grows deferred-free and is used to provide for one's later years. All income taxes are deferred until maturing of the annuity. Capital gains and income accumulate tax deferred. Results in a stream of payments made to the annuitant during his or her lifetime under the annuity agreement. Taxes are paid on the income, interest earned and the capital gains but only to the extent as and when they are received. Currently, there is no annual limit on purchases, but there is no tax credit for purchases. An annuity is not an insurance policy.

Anstalt. A Liechtenstein entity.

AP. Asset protection.

APT. See Asset Protection Trust.

Asset manager. A person appointed by a written contract between the IBC (or the exempt company) or the APT and that person to direct the investment program. It can be a fully discretionary account or limitations can be imposed by the contract under the terms of the APT or by the officers of the IBC. Fees to the asset manager can be based on performance achieved, trading commissions or a percentage of the valuation of the estate under his or her management.

Asset Protection Trust (APT). A special form of irrevocable trust, usually created (settled) offshore for the principal purposes of preserving and protecting part of one's wealth offshore against creditors. Title to the asset is transferred to a person named the trustee. Generally used for asset protection and usually tax neutral. Its ultimate function is to provide for the beneficiaries of the APT.

Authorized capital. With respect to a corporation or company (IBC), the sum value of the aggregate of par value of all shares which the company is authorized to issue. (Also see flight capital.)

Badges of Fraud. Conduct that raises a strong presumption that it was undertaken with the intent to delay, hinder or defraud a creditor.

Bank of Credit & Commerce International (BCCI). An "outlaw" international bank, established by Pakistanis in Dubai some 30 years ago, that failed spectacularly after phenomenal growth, all based on Middle Eastern Oil money. With its principal office in Luxembourg, it had subsidiaries worldwide–for instance, Isle of Man, Cayman Islands and the U K, etc. It was symbolic of a major U.S. and global banking scandal in the early 1990s involving the laundering of offshore and illicit monies and an anti-Israeli agenda by some Arab world countries. Resulted in significant banking failures, financial losses of US$18 billion, criminal prosecutions and major changes in the world's banking system. In 1996, a Federal Reserve judge fined Saudi financier Ghaith R. Pharon, $37 million and barred him from U.S. banking activities.

Bank of International Settlements (BIS). Structured like America's Federal Reserve Bank, controlled by the Basel Committee of the G-10 nations' Central Banks, it sets standards for capital adequacy among the member central banks.

BCCI. See Bank of Credit & Commerce International.

Beneficial interest or ownership. Not a direct interest, but rather through a nominee, holding legal title on behalf of the beneficial owner's equitable interest. Provides privacy and avoids use of one's own name for transactions.

Beneficiary. The person(s), company, trust or estate named by the grantor, settlor or creator to receive the benefits of a trust in due course upon conditions which the grantor established by way of a trust deed. An exception would be the fully discretionary trust. The beneficiary could be a charity, foundation and/or person(s) which or who are characterized by "classes" in terms of their order of entitlement their hierarchy.

BIS. See Bank of International Settlements.

BO. A business organization. Also referred to as a UBO, an unincorporated business organization. This usage is not recommended by the author.

Board of Trustees. A board acting as a trustee of a trust or as advisors to the trustee depending upon the language of the trust indenture. Also see Committee of Advisors.

British public company. See PLC.

British West Indies (BWI). In the Caribbean, including the UK-dependent territories of Anguilla, the British Virgin Islands (BVI), the Cayman Islands, Montserrat and the Turks and Caicos Islands.

Business trust. A trust created for the primary purpose of operating or engaging in a business. It is a person under the Internal Revenue Code (IRC). It must have a business purpose and actually function as a business.

BWI. See British West Indies.

Capital. See authorized capital or flight capital.

CARICOM. Caribbean Common Market. Consists of 14 sister-mem-ber countries of the Caribbean community. Members include: Antigua and Barbuda, Bahamas, Barbados, Belize, Dominica, Grenada, Guyana, Jamaica, Montserrat, St. Kitts and Nevis, St. Lucia, St. Vincent, Surinam, Trinidad and Tobago. They have set as a goal that in 1997 there will be a single market allowing for the free movement of labor. Conspicuous by their absence are the Cayman Islands and the British Virgin Islands, two major players in international banking and finance.

Certified public accountant (CPA). The offshore counterpart is the chartered accountant.

CFC. See controlled foreign corporation.

Committee of Advisors. Provides nonbinding advice to the trustee and trust protector. Friendly towards settlor but must still maintain independence. In cases where there is too close a relationship with the settlor, the committee can be construed as an alter ego of the settlor.

Committee of trust protectors. An alternative to utilizing merely one trust protector. Friendly towards settlor, but must remain independent. See trust protector.

Common Law. The early English system of case law as opposed to statutory law.

Companies Act or Ordinance. Legislation enacted by a tax haven to provide for the incorporation, registration and operation of international business companies (IBCs). More commonly found in the Caribbean tax havens. For a typical example, read the Bahamas' International Business Company Act of 1989.

Company. A restricted corporation, i.e., an IBC or exempt company.

Contingent beneficial interest. An interest given to a beneficiary which is not fully vested by being discretionary. In theory, since they are inchoate interests, not truly gifting, they are unvested, they are not subject to an attachment by the beneficiary's creditor and are not reportable as an IRS form 709 gifting.

Controlled foreign corporation (CFC). An offshore company which, because of ownership or voting control of U.S. persons, is treated by the IRS as a U.S. tax reporting entity. IRC §951 and §957 collectively define the CFC as one in which a U.S. person owns 10 percent or more of a foreign corporation or in which 50 percent or more of the total voting stock is owned by U.S. shareholders collectively or 10 percent or more of the voting control is owned by U.S. persons.

CPA. See certified public accountant.

Creator. A person who creates a trust. Also see settlor and grantor.

Current Account. An offshore, personal savings or checking account.

Custodian. A bank, financial institution or other entity that has the responsibility to manage or administer the custody or other safekeeping of assets for other persons or institutions.

Custodian trustee. A trustee that holds the trust assets in his or her name.

Declaration of trust. A document creating a trust; a trust deed.

Discretionary trust. A grantor trust in which the trustee has complete discretion as to who among the class of beneficiaries receives income and/or principal distributions. There are no limits upon the trustee or it would cease to be a discretionary trust. The letter of wishes could provide some "guidance" to the trustee without having any legal and binding effects. Provides flexibility to the trustee and the utmost privacy.

Donor. A transferor. One who transfers title to an asset by gifting.

EC. The European Commission of the European Union (EU).

Economic Recovery Act of 1981. See the Foreign Investor in Real Property Tax Act of 1980 (FIRPTA).

ECU. European Currency Unit.

EEC. European Economic Community.

Estate. Interests in real and/or personal property.

EU. European Union; replaced by the European Commission (EC).

Ex parte. An application for an injunction filed and heard without notice to the other side to protect assets.

Expat. An expatriate.

Family holding trust. A trust that is created specifically to hold the family's assets consisting of real and/or personal property.

Family limited partnership (FLP). A limited partnership created for family estate planning and some asset protection. It is family controlled by the general partners. A highly appreciated asset is transferred into the FLP to achieve a capital gains tax reduction. Usually, the parents are the general partners holding a 1 to 2 percent interest. The other family members are the limited partners holding the balance of the interest in the partnership.

Family protective trust. A UK term. See Asset Protection Trust (APT).

FIRPTA. See Foreign Investor in Real Property Tax Act of 1980.

Flight capital. Money that flows offshore and likely never returns. Flight is exacerbated by a lack of confidence as government grows without bounds, the cost of government grows out of control and the federal deficit grows (over $5 billion) without the ability of Washington to cap it; it is precipitated further by increasing concerns over invasion of personal privacy, rampant litigation and the threats of further confiscatory direct and indirect taxes.

FLP. See family limited partnership.

Foreign. May be utilized in a geographic, legal or tax sense. When used geographically, it is that which is situated outside of the U.S. or is characteristic of a country other than the U.S.

Foreign Investor in Real Property Tax Act of 1980 (FIRPTA). Under FIRPTA and the Economic Recovery Act of 1981, unless an exemption is granted by the IRS, upon the sale of real property owned by offshore (foreign) persons, the agency, attorney or escrow officer handling the transaction is required to withhold capital gains taxes at the closing of the sale transaction. Unless withheld and submitted to the IRS, the party handling the sale transaction is personally liable for the taxes.

Foreign person. Any person, including a U.S. citizen, who resides outside the U.S. or is subject to the jurisdiction and laws of a country other than the U.S.

Foreign personal holding company (FPHC). Different than a controlled foreign corporation. Discuss with your CPA.

FPHC. See foreign personal holding company.

FPT. See family protective trust. Also see asset protection trust (APT).

Fraudulent conveyance. A transfer of an asset that violates the fraudulent conveyance statutes of the affected jurisdictions.

GmbH. A German form of a limited liability corporation. Gesellschaft mit beschrankte Haftung.

Grantor. A person who creates a trust or transfers real property to another entity. In a U.S. grantor trust, the person responsible for U.S. income taxes on the trust. May have a reversionary interest in a trust.

Grantor trust. A trust created by a grantor and taxed to that grantor (settlor).

High net worth (HNW) person. An individual with more than US500,000 in liquid assets to manage.

HNW. See high net worth person.

Homestead exemption. State or federal bankruptcy laws that protect one's residence from confiscation by a judgment creditor or loss in a personal bankruptcy.

IBC. A corporation. See international business company or exempt company.

IFC. See international financial and banking centre.

Inbound. Coming into the U.S.; onshore; such as funds being paid to a U.S. person from an offshore entity.

Incomplete gift. Where the settlor has reserved the right to add or delete beneficiaries to the trust, it is construed as an incomplete gift. See contingent beneficiary interest.

Independent trustee. A trustee who is independent of the settlor. Independence is generally defined as not being related to the settlor by blood, through marriage, by adoption or in an employer/employee relationship.

INTERFIPOL. International Fiscal Police. The tax crime counterpart to INTERPOL.

International business company (IBC). A corporation formed (incorporated) under a "Company Act" of a tax haven, but *not* authorized to do business within that country of incorporation; intended to be used for global operations. Owned by member(s)/shareholder(s). Has the usual corporate attributes.

International financial and banking centre (IFC). A country identified as being a tax haven.

International trust. A Cook Islands term for a special type of an Asset Protection Trust (APT). Governed by the laws of the Cook Islands.

INTERPOL. International Criminal Police Organization. The network of multinational law enforcement authorities established to exchange information regarding money laundering and other criminal activities. More than 125 member nations.

IRC. The U.S. Internal Revenue Code.

IRS. The U.S. Internal Revenue Service of the Treasury Department.

Layered trusts. Trusts placed in series where the beneficiary of the first trust is the second trust; used for privacy.

Layering. May be achieved with numerous combinations of entities. For example, 100 percent of the shares of an IBC owned by the first trust, which has as its sole beneficiary a second trust.

LC. Another abbreviation for limited liability company. Also l.l.c. and l.c. are authorized in some states.

Letter of wishes. Guidance and a request to the trustee having no binding powers over the trustee. There may be multiple letters. They must be carefully drafted to avoid creating problems with the settlor or true settlor in the case of a grantor trust becoming a co-trustee. The trustee cannot be a "pawn" of the settlor or there is basis for the argument that there never was a complete renouncement of the assets. Sometimes referred to as a side letter.

Limited company. Not an international business company. May be a resident of the tax haven and is set up under a special company act with a simpler body of administrative laws.

Limited liability company (LLC and LC). Consists of member owners and a manager, at a minimum. Similar to a corporation that is taxed as a partnership or as an S-corporation. More specifically, it combines the more favorable characteristics of a corporation and a partnership. The LLC structure permits the complete pass-through of tax advantages and operational flexibility found in a partnership, operating in a corporate-style structure, with limited liability as provided by the state's laws. The LLC may be managed by members but need not be. It may be managed by a professional company manager. A caveat: LLCs are in a state of embryonic evolution, without a clear body of case law and firm guidelines. They will generate much income for the legal community until they become an integral part of our tax, business and legal system.

Living trust. Revocable trust, for reduction of probate costs and to expedite sale of assets upon death of grantor. Provides no asset protection.

LLC. See limited liability company. Also seen in the form of L.L.C., l.l.c., L.C. (Utah) and l.c.

LLP. Limited liability partnership. A form of the LLC favored and used for professional associations, such as accountants and attorneys.

LLLP. Limited liability limited partnership. Intended to protect the general partners from liability. Previously, the general partner was a corporation to protect the principals from personal liability. Under the LLLP, an individual could be a general partner and have limited personal liability.

Ltd. An abbreviation for the word limited.

Mark. Abbreviation for German currency, the Deutche Mark.

Mavera injunction. A court injunction preventing the trustee for a trust from transferring trust assets pending the outcome of a law suit.

Member. An equity owner of a limited liability company ((LLC), limited liability partnership (LLP), limited liability limited partnership (LLLP) or a shareholder in an IBC.

Memorandum. The Memorandum of Association of an IBC, equivalent to articles of incorporation.

MLAT. See Mutual Legal Assistance Treaty.

Money laundering. A process of placing "dirty money" into legitimate banks or business transactions to cleanse the money.

Mutual Legal Assistance Treaty (MLAT). An agreement among the U.S. and many Caribbean countries for the exchange of information for the enforcement of criminal laws. U.S. tax evasion is excluded as not being a crime to the offshore countries. The British Virgin Islands have not executed the Treaty.

Non-grantor trust. Usually an APT created by a NRA person on behalf of the U.S. beneficiaries.

NRA. Nonresident (of the U.S.) alien. Not a U.S. person as defined under the Internal Revenue Code (IRC).

Offshore (OS). Offshore is an international term meaning not only out of your country (jurisdiction) but out of the tax reach of your country of residence or citizenship; synonymous with foreign, transnational, global, international, transworld and multi-national, though foreign is used more in reference to the IRS.

Offshore centre. See international financial and banking centre (IFC). A more sophisticated tax haven.

OS. See offshore.

Outbound. Assets flowing offshore from the U.S.

Ownership. Ownership constitutes the holding or possession of limited liability company legal claim or title to an offshore asset.

Person. Any individual, branch, partnership, associated group, association, estate, trust, corporation, company, or other organization, agency or financial institution under the IRC.

PLC. A UK *public* limited company . Compare with the UK *private* limited company.

Portfolio manager. See asset manager.

Preferential transfer. A disposition of an asset that is unfair to other creditors of the transferor.

Pre-filing notice. Mailed by the IRS to parties (tax payers) who are believed to be participating in fraudulent trust programs. The notice requests that the receiver seek professional counsel before filing their next tax return.

Private banking. OS banking services for high net worth (HNW) persons.

Probate. The legal process for the distribution of the estate of a decedent.

Protector. See trust protector.

Pure equity trust. A special type of irrevocable trust marketed by promoters. The trust assets are obtained by an "exchange" of a certificate of beneficial interest in return for the assets, as opposed to traditional means, such as by gifting.

Pure trust. A contractual trust as opposed to a statutory trust, created under the Common Law. A pure trust is one in which there must be a minimum of three parties–the creator or settlor (never grantor), the trustee and the beneficiary–and each is a separate entity. A pure trust is claimed to be a lawful, irrevocable, separate legal entity.

RA. Reluctant American. *Caution:* Also, resident alien in other literature, but not in this book.

Register. The register of international business companies (IBCs) and exempt companies maintained by the Registrar of a tax haven.

Registrar. The Registrar of Companies, a governmental body controlling the formation and renewal of companies created under their company act.

Revenue Reconciliation Act of 1995. Proposed changes to the Internal Revenue Code affecting foreign trust reporting, among other changes.

RICO. Racketeer, Influence and Corruption Organization Act of 1984.

Rule against perpetuities. A legal limit on remote vesting of assets in the beneficiaries. May be void *ab initio* (from the beginning), a fixed term or determined on a "wait and see" basis.

S.A. See Société Anonyme.

Securities. Shares and debt obligations of every kind, including options, warrants, and rights to acquire shares and debt obligations.

Settle. To create or establish an offshore trust. Done by the settlor (offshore term) or the grantor (U.S. and IRS term).

Settlor. One (the entity) who (which) creates or settles an offshore trust.

Side letter. Same as a letter of wishes.

SIPC. The Securities Industry Protection Corporation. Provides up to $500,000 insurance protection for your U.S. stock brokerage account.

Situs or site. The situs is the domicile or dominating or controlling jurisdiction of the trust. It may be changed to another jurisdiction, to be sited in another country or U.S. state.

Société Anonyme (SA). A limited liability corporation established under French Law. Requires a minimum of seven shareholders. In Spanish speaking countries, it is known as the Sociedad Anonima. Important characteristic of both is that the liability of the shareholder is limited *up to* the amount of their capital contribution.

Sparbuch. An Austrian numbered savings account.

Special custodian. An appointee of the trustee in an APT.

Special investment advisor. An appointee of the trustee in an APT.

Statute of Limitations. The deadline after which a party claiming to be injured by the settlor may (should) no longer file an action to recover his or her damages.

Statutory. That which is fixed by statutes, as opposed to Common Law.

Stiftung. A Liechtenstein form of private foundation.

SWIFT. Society for Worldwide Interbank Financial Telecommunications.

Symbols.
§ section number, singular.
§§ section numbers, plural.
(+) Favorable attribute; (++) very favorable, etc.

(-) Negative attribute; (--) very negative, etc.
~ Tilde–used as part of an Internet URL.

Tax haven. An international banking and financial centre providing privacy and tax benefits.

Tax regimen. The local tax treatment of income tax, foreign source income, nonresident treatment and special tax concessions which, when combined, form complex issues.

TCI. Turks and Caicos Islands.

Tranch. A bond series issued for sale in a foreign country.

Transmogrifying. Conversion of nonexempt assets to exempt assets.

True settlor. The true grantor is not the true settlor, and his or her identity is kept quite private by the trustee. See grantor trust.

Trust. An entity created for the purpose of protecting and conserving assets for the benefit of a third party, the beneficiary. A contract affecting three parties, the settlor, the trustee and the beneficiary. A trust protector is optional but recommended, as well. In the trust, the settlor transfers asset ownership to the trustee on behalf of the beneficiaries.

Trust deed. An asset protection trust document or instrument.

Trust indenture. A trust instrument such as a trust deed creating an offshore trust.

Trust protector. A person appointed by the settlor to oversee the trust on behalf of the beneficiaries. In many jurisdictions, local trust laws define the concept of the trust protector. Has veto power over the trustee with respect to discretionary matters but no say with respect to issues unequivocally covered in the trust deed.

Trust decisions are the trustee's alone. Has the power to remove the trustee and appoint trustees. Consults with the settlor, but the final decisions must be the protector's.

Trustee. A person totally independent of the settlor who has the fiduciary responsibility to the beneficiaries to manage the assets of the trust as a reasonable prudent business person would do in the same circumstances. Shall defer to the trust protector when required in the best interest of the trust. The trustee reporting requirements shall be defined at the onset and should include how often, to whom, how to respond to instructions or inquiries, global investment strategies, fees (flat and/or percentage of the valuation of the trust estate), anticipated future increases in fees, hourly rates for consulting services, seminars and client educational materials, etc. The trustee may have full discretionary powers of distributions to beneficiaries.

Trust settlement document. See trust deed.

UBO. Unincorporated business organization.

UO. Unincorporated business organization.

Uniform Partnership Act (UPA). One of the uniform type of laws adopted by some states or used as a baseline for other states.

United States (U.S.). Comprised of the 50 states, as well as the District of Columbia, the Commonwealth of Puerto Rico, the Commonwealth of the Northern Mariana Islands, American Samoa, Guam, the Midway Islands, the U.S. Virgin Islands and Wake Island.

UPA. See Uniform Partnership Act.

Upstreaming. The process of retaining earnings offshore through the billing process.

URL. Universal resource locator on the World Wide Web. A combination of letters, numbers and punctuation that comprise and "address" for a "home page."

U.S.C. United States Code (of statutes).

USD or US$. United States dollars.

U.S. person. Any person, including a foreign citizen, who resides in the United States or is subject to the jurisdiction of the U.S. tax system (regardless of where the person is situated worldwide).

Variable annuity. An annuity in which you select the investment program that suits your future needs. The ultimate payback is a function of how well your program performs during the intervening period before the maturity of the annuity.

Vetting. It is the process used by the offshore consultant for qualifying the prospective client to determine if he or she is a good candidate for offshore asset protection; as in to "vet" the prospective client.

Web. The World Wide Web (WWW) of the Internet.

World Bank. Formed to be the bank lender and technical advisor to the developing countries, utilizing funds and technical resources from the member nations (the depositors). The headquarters are in Washington D.C.

WWW. The World Wide Web of the Internet.

Appendix C
Some Offshore and Onshore
Publications of Interest

The following list includes both "domestic" and offshore publications which provide significant offshore and asset protection materials.

1.   The International Financial Times Business Enterprises
     Greystone Place
     Fetter Lane
     London EC4A 1ND, England
     Fax: 071 831 2181

        Heavy emphasis on financial and other offshore services for Britons living abroad, including services offered by banks, professionals and others in the Channel Islands, Isle of Man and some Caribbean jurisdictions.

2.   Investment International
     Charterhouse Communications
     4 Tabernacle Street
     London, EC2B 2BH, England

        Contents similar to 1 above.

3.   *The Mouse Monitor*
        c/o Scope International Ltd.
        Forestside House
        Forestside, Rowland's Castle
        Hants PO9 6EE, England
        United Kingdom
        Tel: 44 1705 631 751, fax: 44 1705 631 322
        ⌨ http://www.britnet.co.uk/Scope/

Publishes very diverse offshore subject matter. Scope International may be able to assist you in opening an Austrian Sparbuch Numbered account. Ready-to-use accounts are available, Sparbuch and Wertpapierbucher. Camouflage passport seller.

4.   *International Living*
        824 East Baltimore Street
        Baltimore, MD 21202

A newsletter in the form of a magazine with the theme of living offshore. It covers offshore investing, retirement, travel, employment, health issues, real estate, shopping, etc. Occasional articles on privacy and asset protection as well as some of the tax havens have been noted.

5.   *The Tico Times*
        Costa Rica
        Tel: (506) 222-0040, 222-8952, fax: (506) 233-6378
        e-mail: ttimes@huracan.cr

An English language weekly newspaper for those interested in living, jobs, working, housing markets, or retiring in Costa Rica or Central America.

6. *The Roman Report*
Roman Reports, Inc.
12600 Rockside Road
Suite 107
Garfield Heights, OH 44125

A newsletter reporting on different scams. Write for a sample copy.

7. *Living Easy in Mexico Today*
United Research Publishers
103 North Highway 101
Dept. RA
Encinitas, CA 92024

A practical book on retiring in general and, more specifically, in Mexico for as little as $14 a day. Priced at $15.95, postpaid. 30-day money back guarantee.

8. *Financial Privacy Report*
Michael H. Ketcher, Editor
PO Box 1277
Burnsville, MN 55337
Tel: (612) 895-8757, fax: (612) 895-5526
e-mail: ketcher@ix.netcom.com

Informative and accurate reporting by an astute editor. Written in practical, down-to-earth, nonlegalese language. $144.00 annually.

9. Foreign Tax Law Publishers
PO Box 2189
Ormond Beach, FL 32175-2189
Tel: (904) 253-5785, fax: (904) 257-3003
e-mail: 103076.1764@compuserve.com
🖳 http://www.advernet.com/ftl/

Foreign tax law publishers providing full, consolidated legal texts of over 100 countries translated into English.

10.   *The Jacobs Report on Asset Protection Strategies*
      Vern Jacobs' Financial $olutions
      Financial $olutions On-Line
      Vernon K. Jacobs, CPA, Editor
      4500 West 72nd Terrace
      PO Box 8137
      Prairie Village, KS 66208
      Tel/fax: (913) 362-9667
      e-mail: vkj@rpifs.com
      http://www.rpifs.com

Vern really knows his taxes, and he addresses complex tax and financial concepts into plain English. US$145 annually. As a bonus, new subscribers get three years of back issues.

11.   *The Lawsuit & Asset Protection Letter*
      Brett Kates, Esq.
      Manning Press, Inc.
      PO Box 83
      Swarthmore, PA 19081
      Tel: (610) 328-4933

Easy to read and down to earth. In its fifth year. US$147 annually.

12.   Adam Starchild.[89] Some of his books include:
      a. *Tax Havens: What They Are and What They Can Do for the Shrewd Investor*, Arlington House.
      b. *Tax Havens and Corporations*, Gulf Publishing Co.
      c. *Everyman's Guide to Tax Havens*, Paladin Press.
      d. *The Tax Haven Story*, PPI Publishing.

---

[89] Starchild is an extremely prolific writer of books and magazine articles. This is merely a partial listing. See the Web site for a complete listing of his books.

e. *Tax Planning for Foreign Investors in the U.S.*, Kluwer
Law & Taxation Publishers, the Netherlands.
   f. *The Tax Haven Report*, Scope International, United
Kingdom (see number 3 above).

13.   OFFSHORE ePublishing Company
        930 Tahoe Blvd., Suite 802-326
        Incline Village, NV 89451-9438
        Tel: 1-800-823-0080

   Publishers of *OFFSHORE*, an *eJournal*, and numerous
books, including *Offshore for Newbies: How to Go Offshore and
Reclaim Your Privacy*, by this author.

14.   The Internal Revenue Service
        See their toll free 800 phone number in your telephone
book.

   Order any of the forms listed in Chapter 11 by telephone.
Use the name of John (Jane) Smith please (not mine!) when
ordering so many foreign forms. Don't forget to also request
Publication Number 953, "International Tax Information for
Business". Also order Publication Number 54, "Tax Guide for
U.S. Citizens and Resident Aliens Abroad."

15.   Lorne House Report
        Lorne House Trust Limited
        Attn: Colin Peters
        Lorne House
        Castletown, Isle of Man
        British Isles
        Tel: +44 1624 823579, fax: +44 1624 822952
        e-mail: colin@lorne-house.com
        http://www.lorne-house.com/ackno.html

   Also provides an excellent and conservative international
investment newsletter and advice on global asset management.

16.   *Pitfalls of Using Foreign Corporations for U.S. Families,*
        by William E. Comer.
        Research Press, Inc.
        PO Box 8137
        Prairie Village, KS 66208
        Tel: (913) 362-9667, fax: (913) 362-4922
        e-mail: vkj@rpifs.com

        Available at US$49.95 from number 16 below.

17.   Camouflage Passports from 13 countries.
        Safeguard Services
        Dept. RA
        1305 Grand #500
        Nogales, AZ 35621
        Tel/fax: (520) 287-5161

        Available at US$160, one week delivery.

18.   TSB Bank Channel Islands Limited
        PO Box 597
        St. Helier
        Jersey JE4 8XW
        Channel Islands
        Tel: 44 1534 503909, fax: 44 1534 503211

        Offshore Banking and Visa Credit Card.

19.   Camouflage Passports
        International Documents Services
        Dept. RA
        PO Box 66712
        Houston, TX 77019
        Tel: (713) 523-3722, fax: (713) 523-3760

        Another source for camouflage passports. (Also see
number 17 above.)

20.   *Dictionary of International Business Terms* by Capela and Hartman.
     A *Barron's Business Guide.*

     Available at bookstores at US$12.95. Contains and defines abbreviations, acronyms and internet terminology, also.

Appendix D
Some Selected and
Representative
Offshore Service Providers

There are numerous, highly qualified professionals located worldwide; the following is merely a representative list of different types of service providers.

1.   Universal Corporate Services, Inc.
      PO Box 211533
      Bedford, TX 76095
      Tel: (800) 551-2141, (817) 595-4777,
      fax: (817) 595-4477
      e-mail: offshore@onramp.com
      ⌨ http://www.ifu.net/ucs/
      Contact: Paul Petit

      Corporate formations in the Bahamas, the British Virgin Islands and the Cayman Islands. Corporate services. International Visa secured credit cards.

2.   Offshore eAssets Reconciliation Limited (OAR)
        55 Frederick Street
        PO Box CB-13039
        Nassau, Bahamas CB13039
        Tel*: (809) 356-2093, fax: (809) 356-2095
        e-mail: ucs@bahamas.net.bs
        🖳 http://www.dnai.com/offshore/offshore.html
        Contact: Nancy Lake, Office Manager

        Corporate (IBC) and APT formations in the Bahamas, the
British Virgin Islands and the Cayman Islands. Corporate services
for ongoing company services, APTs, private banking, Visa credit
cards, asset management, escrow services and asset and financial
movement *using PGP encryption.* The first Nassau company to use
PGP in this manner.

Area code (809) changes to (242) effective October 1, 1996.

3.   Grand Cayman Banccor Limited
        Marlborough House
        Cumberland & Bay Streets
        PO Box N-1201
        Nassau, the Bahamas N1201
        Contact: Dennis J. Sutton, Director
        Tel: (809) 356-0107, fax: (809) 322-1612
        e-mail: itiltd@bahamas.net.bs

        Company formations, company management, formation of
trusts, private banks, mutual funds and private foundations.

4.   Markus H. Mage, Hendrix Andersson, Ole Schmidt
      Saming 11
      4785 Haibach
      Austria
      Tel/fax.: +43 77 13 84 82
      e-mail: 100022.1345@compuserve.com,
      p2maeg01@fsrz1.rz.uni-passau.de

A contact for opening a Sparbuch Austrian numbered savings account.

5.   Libertarian Corporate Services
      59 Bath Street
      Ilkeston, Derbyu
      England DE7 8AH
      Tel: +44 115 932 2436, fax: +44 115 932 1577

Libertarian Corporate Services is an organization that subscribes to strict Libertarian principals regarding your rights to privacy and confidentiality in personal and business matters.

6.   William R. Storie & Company Ltd.
      18 Reid Street
      Hamilton, Bermuda
      PO Box HM 2386
      Hamilton HMJX Bermuda
      Tel: (441) 295-3987, fax: (441) 295-1470
      e-mail: wrsl@ibl.bm
      💻 http://www.webcom.com/~wrsl/

Offshore insurance, captive insurance and re-insurance, company formation and management. *Ils parlent français mais je parle seulement un petit peu.*

7.   Vernon K. Jacobs, CPA.
        PO Box 8137
        Prairie Village, KS 66208
        Tel: (913) 362-9667, fax: (913) 362-4922
        e-mail: vkj@rpifs.com
        🖳 http://www.rpifs.com/ostax

        A U.S. tax advisor with an interest in helping U.S. citizens
avoid problems with the IRS. Vern is also editor and publisher of
the *Asset Protection Strategies Newsletter.*

8.   David S. Lesperance, Attorney at Law
        762 Upper James
        Suite 196
        Hamilton, Ontario L9C 3A2
        Canada
        Tel: (905) 627-2263, fax: (905) 627-2572
        e-mail: relocate@netaccess.on.ca

        A Canadian attorney quite conversant in renunciation of
U.S. citizenship, U.S. and Canadian expatriation tax and legal
issues, second citizenships and passports.

9.   Bermuda Mailing Addresses
        Tel: (441) 292-6563, fax: (441) 292-6587

        Popular international street mailing address, telephone,
fax, mail forwarding and courier services. Starts at US$8/month.

10.   International Trade & Investments Limited
        Marlborough House, Third Floor
        Cumberland Street
        P.O. Box N-1201
        Nassau, Bahamas N1201
        Contact: Roy Bouchier
        Tel: (809) 356-2036, fax: (809) 356-2037
        e-mail: ITILTD@bahamas.net.bs

Company formation and asset management.

11.   Kiwi Maildrops
        Rockford R.D.
        Oxford
        North Canterbury
        New Zealand

        Secure mail drop available in New Zealand. Send NZ$500
for one year plus NZ$200 for initial postage.

Appendix E
What to Do with Offshore Assets

There is a literal smorgasbord of investment opportunities available to the offshore entity (APT, IBC, LLC, foundation, etc.), that is not available in the U.S. for a U.S. person. For an investment to be offered in the U.S., it has to meet rigorous federal and/or state disclosure requirements and financial criteria. The qualification process (U.S. regulatory approval) is quite expensive and time consuming. If an offshore issuer cares not to expend these resources, you will never see it offered in the U.S. Selected offshore investment opportunities can certainly be found that meet quality standards equivalent to their U.S. counterparts, which an OS APT or IBC may purchase. It is just that the offshore issuer, seller or marketer has no need or interest in offering the investment directly to U.S. investors as an American Depositary Receipt (ADR).

"1995 World Investment Report"

In late 1995, the United Nations issued an interesting report out of Geneva. Some of its more interesting and applicable items were:

• The U.S. and China are the top attractions for offshore investors.

- It appears likely that the high level of direct offshore investment will continue to rise in the coming years.
- There are 40,000 transnational corporations with 250,000 foreign affiliates. (Suggest to your son or daughter that they get an MBA in international business!)
- Investments in South and East Asia totaled US$59 billion in 1994, up from $48 billion in 1993.

Offshore Stock and Commodity Markets

Around 62 percent of the global equity investment opportunities are offshore. Over the past 10 years, seven foreign stock markets outperformed the U.S. markets. Markets outperforming the U.S.'s 10-year average of 12.85 percent went from a high of 25.8 percent for Hong Kong to 13.2 percent for Denmark. See Table E-1.

Table E-2, which is far from complete, lists some global stock and commodity exchanges, as well as U.S. exchanges, available for your consideration. At my last count, there were more than 250 stock or commodity exchanges in 65 countries so Table E-2 is a mere sampling, only about one-fifth, of what is available to non-U.S. persons. Use you imagination as to where your funds can be concealed onshore and offshore for asset protection and privacy. Capitalize on investors' markets other than in the U.S.

TABLE E-1: Offshore Stock Market Averages

Average Annual Return for a 10-Year Period Ending March 31, 1996

Stock Market	Average Return (%)
1. Hong Kong	25.8
2. Singapore/Malaysia	21.8
3. Netherlands	17.6
4. Sweden	16.9
5. Switzerland	16.2
6. Belgium	16.1
7. Denmark	13.2
8. United States	12.9

TABLE E-2: A Partial Listing of the World's Investment Exchanges (Bourses)

- Africa, Continent of. Has more than 25 public stock markets.
- †American Stock Exchange
- 🖥 http://www.amex.com
- †Amsterdam Stock Exchange
- Athens Stock Exchange
- Australian Options Market
- †Australian Stock Exchange
- Belgian Futures and Options Exchange
- Boston Stock Exchange
- Chicago Board Options Exchange
- Chicago Board of Trade
- 🖥 http://www.cbot.com
- Chicago Mercantile Exchange
- 🖥 http://www.cme.com
- †Chicago Stock Exchange
- Coffee Sugar & Cocoa Exchange
- Commodity Exchange, Inc.
- Commodity Exchange of New York
- Copenhagen Stock Exchange & Gfdof
- †Deutsche Terminborse, DTB—Frankfort
- †Dublin Stock Exchange
- European Options Exchange
- Financiele Termijnmarkt Amsterdam
- Finex
- Frankfurter Wertpapierborse
- FUTOP Copenhagen
- Guarantee Fund Danish Options & Futures
- Hong Kong Futures Exchange
- †Hong Kong, Stock Exchange of
- International Monetary Market
- International Petroleum Exchange

- Irish Futures & Options Exchange
- Johannesburg Stock Exchange
- Kansas City Board of Trade
- Korean Stock Exchange
- Kuala Lumpur Commodity Exchange
- Lisbon Stock Exchange
- London Future/Options Exchange
- London International Financial Futures and Options Exchange
-   (LIFFE)
- London Metals Exchange
- London Metals and Terminal Markets
- †London Stock Exchange
- London Traded Options Market
- †Luxembourg Stock Exchange
- Marche A Term International De France
- MEFFSA
- Madrid Financial Futures Exchange
- Mexico Stock Exchange.
- MidAmerica Commodity Exchange
- Midwest Stock Exchange
- Minneapolis Grain Exchange
- †Montreal Stock Exchange
- †Nagoya Stock Exchange
- †NASDAQ Stock Exchange
-    🖳 http://www.nasdaq.com
- New York Coffee, Sugar, and Cocoa Exchange
- New York Cotton Exchange
- New York Futures Exchange
- New York Mercantile Exchange
- †New York Stock Exchange
-    🖳 http://www.nyse.com
- New Zealand Stock Exchange
- New Zealand Futures Exchange
- Nikkei Over-the-Counter Market
- Oporto Stock Exchange

- †Osaka Stock Exchange
- Pacific Stock Exchange
- †Paris Stock Exchange
- Paris Stock Options Market
- Philadelphia Stock Exchange
-      💻 http:www.libertynet.org/~phlx/
- Rio de Janeiro Stock Exchange
- Rotterdam Energy Futures Exchange
- São Paulo Stock Exchange
- Singapore International Monetary Exchange
- †Singapore Stock Exchange
- Soffex
- Stockholm Options Market
- Stockholm Stock Exchange
- Suomen Option Porssi
- Swiss Exchange
- Swiss Option & Financial Futures Exchange
- Sydney Futures Exchange
- †Taiwan Stock Exchange
- Thailand, Stock Exchange of
- Tokyo Grain Exchange
- Tokyo International Financial Futures Exchange
- †Tokyo Stock Exchange
- Toronto Futures Exchange
- †Toronto Stock Exchange
- Vancouver Stock Exchange
- Warsaw Stock Exchange
- Winnipeg Commodity Exchange
- Winnipeg Grain Exchange
- †Zurich Stock Exchange

Table Note: For free quotes and charts on about 60,000 different stocks, try Teleserv in the UK. There are no access restrictions.
💻 http://www.teleserv.co.uk/stock/

† Permitted investment bourses under the Bahamian Mutual Funds Act of 1995.

The "New" Time Sharing: Vacation Ownership

From the pages of *OFFSHORE, an eJournal.*™

    OFFSHORE has monitored the past concept of Time Shared Ownership for years and found it to have been previously seriously flawed. Past problems were:

> 1.   Loss of ownership interest if the resort developer failed or filed for bankruptcy. Many were merely a right to use and not deeded ownership.

> 2.   No (U.S.) tax benefits such as deductibility of real property taxes and interest paid as a second home under current tax laws.

> 3.   Rigidity such as the necessity of utilizing the third week of March every year in Maui, Hawaii. Use it or lose it!

> 4.   Reversion of the property after X number of years to the landowner or the developer.

> 5.   Title-holder restrictions having to be circumvented because of limitations of foreign ownership in the country where the time share is located.

> 6.   Limited ability to transfer interests to heirs. If you can't "will it," it fails one of our tests.

    But now, if the OS APT buys a quality vacation ownership (VO), in a 5-star[90] resort, one in demand 52 weeks a year (*red* 52 weeks, in the parlance of this industry), it doesn't matter where one owns if it is being purchased primarily to exchange worldwide. If you really want to save money, *never buy at retail from the developer!* The APT can purchase a time share resale on the secondary market for a 25 to 75 percent discount. The

---

[90] The star rating system is suspect. Insiders disclose that a developer can "buy" a five-star rating.

repurchase price is *very* negotiable, usually because of a divorce, financial problems or lack of interest in the time share. If you are buying for personal use at the home resort, at times, then buy one at the resort where you would use it.

Our latest analysis finds that all of the above problems have been remedied in some current types of offerings we have recently reviewed. *The current OFFSHORE position is buy the right situation.* If you like it, would use it and find it affordable, it is the modern way to vacation and travel.

The new time sharing VO is the second fastest growing phenomenon in the world with somewhere between 2 and 3 million people worldwide now participating. (Cellular phones are the fastest growing industry.)

You should inquire at this point, what is the right situation? The following analysis attempts to educate you:

1.   Some people utilize offshore funds to acquire a "quality vacation ownership" (VO) in the name of an OS IBC or trust. The Global Group can assist you by answering your questions and helping you acquire the best situation for your needs.

2.   Buy only a floating week (not a fixed week per year), and buy a deeded interest which provides a Grant Deed and Title Insurance. It's then yours forever.

3.   Buy only an interest in a quality, 5-star resort, and one in demand–red hot–52 weeks a year. 5-star ownership gives you priority in the exchange system.

4.   Buy only a resort which trades (exchanges) with a quality, well established firm, such as Interval International (II) or RCI.

5.   Buy from an established resort developer with at least a 10-year history of development. Too many newcomers are racing to join this new growth industry.

6.   Do not expect to make money on the future sale of the VO. Buy it to use, enjoy or exchange. Don't buy it as an investment.

Here is how the modern VO works:

1.   You purchase a VO to use it, loan it, rent it, gift it, put it in your trust, "will it" to your family forever, sell it or do what around 85 percent of the owners do, *exchange it* for a different vacation location each year.

2.   If the VO is not to be used, it is put into the exchange program, given to II to provide to other members of II. It is banked. II currently charges an annual membership fee of US$64 per year. With over 1,500 resorts in 60 countries, you should always find something new to enjoy. Your week can be saved until the next year for two weeks, or one can borrow from the future and take three weeks for that long vacation trip. For example, II charges an exchange fee of US$89 for a traded week in the U.S. for another U.S. property (i.e., Las Vegas to Hawaii). II charges an exchange fee of US$109 for a traded week from the U.S. to a non-U.S. resort (i.e., Lake Tahoe to Nassau).

3.   II will allow you to purchase additional weeks for you, your family or friends for a fee from between US$129 to $569 per week (typically around $280 a week). These weeks are available from 24 hours to 60 days before you need them.

4.   Through II's travel agency, discount airfares, hotels, cruises, and car rentals are also available. They may also be used for your business purposes.

5.   Many resorts allow daily use rentals through II.

6.   Over 3,200 hotels worldwide offer II members the lowest room rates.

7. There are only 177 5-star resorts worldwide, and almost all participate in the II program.

8. One can take long weekend vacations (mini-vacations) at highly discounted prices.

Vacation ownership has come of age. It allows one to prepay for future vacations and get more luxury (5-star or 4-star quality) for less money. We are now seeing people acquire more than one week of VO. We are seeing grandparents and parents buying (gifting) VO for their children and grandchildren. Since they can be in some cases purchased for less than US$10,000, it is a U.S. tax-free gift. Everybody wins. The resort or hotel fills up empty rooms and hopes that you dine in their restaurant and buy in their gift shops. The lower costs encourage one to vacation more frequently, which fills up vacant airline seats.

The VO program is so flexible that it may be right for you if you take a real one-week vacation each year or multiple week vacations every other year. If you have offshore funds to acquire a VO interest or if you think it may be beneficial for you or if you merely have some further questions, e-mail to: offshore@dnai.com

Offshore Mortgage Financing

Provide funds to an offshore mortgage finance company to lend out offshore or onshore. These funds can earn at 10 to 11 percent or higher on *first* mortgages, for example, in the Turks and Caicos Islands.

Other Examples of OS Investment Opportunities

1. Offshore Accounts Receivable Financing

2. Offshore Irrevocable Letters of Credit Financing

3. Offshore Consulting Company

4.   Offshore Fulfillment Organization

Discussion of these topics are planned for inclusion in our "Quarterly Update Service" described on the last page.

Index

A

Abbreviations. *See* Glossary
Abu Dhabi, 201
Acceptance fee, 107
Accounts. *See* Chop Block
    Account; Numbered accounts;
    Private accounts; Sparbuch
    (Savings) Account
Actionable fraud, 102-104
Administrative fee, 114
Adobe Acrobat Reader, 207
ADR. *See* American Depositary
    Receipt
Advanced pricing agreements, 7
Adverse trustee, 215
Agent's fees, 78
Air transportation companies, 74
Alderney, 48
AM & G-Accountants and
    Consultants, 207
American. *See* Reluctant
    American; Ugly American
American Bar Association, 128
American Depositary Receipt
    (ADR), 216, 247
American Express Bank, 111
Andorra, 12, 48, 163
Anguilla, 37, 48
Annual audits, 183
Annual fees, 26, 48, 107

Annual reporting, 107
Annual Return of Foreign Trust
    with U.S. Beneficiaries, 169
Annual returns, 77
Annuitant, 68, 121, 122, 164,
    215
Annuities, 68, 121-125, 145,
    215-216. *See also* Deferred
    annuities; Offshore annuity;
    Private annuity; Swiss annuity;
    Variable annuity
    background, 121-122
Annuity contract, 124
Annuity distribution, 123
Annuity income, 164
Annuity proceeds, taxes, 163-164
Annuity variation, 21
Anstalt, 216
Anticonduit financing rules, 7
Anti-expatriation rules, 164
Antigua, 38, 49, 186, 205
AP. *See* Asset protection
Appendices, 201-256
Application. *See* Learning
Application for Taxpayer
    Identification Number, 166
APT. *See* Asset Protection Trust
Arbitrage, 32
Arendt, Hannah, 130
Argentina, 137
Aruba, 37, 38, 42, 49
    Travel Information, 205

Asset disposition, 97
Asset jurisdiction, 94
Asset locators, 111
Asset management, 116
Asset manager, 22, 42, 63, 93,
    98, 107, 117, 154, 182
Asset placement, where/how,
    35-59
Asset Preservation Plan. *See*
    Bankruptcy
Asset protection (AP), 3, 10, 77,
    85, 92, 108, 123, 139, 142,
    143, 154, 197, 198, 208, 216
    specialty, 26
    strategies, 129
    tool, 14, 88, 138. *See also*
    Family Limited Partnership;
    Real property equity stripping
Asset Protection Trust (APT), 8,
    14, 16, 21, 22, 27, 36, 48, 50-
    53, 57, 66, 163, 166-170, 176,
    185, 188, 209, 216, 247. *See
    also* Grantor APT; Offshore
    Asset Protection Trust; Tax
    neutral APT
    Act, 187
    costs, 59
    legislation, 44, 50-52, 54-56
    need, 92-94
    parties, 94-98
Asset transfer, 99
Asset trustees, 93
Assets. *See* Offshore assets
    disposition, 105
    protectors, 6
    transfer, 58-59
ATM, 201
    cards. *See* Offshore ATM
    cards
Austria, 12, 49, 114

Austrian Ueberbringer Sparbuch.
    See Sparbuch account
Author note, 1-10
Authorized capital, 216
Automatic flight, 106
AutoPGP, 203

B

Babcock, Mike, 203
Bacard's Privacy Page, 204
Badges of fraud. *See* Fraud
Bahamas, 26, 36, 41, 42, 49, 51,
    57, 58, 66, 74, 79, 83, 84, 100,
    101, 112, 128, 171, 182, 187
Bahamas Telephone Company
    (Batelco), 174
Bahamian Exchange Control
    Legislation, 83
Bahrain, 12, 49
Bank account establishment, 78
Bank of America (BofA), 110,
    196
Bank of Credit & Commerce
    International (BCCI), 216-217
    money laundering, 111
Bank of England, 48, 50, 185
Bank of International Settlements
    (BIS), 217
Bank laundering, 55
Bank trustee, 188
Bankers, 6
Banking, 44
Banking cards. *See* Offshore
    banking cards
Banking fees, 107
Banking privacy, 52, 111
    laws, 109-110
Banking protection, 29
Banking rules, 110-111
Banking secrecy, 187

Banking services, 32, 38, 72, 78
Banking stability, 136
Banking transactions, 32
Bankruptcy, 32, 57, 130, 141, 151, 252
  Asset Preservation Plan, 156-158
  Code, 103, 157. *See also* U.S. Bankruptcy Code
  Court, 156
  fraud, 4
  insolvency test, 91
  statutes, 88
  trustee, 51, 157
Barbados, 49, 209
Barber, Hoyt L., 8
Barbuda, 49
Barclays bank, 110, 193
Barron's Online, 213
Batelco. *See* Bahamas Telephone Company
BCCI. *See* Bank of Credit & Commerce International
BCE. *See* Before the Common Era
Bearer shares, 21, 55
Before the Common Era (BCE), 89
Belgium, 137
Belize, 25, 44-45, 49, 132, 201
Beneficial interest, 217
Beneficial owner, disclosure, 79
Beneficial ownership, 217
Beneficiaries, 97, 153, 180, 188, 217
Bermuda, 43, 50, 51, 98, 100, 171, 180, 182
Bermuda Sun, 212-213
BIS. *See* Bank of International Settlements
Bloomberg Exchange Rates, 205

BO. *See* Business organization
BofA. *See* Bank of America
Bogus passports, 132
Bookkeeping test, 91
Branch profits, 7
Brazil, 132, 137
British Honduras, 25, 44, 132
British Telecon, 201
British Virgin Islands (BVI), 8, 42, 44, 50, 74, 98, 99, 128, 163, 171, 175, 185, 187
British Virgin Islands Act (BVI Act), 49
British West Indies (BWI), 48-50, 52-54, 56, 218
Brokerage accounts, 63, 107, 130. *See also* U.S. stock brokerage accounts
Brokerage fees, 22
Brokerage firm, 63
Brokerage houses, 30
BTO. *See* Business Trust Organization
Burdick, Eugene, 1
Burke's Offshore Tax Haven, 205
Business associates, 176
Business failure, 32
Business interests, 86
Business organization (BO), 21, 217. *See also* Unincorporated business organization
Business trust, 151, 154
Business Trust Organization (BTO), 21
BVI. *See* British Virgin Islands
BWI. *See* British West Indies

C

Caicos Island, 10. *See also* Turks and Caicos Islands

Camoflage passports, 132, 234, 238

Canada, 36, 133, 174. *See also* New Brunswick

Canadian Business InfoWorld, 211

Canadian Imperial Bank of Commerce, 112

Canary Islands, 38, 41, 50

Cape Verde, 135, 137

Capital gains, 123, 160, 182
taxes, 46, 50, 64, 65, 72, 124, 164, 168

Capital transfer taxes, 47

Capitalization, 55, 76

Captive insurance
company, 21, 47, 72, 179-184. *See also* Offshore captive insurance company
costs, 183
definition, 179-183
market, 54
statutory requirements, 183

Caribbean Common Market (CARICOM), 218

CARICOM. *See* Caribbean Common Market

Case study, 185-187

Cash disbursements, 165

Cash flow, 181

Cayman Islands, 36, 38, 41, 43, 44, 50-51, 57, 74, 100, 101, 160, 171, 174, 179-183

CBI. *See* Certificate of beneficial interest

Central America, 44, 45

Central Bank of Nigeria, 192

Central Intelligence Agency (CIA), 211

Certificate of beneficial interest (CBI), 145, 155

Certified Public Accountant (CPA), 4, 13, 14, 41, 88, 92, 134, 154, 199, 218

Ceylon. *See* Republic of Ceylon

CFC. *See* Controlled foreign corporation

Chad, 137

Chagall, Marc, 130

Channel Islands, 51, 74, 89, 171, 238

Charitable foundations, 21. *See also* Offshore charitable foundations

Chartered accountants, 42, 76

CHC. *See* Contract hybrid company

Chile, 137

Choice of Governing Law, 58

Choice of Law, 101, 108

Chop Block Account, 112-114

CIA. *See* Central Intelligence Agency

CIS. *See* Congress of Independent States

Citizenship, 62, 129-134. *See also* Second citizenship; U.S. citizenship

C-note, 30

Commerce, engagement, 72

Commercial bankers, 196

Commercial property, 92

Commissions, 63, 73

Committee of Advisors, 218-219

Committee of Trust Protectors, 219

Commodity exchanges, 248

Commodity trading advisor (CTA), 196

Commodity trading company, 72

Common Law, 21, 150, 219
contract, 150

Common Law, *Cont'd*
  instrument, 151
  jurisdiction, 53. *See also*
    English Common Law
    jurisdiction
Communications, 38-40, 73, 165,
  186. *See also* E-mail;
    Facsimile communications;
    Internet; Offshore
    communications; Voice
    communications
  quality. *See* International
    Business Company
Community markets. *See*
  Offshore community markets
Companies Act or Ordinance,
  219
Company. *See* Contract hybrid
  company; International
  Business Company; Offshore
  company
  act, 71
  formation/agreement,
    application, 77-78
  limited lifetime, 128
  management, 78
  managers, 42
  name restrictions, 79
Compensation, 95
Complicity, 3
Comptroller of the Currency. *See*
  U.S. Comptroller of the
  Currency
Computer files, 176
Concerns,
  recognition/overcoming, 19-27
Conclusion, 185-199
Confidentiality, 31
Congress of Independent States
  (CIS), 112
Connected Traveller, 211

Conservatorship, 89
Consulting companies, 74
Contempt of court, settlor, 105-
  106
Contingent beneficial interest,
  219
Contingent fee, 157
Contract hybrid company (CHC),
  128
Controlled foreign corporation
  (CFC), 64, 72, 73, 78, 162,
  218, 219
Cook Island Trust Act, 51
Cook Islands, 36, 42, 45, 51-52,
  57, 59, 100, 101, 187
CoolTalk, 174
Corporate bearer shares, 54
Corporate books/records, 165
Corporate income taxes, 47
Corporate management, 165
Corporate seal, 78
Corporate shares, taxes, 47
Corruption, 46
Cost efficiency, 181
Costa Rica, 38, 44, 45, 52
Côte d'Azur, 199
Co-trustee, 96, 97
Couriers, 213
Coverage, unavailability, 181
CPA. *See* Certified Public
  Accountant
Creation of or Transfers to
  Certain Foreign Trusts, 169
Credit cards, 173. *See also*
  Offshore credit cards
  business, 109
  issuers, 32
Credit reporting bureaus, 32, 110
Credit Suisse, 193
Creditor claims, 57
Creditors, types/classes, 99-100

Criminal liability, 3-4
Criminal penalties, 79
Cross-cut shredder, 175-176
Crown jewel, 21
Cryptography, 203
CTA. *See* Commodity trading
    advisor
Cuba Clause, 106
CubaWeb, 212
Curaçao, 38
Currency exchange rates, 163,
    205
Currency regulations, 42
Current account, 220
Custodian, 220
    trustee, 220
Cybercash, 201, 210
CyberShore, 9, 201-213
Cylink, 39
Cypherpunks 15th Archive, 204
Cyprus, 36, 51, 52, 100, 128, 163

D

Daily Record, 213
Databases, 32, 33
De novo action, 106
Death duties, 47
Debit cards. *See* Offshore debit
    cards
Declaration of Trust, 150, 220
Deferred annuities, 197
Departure tax planning, 16
Dependent territory, 38
Deutsche Bank, 193
Deutsche mark, 123
DHL, 56, 107
DigiCash, 117, 201, 210
Disclosure requirements, 30, 48
Discretionary flight, 106
Discretionary trust, 220

Disintermediation, 29
Divorce, 31, 130, 151
Doctrine of Euro-compatible,
    114
Domicile, 62, 83, 99, 129-134,
    180
Domicile of choice, 131
Domicile of origin, 131
Domicilliary fees. *See*
    International Business
    Company
Dominica, 47, 52, 137
Dominican Republic, 137
Donor, 220
Double tax agreement, 53
Double tax treaty, 49, 187
Double taxation, 10
Dual tax treaty, 95
    aspects, 75
Due diligence, 23, 196-197
Duress provisions, 104
Dynastic settlements, 99

E

EA. *See* Enrolled Agent
Earnings stripping, 2, 7
Eavesdropping, 77
EC, 135, 186, 220
EC community, 163
EC country, 12
EC directive, 47
E-cash, 117
    companies, 210
Economic passport, 134
Economic Recovery Act of 1981,
    65, 220
Economic stability. *See* Long-
    term economic stability
Economist, 212
ECU, 123

EEC, 220
EIN. *See* Employer Identification
    Number
Electronic cash, 117
Electronic Privacy Information
    Center Home Page, 204
E-mail, 76, 175, 176
    communications, 40
Employer Identification Number
    (EIN), 166
Encryption, 40, 177, 201. *See*
    also Pretty Good Privacy;
    Voice encryption
English common law, 90, 108
English Common Law
    jurisdiction, 49, 56, 98, 100
Enrolled Agent (EA), 166
Entity structure, 20
Equity, 92
Equity stripping, 8, 99. *See also*
    Real property equity stripping
    company, 66
Equity trust. *See* Pure equity trust
Eritrea, 133, 160
Escrow account, 68
Escrow company, 66, 170
Estate duties, 50
Estate planner, 13
Estate planning, 6, 16, 30, 93,
    108, 140, 213. *See also* Global
    estate planning; International
    estate planning
    tool, 138
Estate taxes, 87, 93, 129, 140,
    188
EU, 136
European Commission, 112
European Economic Community,
    186
European Union, 114
European Union Bank, 208

Ex parte, 220
Excelsior Bank, 209
Exchange controls, 30, 42, 77,
    115
Exchange fee, 254
Excise tax, 122, 163
Exempt assets, 91, 145
Exempt company, 27, 48, 62, 71-
    84, 125, 188. *See also*
    Offshore exempt company
Expatriation planning, 16
Export Today (magazine), 212

F

401(k), 121, 164
Facsimile communications, 39-
    40
Fair market value, 139
Family foundation, 54
Family holding trust, 221
Family Limited Partnership
    (FLP), 138-143, 155, 221. *See*
    also Real estate FLP
    AP tool, weakness, 141-142
    checklist, 143
Family partnership, 24
Family protective trust, 21, 94,
    221, 222
Family settlement trust, 21, 94
Family Trust cases, 150
FDIC. *See* Federal Deposit
    Insurance Corporation
Feasibility study, 116
Federal Deposit Insurance
    Corporation (FDIC), 29, 136
Federal Express (FedEx), 56,
    107, 213
Federal Reserve Board, 209
Federal Reserve wire transfer
    system, 59

FedEx. *See* Federal Express
Fellowes (shredder), 175
Feuchtwanger, Leon, 130
Fiduciary, 87
File transfer protocol (FTP), 40
Filing fee, 76
Financial centres, 89
Financial community, 46, 61
Financial planning, 10, 16, 30
Financial privacy, 13, 31
Financial Privacy Report, 235
Financial profile, 92
Financial ratios, 183
Financial reports, 165
Financial Resource Guide, 210
Financial security, 31
Financial services, 32
    industry, 42
Financial Services Commission,
    56
Financial statements, 183
Financial transactions, 32
First Virtual Holding, Inc., 210
FIRPTA. *See* Foreign Investor in
    Real Property Tax Act of 1980
Fiscal independence, 185
Fixed fee, 63
Fleet Clause, 106
Flight, provisions, 106
Flight capital, 7, 32, 45, 115
Flight jurisdiction, 52
FLP. *See* Family Limited
    Partnership
FMV, 91
Forced heirship, 101
Ford Foundation, 156
Foreclosure, 142
Foreign Asset Protection Trust.
    See Offshore Asset Protection
    Trust
Foreign corporation, 11

Foreign Investor in Real Property
    Tax Act of 1980 (FIRPTA),
    64-65, 220-222
Foreign judgments, enforcement,
    106
Foreign personal holding
    company (FPHC), 162, 222
Foreign Tax Law Publishers, 235
Foreign trust, 11-12, 168
Forfeiture laws, 33
Form 1099 income, 154
Formation costs, 76
Forms. *See* Internal Revenue
    Service
Fortune (magazine), 212
Foundations. *See* Offshore
    charitable foundations; Private
    foundations
FPHC. *See* Foreign personal
    holding company
France, 52
Franchise taxes, 47
Fraud, 99, 106. *See also*
    Actionable fraud; Bankruptcy;
    Mail fraud
    badges, 100, 102-104, 198,
    216
Fraudulent conveyance, 222
    statutes, 88
Fraudulent transfer, 99, 108
Free Trade Zone, 54. *See also*
    Halo FTZ
Freebooter Newsletter, 205
Freezone, 49
French Territories, 37
Frequent Flyer Programs, 175
Fry, Varian, 130
FSLIC, 29
FTC. *See* Futures Trading
    Commission
FTP. *See* File transfer protocol

FTZ. *See* Free Trade Zone; Halo FTZ
Full Disclosure Live, 203
Fund management, 116
Fund manager, 117
Futures Trading Commission (FTC), 196

G

General partner (GP), 138, 139, 143
Geographic considerations, 185
Geographic diversity, 13, 15, 56
Georgia Uniform Partnership Act (UPA), 140
Ghost investment, 196
Gibraltar, 12, 36, 52-53, 74, 100, 101, 128
Ginsburg, Anthony S., 8
Global business, 210-212
Global community, 11, 47
Global equity investment opportunities, 248
Global estate planning, 16
Global fund, 12
Global Group, 204
Global insurance resource. *See* World Wide Web
Global Risk Management Network, 212
Global village, 11
Globalink, 37
Globalization, 7, 90
Glossary, terms/abbreviations, 215-232
GmbH, 222
Governing Law Act, 58
GP. *See* General partner
Granada, 53

Grand Cayman Banccor Limited, 242
Grantor, 101, 150, 168, 222
Grantor APT, 167
Grenada, 12
Grisham, John, 2
Guadeloupe, 47
Guarantees alert, 189
Guaranty/hybrid company, 21
Guatemala, 137
Guernsey, 43, 47, 51, 53, 180, 211

H

Halo FTZ, 54
Hard fraud, 103
Hedge fund, 21
High net worth (HNW), 115, 116, 222
High-risk profession, 15
child provision, 155-156
HNW. *See* High net worth
Holding companies, 54, 62, 72-74. *See also* Offshore holding company
Homestead allowance, 68
exemption, 223
laws, 158
value, 68
Honduras, 137
Hong Kong, 36, 53, 74, 112, 114, 128, 171, 201
House of Lords, 51
HSBC Investment Bank Asia Holding, 116
Hype marketing, 190

I

IBC. *See* International Business Company
Identifying numbers, 169
IFC. *See* International financial centre
IFSC. *See* International Financial Services Centre
II. *See* Interval International
Illness, 32
IMF, 6
In rem jurisdiction, 102
Income accumulation, 99
Income tax rate, 30, 164
Income taxes, 46, 50, 53, 164, 199. *See also* Corporate income taxes; Personal income taxes
rates, 121
Incomplete gift, 167, 223
Indemnification, 143
Independent country, 38
Independent trustee, 223
India, 54
Inflation rate, 30
Information exchange, 41
Information Exchange Agreement, 52
Informational Return on U.S. Persons with Respect to Certain Foreign Corporations, 170
Information-sharing agreement, 48
InfoSeek, 202
Inheritance taxes, 47, 50
Injunctive order. *See* Mareva injunctive order, 94
Insolvency, 32, 88

Institute of Chartered Accountants, 206
Insurance. *See* Captive insurance resource. *See* World Wide Web
InsureWeb, 184
Inter vivos declaration, 154
Inter vivos trust, 87
Interest rate, 68
Internal Revenue Code (IRC), 12, 62, 64, 124, 151, 164, 165, 167, 169, 182, 224
compliance, 23
IRC of 1986, 164
Internal Revenue Service (IRS), 2, 14, 16, 24, 31, 32, 48, 52, 54, 86, 93, 109, 123, 133, 139, 159, 160, 162-164, 166, 176, 197, 206, 224, 237, 244
audit, 140
Form SS-4, 166
Form 56, 166-167
Form 709, 167
Form 926, 167-168
Form 1040, 160, 168-169
Form 1041, 167, 169
Form 3520, 169
Form 3520-A, 169
Form 5471, 170
Form 8288, 170
Form 8288-A, 170
forms, 12, 166-170
pre-filing notice, 155
purchasing agent, 16
reporting requirement, 78
reporting scenario, 11
requirements. *See* Offshore principal office
Revenue Ruling 69-70, 78
tax compliance, 166
Tax Forms, 207

International Air Mail Service, 211

International banking centre, 20, 35

International Business Companies Act, 49

International Business Company (IBC), 16, 19, 21, 22, 27, 36, 43, 45, 48, 50, 52, 53, 55, 56, 62, 64, 68, 94, 106, 108, 116, 124, 125, 128, 164, 170, 188, 216, 223, 242, 247. *See also* Offshore IBC

  capabilities, 72-74

  Caribbean style, 71-84

  communications quality, 75-76

  comparison checklist, 78-84

  considerations, 74-75

  costs, 76

  domicilliary fees, 76

  features, 74-77

  investing. *See* U.S. stock market

  language, 76

  management fees, 76

  monetary controls, 77

  name restrictions, 77

  operations, simplicity/flexibility, 75

  privacy, 76-77

  registration fees, 76

  stock, marketing/solicitation, 165

  structure, 77

  tax regimen, 75

International estate planning, 3, 10

International financial centre (IFC), 3, 29, 35, 44, 47, 50, 53, 106, 170, 185, 223, 226

  discussion, 44-48

International Financial Services Centre (IFSC), 53

International Financial Times Business Enterprises, 233

International Fiscal Police (INTERFIPOL), 223

International Living, 234

International Money Fund, 209

International operating company, 71

International Police (INTERPOL), 223, 224

International services, set-up/servicing, 26-27

International Tax Resources, 206

International Trade Administration, 211

International Trade & Investments Limited, 244

International trust, 223

Internet, 9, 17, 37, 58, 76, 117, 135, 184, 192

  communication, 40

  Income Tax Information, 208

  offshore related sites, 201-202

  resources, 201-213

INTERFIPOL. *See* International Fiscal Police

INTERPOL. *See* International Police

Interval International (II), 253-255

Investment activity, 101

Investment exchanges, 249-251

Investment International, 233

Investment management, 25

Investment opportunities, 15, 93. *See also* Offshore investment opportunities

Investment report. *See* World Investment Report

Investment trust, 154
IRA, 121
Iran Contra scandal, 111
IRC. *See* Internal Revenue Code
Ireland, 12, 53, 128, 137, 1711
Irish Tax Site, 206
Irish-non-resident companies, 53
IRS. *See* Internal Revenue
  Service
Isle of Man, 41, 53, 74, 98, 128,
  157, 174
Israel, 137
Issuer test, 189
Italian Taxation System, 207
Italy, 132

J

Jacobs, Vernon K., 88, 236, 244
Jacobs Report, 236
Java, 9
Jersey, 51, 53, 185, 211
Joint trustees, 96
Jones, Michael Arthur, 111
J.P. Morgan. *See* Morgan
Judgment creditor, 143
Judgment Purchase Corporation,
  26
Jury awards, 6

K

Keogh plan, 164
Kiwi Maildrops, 245
Koblas Currency Converter, 205
KPMG Tax Online, 207

L

Labuan, 53

Lao-tzu, 19
Lawsuit & Asset Protection
  Letter, 236
Layered trust, 224
Layering, 56, 224
LC. *See* Limited liability
  company
Learning, application, 185-199
Leasing, 73
Lederer, Bill, 1
Legal settlor, 85
Lender, 73
Lesperance, David S., 244
Letters of wishes, 93, 95, 224
Liberia, 53
Libertarian Corporate Services,
  243
Library Map Collection, 211
Licensing companies, 74
Liechtenstein, 12, 37, 43, 54, 156
  laws, 55
Lifschitz, Jacques, 130
Limited company, 224
Limited duration company, 21
Limited liability company (LLC)
  (LC), 21, 75, 94, 163, 148,
  180, 224-225, 247
Limited liability limited
  partnership (LLLP), 225
Limited liability partnership
  (LLP), 163, 225
Limited life company, 21
Limited partner (LP), 138-142.
  See also Offshore LP
Limited partnership, 64, 65, 143
Liquid assets, 115
Liquidating loan, 195. *See also*
  Self-liquidating loans
Liquidating trust, 154
Liquidation values, 91

Litigation, 6, 13-15, 31, 33, 66, 90-93, 103, 144
Living trust, 138, 225. *See also* U.S. living trust
LLC. *See* Limited liability company
LLLP. *See* Limited liability limited partnership
LLP. *See* Limited liability partnership
Local customs, 43
Local jurisdictions, 108
   tax concessions, 163
Local politics, 44
Local professionals, 42
Long-term economic stability, 42-43
Look back period, 158
Loren, Karl, 145, 148
Lorne House Report, 237
Loss reserve practices, 183
LP. *See* Limited partner
Lump-sum disability, 32
Luxembourg, 12, 43, 54
Lycos, 202
   Web search, 9

M

Macao, 163
Madeira, 54, 171
Mage, Markus H., 243
Mail fraud, 4
Maintenance services, 107
Malaysia, 54
Malaysian Business Pages, 210
Malta, 54
Management fees, 22, 116. *See also* International Business Company
Management trust, 151

Mareva injunctive order, 94
Margins, 183
Mark Twain Bank, 117, 209, 210
Marshall Islands, 54
Massachusetts Trust, 21
Mauritius, 51, 54, 57, 100, 101
Mavera injunction, 225
McDonald's, 90
McKinley Internet Directory, 202
Media, 212-213
Melding Obgebruikelijke Transacties, 49
Mexico, 137
   Doing Business, 210
   Living Easy, 235
MGA, 184
Microsoft Windows, 203
Midland Bank, 201
Minority ownership, 140
MLAT. *See* Mutual Legal Assistance Treaty
MLM. *See* Multilevel marketing
Modem-to-modem data transmission, 40
Monaco, 12, 15, 54
Mondex, 201
Monetary controls. *See* International Business Company
Monetary policies, 115
Money Launderer, 205
Money laundering, 4, 226
Monserrat, 54
Morgan, J.P., 193
Mortgage financing. *See* Offshore mortgage financing
Mouse Monitor, 234
Multilevel marketing (MLM), 45
   marketing program, 209
Mutual funds, 84. *See also* Offshore mutual funds

Mutual Legal Assistance Treaty (MLAT), 41, 226

N

1995 World Investment Report. *See* World Investment Report
Name restrictions. *See* International Business Company
Nassau, 25, 58, 112, 119
National Network of Estate Planning, 213
National Trade Databank, 212
National Westminster, 201
Nationality, 62
Nauru, 12, 54, 163
Netherlands, 12, 43
Netherlands Antilles, 38, 43, 54, 66, 171, 174
Netherlands West Indies (NWI), 48
Netscape, 37, 62, 117, 119
    Communication, 174
    Communication Corp., 210
    Navigator Web, 174
Nevada (US), 47-48, 54
Nevada corporation, 21
Nevis, 36, 46, 54, 55, 100, 101, 136, 138
New Brunswick (Canada), 54, 180
New Zealand, 51, 54
Newbie, 36
Nigeria, 137
Nigerian National Petroleum Corporation (NNPC), 191, 192
Nigerian scam, 190-193
Niue, 45-46, 55

NNPC. *See* Nigerian National Petroleum Corporation
No-fault settlement, 32
Nominee settlor, 85
Nominees, 6, 26
Non-annuity withdrawals, 164
Non-APT trust, 138
Noncitizenship passports, 133
Noncompliant claims, 45
Nongrantor foreign trust, 166
Nongrantor trust, 85, 86, 226
Nonresident alien (NRA), 3, 78, 85, 86, 96, 160, 226
Non-United Nations, 137
Normandy Cherbourg, 47
No-tax jurisdiction, 75
Notice Concerning Fiduciary Relationship, 166-167
NRA. *See* Nonresident alien
Numbered accounts, 111-115
NWI. *See* Netherlands West Indies

O

OAR. *See* Offshore eAsset Reconciliation
OFFSHORE, 193, 195, 237, 252, 253
Offshore Accounts Receivable Financing, 255
Offshore annuity, 68
    issuers, 122
Offshore asset managers, 6
Offshore (Foreign) Asset Protection Trust (OS APT), 85-108, 148, 163, 167, 188, 247, 252
    costs, 106-107
    technicalities, 108

Offshore assets, 29, 35, 188
   usage, 247-256
Offshore Assets Reconciliation
   Limited, 110
Offshore ATM cards, 201
Offshore bank account, 130
Offshore banking cards, 208-209
Offshore banks, 14, 109-119
Offshore bankers, 109
Offshore banking services, 109-
   119
Offshore brokerage houses, 22
Offshore capital outflow, 122
Offshore captive insurance
   company, 181
Offshore centre, 226
Offshore charitable foundations,
   156
Offshore communications, 173-
   177
Offshore community, 14
   markets, 248-251
Offshore company, 140
   limited by guaranty, 21, 127-
   128
Offshore consultant, 24, 68, 78,
   97, 122
Offshore Consulting Company,
   255
Offshore Corporate Law, 49
Offshore credit cards, 109-110,
   208-209
Offshore debit cards, 109-110
Offshore eAsset Reconciliation
   (OAR), 119, 201, 210, 242
Offshore entities, 62-69, 94, 108,
   162
Offshore Entrepreneur, 204
Offshore exempt company, 127-
   129
Offshore fees, 107

Offshore Fulfillment
   Organization, 255
Offshore funds, 62, 64
Offshore holding company, 65
Offshore IBC (OS IBC), 63, 95,
   123, 124, 162, 253
Offshore income, 160, 162
Offshore incorporation, 16
Offshore Insurance, Re-
   insurance, Captive Insurance,
   211
Offshore investment
   opportunities, examples, 255-
   256
Offshore Irrevocable Letters of
   Credit Financing, 255
Offshore living trust, 97
Offshore LP, 141
Offshore manufacturing, 74
Offshore materials, 204-206
Offshore mortgage financing,
   255
Offshore movement, 122-123
   reasons, 29-33
Offshore mutual fund, 21, 50, 53,
   54
Offshore operating entity, 43
Offshore operations, 26
Offshore options
   evaluation guidelines, 36-44
   governing law, choice, 37
   language, 37-38
Offshore planners, 30, 108, 159,
   164
Offshore principal office, IRS
   requirements, 165
Offshore privacy, 173
Offshore private annuity contract,
   124
Offshore private bank, 115
Offshore professional, 8, 23

Offshore profit, 79
Offshore publications, 233-239
Offshore related sites. *See*
    Internet
Offshore scams, avoidance, 188-
    197
Offshore service providers, 35,
    164, 241-245
Offshore stock markets, 248-251
Offshore structure, 42, 43, 61,
    198
    set-up costs, 25-26
Offshore tax havens, 98
Offshore tax planning, 159
Offshore taxes, 159-164
Offshore trust, 87, 97, 99, 145,
    155
Offshore trustee, 22, 23, 102,
    104, 166
Offshore Visa Card, 209
Onshore assets/investing, 33
Onshore corporation, 77
Onshore credit cards, 109
Onshore movement, reasons, 29-
    30
Onshore planning, 30
Onshore portfolio manager, 63
Onshore publications, 233-239
Onshore services, 23
Operating company, 62, 66
Operating structure, 20, 62
Ordinary trust, 154
OS APT. *See* Offshore Asset
    Protection Trust
Ostrich syndrome, 14
Ownership, 226
    interest, 139

P

PA. *See* Private annuity

Pacific Rim, 47, 51
    Job Opportunities, 210
Palau, 55
Panama, 38, 55, 74, 75, 133, 137,
    171
Paraguay, 137
Paribas, 193
Participants, 22-25
Partnership, 94, 141, 142, 163,
    180. *See also* Family Limited
    Partnership; Limited
    Partnership
    dissolution, 130
Passports, 129-133. *See also*
    Bogus passports; Camoflage
    passports; Economic passport;
    Noncitizenship passports;
    Second passport
    review, 174-175
Performance-based fee, 63
Personal identification number
    (PIN), 173
Personal income taxes, 48
Personal injury, 32
Personal privacy, 31
Personal property, 86, 92
Peru, 138
PGP. *See* AutoPGP; Pretty Good
    Privacy
Phantom income, 139
    tax recapture, 139
Philippines, 133, 160
PILL. *See* Prosper International
    League Ltd.
PIN. *See* Personal identification
    number
PLC. *See* Public limited company
Pocket expenses, 107
Political independence, 185
Political instability, 7, 129, 135
Political stability, 41, 135, 186

Politics. *See* Local politics
Ponzi scheme, 189
Portfolio managers, 6, 22, 42, 63, 98, 227. *See also* Onshore portfolio manager
Portugal, 138
Preference transfer, 158
Preferential transfer, 227
Pre-filing notice, 227
Pretty Good Privacy (PGP), 40, 119, 176, 198, 201, 203. *See also* AutoPGP
   encryption, 76, 242
Prime bank guaranty scam, 193-197
Prime bank scam, 193-197
Privacy, 31, 59, 76, 92, 93, 109, 117-119, 136, 173-177, 198, 203. *See also* Banking privacy; Financial privacy; International Business Company; Offshore privacy; Personal privacy; Pretty Good Privacy
   level, 41
   publications, 203-204
   tool, 73-74
Private accounts, 111-115
Private annuity (PA), 8, 21, 123-125
Private bank, 21, 54, 116-117. *See also* Offshore private bank
Private bankers, 116
Private banking, 47, 115-117, 227
Private family, 21
Private foundations, 156
Private insurance, 30
Privy Council, 51

Probate, 87, 227
   avoidance, 73-74
   costs, 138
Professional diversity, 13
Professional planner, 4
Professionals. *See* Local professionals; Offshore professional
Promissory note, 68
Proprietary Triple Trust Structure, 145-148
Prosper International League Ltd (PILL), 209
Public limited company (PLC), 227
Public policy, 86
Puerto Rico, 185
Pure Contractual Trust, 150
Pure equity trust, 154-155, 227
Pure trust, 21, 150-154, 227
   definition, 150-154
Purpose Trust, 99
Pyramid scheme, 189

Q

Quadralay Cryptography Archive, 203

R

RA. *See* Reluctant American; Resident alien
Racketeer, Influence and Corruption Organization Act of 1984 (RICO), 228
   racketeering statutes, 4
RCI, 253
Real estate, 44, 73, 141, 144
Real estate FLP, 21

Real estate ownership, 43
Real property, 86, 99, 142, 144
  transactions, 170
Real property equity stripping,
  AP tool, 144-145
Reference letter, 112
Register, 228
Registered agents, 26
Registered insurers, 184
Registrar, 228
  fees, 78
Registration fees. *See*
  International Business
  Company
Reinsurance, 180
Re-insurance business, 84
Re-insurance services, 72
Reinsurers, 184
Reliable Office Supply, 175
Reluctant American (RA), 7, 11-
  17, 23, 25, 37, 48, 68, 76, 77,
  121, 124, 165, 166, 201, 228
  farewell, 197-199
  identification, 13-17
Re-mailing services, 78
Report of Foreign Bank and
  Financial Account, 167
Report of International
  Transportation of Currency or
  Money Instruments, 169-170
Reporting requirements, 48
Republic of Ceylon, 132
Residence, 129-134
Residency, 62
Resident alien (RA), 2
Retirement, 32, 93
  age, 61

Return by a Transferor of
  Property to a Foreign
  Corporation, Foreign Estate or
  Trust, or Foreign Partnership,
  167-168
Reuters Newsmedia, 213
Revenue Reconciliation Bill of
  1995, 128, 129, 159, 228
Revenue Ruling. *See* Internal
  Revenue Service
Revocable trust, 138
RICO. *See* Racketeer, Influence
  and Corruption Organization
  Act of 1984
Rights of Settlement, 99
Risk investments, 29
Roam phone, 39
Roberts, Glen L., 203
Rockefeller Foundation, 156
Roll program scam, 193-197
Roman Report, 235
Roosevelt, Eleanor, 130
Rule Against Perpetuities, 98-99,
  228
Russia, 30

S

SA. *See* Société Anonyme
Safe haven, 29, 30, 53
Safety test, 189
San Juan, 186
Savvy Search, 9, 202
Scam. *See* Nigerian scam; Prime
  bank guaranty scam; Prime
  bank scam; Roll program scam
  avoidance. *See* Offshore scam

Scope International Ltd., 8, 204
SCZ. *See* Special Canary Zone
Sea-First Bank, 196
SEC. *See* Securities Exchange Commission
Second citizenship, 135
  acquisition, 43
Second passport, 134, 135
  acquisition, 43
Securities Exchange Commission (SEC), 195, 196
Securities Industry Protection Corporation (SIPC), 30, 229
Self-liquidating loans, 195
Service providers, 4, 35, 97, 108, 173. *See also* Offshore service providers; Telecommunications service providers
Settlor, 57, 85-108, 138, 145, 150, 152, 167, 168, 228. *See also* Contempt of Court; Legal settlor; Nominee settlor; True settlor
Seychelles, 55
SFR. *See* Swiss franc
Share certificates, 78
Ship ownership, 84
Shipping companies, 74
Side letter, 228
Sierra Leone, 138
Signatory authority, 167, 168
Singapore, 55
SIPC. *See* Securities Industry Protection Corporation
S/L. *See* Statute of Limitations
Smell test, 103
Snickers Test, 25
Social environment, 43
Social security number, 169
Social Security System, 93

Social stability, 42-43
Société Anonyme (SA), 229
Society for Worldwide Interbank Financial Telecommunications (SWIFT), 229
Soft fraud, 103
Sole proprietorship, 94
Solvency, 88
South Africa, 46-47, 54, 138
Soviet Union, 36
Spain, 138
Sparbuch (Savings) Account (Austrian Ueberbringer Sparbuch), 112, 114-115, 229, 234, 243
Special Canary Zone (SCZ), 50
Special custodian, 229
Special investment advisor, 229
Spendthrift Clause, 56-57, 155
Spendthrift provisions, 87, 141
Sri Lanka, 55
St. Christopher, 36, 47, 55, 138
St. John, 185
St. Kitts. *See* St. Christopher
St. Lucia, 47
St. Thomas, 185
St. Vincent, 55
Staging, 26
Standby trustee, 95
Starchild, Adam, 8, 236
State Farm Mutual Automobile Insurance Company, 90-91
Statute of Elizabeth, 53, 96, 100-101, 108, 158, 187
Statute of Limitations (S/L), 49, 50-52, 57, 229
Statutory filings, 183
Statutory law contract, 150
Statutory requirements. *See* Captive insurance
Statutory trust, 48

Stiftung, 156, 229
Stock brokerage firm, 164
Stock exchanges, 15, 249
Stock markets. *See* Offshore
    stock markets; U.S. stock
    market
Stockholders, names, 48
Storie, William R., 243
Strategies, 125-158
Straw man, 94
Structure. *See* Offshore structure;
    Proprietary Triple Trust
    Structure; Three-tier structure
    selection, 61-69
Structures, 20-21, 125-158
Sublicensing companies, 74
Subpoena duces tecum, 110
Successor trustees, 153
SundayMail, 213
SWIFT. *See* Society for
    Worldwide Interbank
    Financial Telecommunications
    banking system, 58, 59
Swiss annuity, 42, 122-123
Swiss banking, 111
Swiss franc (SFR), 123
Switzerland, 12, 43, 55, 174

T

Tax avaison, 16, 197
Tax avoidance, 129, 148, 160,
    197
Tax Bullets, 207
Tax concessions. *See* Local
    jurisdictions
Tax deferral, 93, 121, 160, 197
Tax Discussion Groups, 207
Tax domicile, 43
Tax evasion, 16, 125
Tax exemptions, 89

Tax fraud, 176, 197
Tax havens, 3, 6, 8, 12, 21, 29,
    30, 35, 41, 44, 45, 47-56, 72,
    100, 102, 106, 108, 110, 111,
    136, 160, 175, 186, 208, 230.
    See also Offshore tax havens
    laws, 187
    reputation/quality, 36-37
    tax attributes classification,
    170-171
Tax ID, 151
    number, 169
Tax implications. *See* U.S.
    person
Tax information, 206-208
Tax liability, 123, 125, 134, 162
Tax neutral APT, 166
Tax neutral structures, 197
Tax News Groups, 208
Tax Notes NewsWire, 207
Tax payment, 7
Tax regimen, 42, 47, 160, 230.
    See also International Business
    Company; Zero-tax regimen
Tax residence, 43
Tax shelter, 2
Tax status, 89
Tax treaties, 41, 46
Tax treatment
    deferral, 159-171
    ramifications, 159-171
Taxation, 181. *See also* Double
    taxation
TaxBombers, 204
Taxes. *See* Annuity proceeds;
    Excise tax; Offshore taxes;
    U.S. citizenship; U.S. stock
    market; U.S. trustee
TAXFAX, 206
Tax-free income, 45
Tax-free transfer, 145

Tax-neutral funds, 122
Tax-neutral money, 130
TaxSites, 206
TCI. *See* Turks and Caicos
  Islands
Telecommunications service
  providers, 39
Telephone records, 175
Temporary restraining order
  (TRO), 94
Terminology, 11-12, 56-58
Terms. *See* Glossary
Test, 187-188
Testamentary disposition, 85
Testamentary distributions, 93
Testamentary trust, 89, 97
Third-party obligations, 83
Three-tier structure, 148-149
Tico Times, 234
Time (magazine), 212
Time share resorts, 21
Time sharing, 252-255
Time zone. *See* User-friendly
  time zone
Token tax, 170
Tort reform, 16
Trading company, 73
Transaction costs, 78
Transactional fees, 76
Transfer pricing, 7
Transmogrifying, 158, 230
Travel Agent Records, 174-175
Treaty shopping, 75
TRO. *See* Temporary restraining
  order
True settlor, 85, 230

Trust. *See* Business trust;
  Massachusetts Trust; Offshore
  Asset Protection Trust; Pure
  trust; U.S. living trust
  assets, 22, 51, 151
  bank, 107
  business, 84
  characteristics, 155
  corpus, 95
  deed, 58, 94, 96, 98, 230
  evolution, 89-92
  indenture, 27, 94, 230
  laws, 50
  management, 154
  nomenclature, 98-106
  organization. *See* Business
  Trust Organization
  protector, 22, 59, 87, 96, 101,
  104, 106, 230-231
  question, 23-25
  services, 72
  settlement document, 231
  structure. *See* Proprietary
  Triple Trust Structure
Trust Act (1994), 54
Trustees, 22, 27, 42, 50, 59, 85-
  108, 145, 150, 152, 157, 231.
  See also Adverse trustee; Bank
  trustee; Bankruptcy; Co-
  trustee; Custodian;
  Independent trustee; Joint
  trustees; Offshore trustee;
  Standby trustee; Successor
  trustees; U.S. trustee
  owner, 53
Trusts, 85-87

TSB Bank, 238
Turks and Caicos Islands (TCI),
12, 36, 38, 41-43, 56, 71, 100,
171, 230
Turnkey, 78

U

UBI. *See* Units of beneficial
interest
UBO. *See* Unincorporated
business organization
Ugly American, 1
UK. *See* United Kingdom
Ultra vires activities, 83
Uniform Fraudulent Conveyance
Act, 100
Uniform Fraudulent Transfer
Act, 100
Uniform Partnership Act (UPA),
231
Unincorporated business
corporation (UBO), 21, 145,
217, 231
Unincorporated organization
(UO), 145, 231
filing, 148
United Arab Emirates, 56
United Kingdom (UK), 47, 114,
160, 174, 185, 186
United Nations, 247
United Parcel Service (UPS),
107, 213
United States Code (U.S.C.), 4
Units of beneficial interest (UBI),
155
Universal Corporate Services,
Inc., 241
Universal Resource Locator
(URL), 9, 232
Unsecured contract, 123

UO. *See* Unincorporated
organization
UPA. *See* Georgia Uniform
Partnership Act; Uniform
Partnership Act
Up-front fees, 195
UPS. *See* United Parcel Service
Upstreaming, 2, 231
Uruguay, 133, 138
URL. *See* Universal Resource
Locator
U.S. attribution rules, 162
U.S. banking system, 31, 32, 58,
201, 160
U.S. Bankruptcy Code, 158
U.S. citizenship
renouncement, 133-138
taxes, 164
U.S. Comptroller of the
Currency, 196
U.S. Congress, 90, 159
U.S. Council for International
Business, 211
U.S. currency, 30
U.S. Customs, Form 4790, 169-
170
Officer, 170
U.S. dollars (USD), 42, 58, 59,
123, 186, 232
transfers, 110
U.S. Federal Reserve
Bank, 160, 217
wire transfer system, 59, 77, 110
U.S. Fiduciary Income Tax
Return, 169
U.S. Gift (and Generation-
Skipping) Tax Return, 167
U.S. government securities, 160
US Income Tax Law--GPO
Access, 207
U.S. judgment creditor, 51

U.S. living trust, 87-89
U.S. person, tax implications, 162
U.S. Post Office, 211
U.S. Secret Service, 192
U.S. stock brokerage accounts, 30
U.S. stock market, 162
  IBC investing, U.S. taxes, 164
U.S. tax code, 62, 206
U.S. tax laws, 64, 95
U.S. taxes. *See* U.S. stock market
U.S. Treasury Department, 93, 168
  Form TD 90-22.1, 167
U.S. trustee, tax, 163
U.S. voting process, 15
U.S. Virgin Islands, 3, 71, 185
U.S.C. *See* United States Code
USD. *See* U.S. dollars
UseNet, 208
User-friendly time zone, 41

V

Vacation ownership (VO), 252-255
Valuation discount, 139, 140
Value added
  basis, 3
  phenomena, 25
Vanuatu, 12, 36, 47, 56
Variable annuity, 232
VAT, 47
Venezuela, 49, 138
Vesting period, 99
Vetting, 232
ViaCrypt, 40
Villanova Tax Law
  Compendium, 206
Virgin Gorda, 175

Visa card, 209
Visa-free traveling, 135, 136
VO. *See* Vacation ownership
Voice communications, 39, 174
Voice encryption, 39
Voice scramblers, 40
Voting stock, 64

W

Wait and see test, 49
Wall Street Journal (newspaper), 212
Wardley, 116
Wealth preservation, 16
Wealth conservation, 16, 198
Web. *See* World Wide Web
  site, 202, 203
WebCrawler, 202
Wertpapierbuch account, 115, 234
West Indies, 47
Western Samoa, 56
Westminster Model, 37
Wholesalers, 184
Windfall test, 189
Wire transfer fees, 107
Wire transfer system. *See* U.S.
  Federal Reserve
Wire transfers, 30, 40
Withholding tax, 50, 164
Work permit, 43
Workman's compensation, 32
World Bank, 209, 232
World Citizenships, 138
World Currency Converter, 211
World Fact Book, 211
World Investment Report (1995), 247-248
World Stock and Commodity
  Exchanges, 211, 249

World War II, 130
World Wide Web (Web), 9, 40,
    154, 174, 177, 201, 206, 232
    global insurance resource, 184
    search engines, 202
    sites, 203-204

Y

Yahoo, 9, 202

Z

Zero tax, 170
Zero-tax jurisdictions, 170
Zero-tax regimen, 148
Zimmerman, Paul, 198

WHAT'S ON THE FLOPPY DISC

To assist you in "surfing the web" or corresponding with OS resource providers, the disc contains four text files:

1.   a.txt–Appendix A: Universal Resource Locators (URLs) for "surfing the Web."
2.   b.txt–Appendix B: Glossary of Terms and Abbreviations. Refer to it and add to it as time progresses.
3.   c.txt–Appendix C: Offshore Resources for faxing, mailing, calling or e-mailing.
4.   d.txt–Appendix D: Service Providers for faxing, mailing, calling or e-mailing.

And four Word for Windows files:

1.   a.doc–Appendix A: Universal Resource Locators (URLs) for "surfing the Web."
2.   b.doc–Appendix B: Glossary of Terms and Abbreviations. Refer to it and add to it as time progresses.
3.   c.doc–Appendix C: Offshore Resources for faxing, mailing, calling or e-mailing.
4.   d.doc–Appendix D: Service Providers for faxing, mailing, calling or e-mailing

QUARTERLY UPDATE SERVICE

Keep up to date on offshore financial and tax haven matters with our quarterly update reports.

Stay current on:

- ✓ **New scams with *Scam Alerts***
- ✓ **Tax haven changes and new tax havens**
- ✓ **Tax laws changes**
- ✓ **New asset protection strategies**
- ✓ **Secrets from the experts**
- ✓ **How not to waste money**
- ✓ **Travel tips**
- ✓ **Seminar alerts**
- ✓ **And much more to enhance your education of offshore matters**

Sign up *now!*

YES, I would like to keep my copy of *The Offshore Money Book* current with this valuable, yet affordable, quarterly offshore service! Please send my update via:

Please tick one:

___ 🖅Post   ___ 🖳 e-mail (*address:* _____)
___ 🖫 Post, on 3 1/2" floppy disc, DOS format, text (.txt) file.

Please print clearly.
Subscriber's name: _____

Address: _____

_____

Country/Postal Code: _____

Make checks payable to **The Global Group Limited** for US$100 (U.S. dollars only) for four issues per year and send by air post to:

The Global Group Limited	Tel: (809) 356-2093
PO Box CB 13039	Fax: (809) 356-2095
Nassau, Bahamas CB 13039	e-mail: 0ffshore@bahamas.net.bs